THE
COLOR
OF
CHURCH

THE
COLOR
OF
CHURCH

RODNEY M. WOO

ACADEMIC

NASHVILLE, TENNESSEE

A BIBLICAL AND PRACTICAL PARADIGM FOR MULTIRACIAL CHURCHES

ISBN: 978-0-8054-4839-9

Published by B&H Publishing Group
Nashville, Tennessee

Dewey Decimal Classification: 261.83
Subject Heading: CHURCH WORK WITH RACIALLY MIXED
PEOPLE\MULTICULTURALISM\CHRISTIANITY AND CULTURE

Unless otherwise noted, Scripture quotes are from the *Holman Christian Standard Bible* ® Copyright © 1999, 2000, 2002, 2003 by Holman Bible Publishers. Used by permission.

Scripture quotations marked NASB are from the *New American Standard Bible*. © The Lockman Foundation, 1960, 1962, 1963, 1968, 1971, 1972, 1973, 1975, 1977. Used by permission.

Printed in the United States of America
1 2 3 4 5 6 7 8 9 10 11 12 • 17 16 15 14 13 12 11 10 09
VP

C O N T E N T S

120542

P R E F A C E

his book supplements *People of the Dream*,[1] which is an interaction between a sociologist and a pastor as they compare and contrast churches across the nation and a local congregation in Houston, Texas. *The Color of Church* expounds on this one church's journey as it applies the biblical model of racial reconciliation to its everyday walk.

Rodney Woo has served for more than 17 years at Wilcrest Baptist Church, which is located in Alief, a racially diverse suburb in southwest Houston. The church has adopted the mission statement, "Wilcrest Baptist Church is God's multiethnic bridge that draws all people to Jesus Christ, who transforms them from unbelievers to missionaries." This vision underlies the transformation of a formerly all-white church to a congregation now represented by 44 different countries with a white population of less than 40 percent. *The Color of Church* adopts the definition that a *multiracial congregation is composed of racially diverse believers united by their faith in Christ, who make disciples of all the nations in the anticipation of the ultimate racial reunion around the throne of God.*

The Color of Church also unfolds the story of how God has helped Wilcrest understand the biblical principles of a multiracial church that He has progressively revealed in Scripture. Each chapter will parallel two perspectives: (a) the biblical model or mandate and (b) the Wilcrest transformation story from a uniracial congregation to a multiracial congregation. There will be a comparison of the Bible's stance concerning racial reconciliation and an in-depth interaction with how Wilcrest has succeeded or failed in a contemporary urban setting in the Deep South. Based on the biblical accounts, this book contends that it is God's will for all churches to move toward crossing any racial and ethnic lines that have been established in their immediate communities. At a bare minimum each church should reflect the diversity of its surrounding community; but ultimately each church

---

[1] Michael O. Emerson, with Rodney M. Woo, *People of the Dream: Multiracial Congregations in the United States* (Princeton: Princeton University Press, 2006).

should project the heavenly image of all nations worshipping together at the throne.

The Color of Church is divided into three sections and then concludes with the challenge to multiply the multiracial vision. The first section (chaps. 1–4) establishes the biblical foundation for multiracial ministry. It provides an overarching biblical perspective of God's call to the nations, the importance of having a biblical vision of reaching the nations, the theology of unity in the midst of diversity, and the biblical model of repentance from racism. The second section (chaps. 5–8) provides a clear picture of current reality, depicting relationships among the races in our society and churches. A church that captures the vision for multiracial ministry must decide their willingness to pursue this vision despite numerous obstacles from both within and outside the church. This section also helps the readers to assess their progress in the process and to give them insight concerning the costs of this multiracial vision. The third section (chaps. 9–12) offers practical guidance, with help to implement multiracial ministry. It also includes specific rules of engagement as the spiritual battle for reaching all the races ensues. The key battlefields of worship, leadership, and missions will be addressed through the lenses of multiracial ministry. The final section (chap. 13) deals with the question of whether the multiracial vision can be reproduced in a variety of racial and cultural settings.

The primary audience of *The Color of Church* consists of local pastors, seminary professors, denominational leaders, and lay leaders with a heart for multiracial ministry within the evangelical context. Since this story is told by a pastor of a local congregation, there will be helpful insights that will assist and prepare the church leader for the transformational process of becoming a multiracial congregation. The book's goal is to provide an interactive study that will take individuals and local congregations step-by-step through this transformational process. Prompting questions at the end of each chapter offer assistance to any study group or class for further dialogue and inquiries concerning multiracial ministry.

The purpose of *The Color of Church* is not to do an in-depth, systematic study of all the biblical texts dealing with multiracial ministry. Rather, this book examines various texts throughout its entirety, in a progressive manner as God has enabled Wilcrest to understand the multiracial vision. For a more exhaustive and comprehensive study of the biblical texts, please refer to the bibliography.

Michael O. Emerson
Allyn and Gladys Cline Professor of Sociology
Founding Director, Center on Race, Religion, and Urban Life
Author, *People of the Dream* and *Divided by Faith*

BIBLICAL BASIS

CHAPTER 1

THE BEGINNING, THE END, AND EVERYTHING BETWEEN

"After this I looked, and there was a vast multitude from every nation, tribe, people, and language, which no one could number, standing before the throne and before the Lamb" (Rev 7:9a).[1]

From the time we open the Bible and read the first words written to us, we quickly realize that God is concerned about "beginnings." One can characterize the whole book of Genesis as a book about beginnings. It was the beginning of creation, humankind, nations, and in particular, the nation of Israel. Therefore, it is vital that we get a clear picture of what exactly takes place in the beginning. The Bible begins, "In the beginning God created the heavens and the earth" (Gen 1:1). In this initial interaction between the divine and the human, we see a close correlation among God, the beginning, and creation. God reveals to us from the beginning that all the heavens and humanity ultimately derive their origin from God. Everything begins with God. Once humanity arrives on the scene, we see that it is God, our creator, who purposefully places us here. In this journey, we will discover not only the purpose of our existence as God's creation, but also our identity and relationship with God and those around us.

THE BEGINNING

The beginning of anything is often an emotional experience. There are many examples of beginnings in our lives. The birth of a newborn baby represents an abrupt departure from the mother's womb to an

---

[1] All biblical references are from the Holman Christian Standard Bible unless otherwise noted.

unknown world. The first day of school is both a terrifying and exhilarating experience. Acquiring a driver's license opens an entirely new dimension, both for the teenager and the parents. Graduating from high school or college closes one chapter and opens another. The wedding day dramatically changes one from being single to being married with the simple words, "I do." A new job, promotion, or relocation—all signify new stressful beginnings. In addition to the beginnings in the physical sphere, there are also new "spiritual beginnings," such as one's conversion to Christ, baptism, joining a local church body, responding to the call to ministry, sharing one's faith, serving in a ministry at church, or going on one's first mission trip.

This study may also represent a new beginning for you in the area of race relations and racial reconciliation. Perhaps God has already started to deal with you, your ministry, and your church in this potentially volatile area. Or you may be unaware of the magnitude of the racial divide in churches across the United States. Wherever you are spiritually in this delicate and explosive process, God may be calling you to a new beginning. Your beginning may simply involve becoming aware of what is going on racially across our country and more specifically in your local context. You may need to learn how to leave your racial comfort zone and begin to establish new relationships with people who belong to different races. In addition, your congregation may need a new beginning in the manner and target of their ministry. Enlarging your racial, cultural, and ethnic boundaries may need to take on an entirely new dimension. I am convinced that God is doing a new work in the area of racial reconciliation and that His initial target is the heart of His children, the body of Christ. Once the heart of creation beats with the heart of the Creator of all the nations, it will be impossible to remain silent. We then can join with the apostles Peter and John when they say, "We are unable to stop speaking about what we have seen and heard" (Acts 4:20). Initially I was unaware of God's holy pulse that ran through my spiritual veins in the area of multiracial ministry, and then God begin to stir my heart. But then I felt the resounding heartbeat of God's purpose through a variety of events in my life.

MY BEGINNING

I have served as the senior pastor of Wilcrest Baptist Church in Houston, Texas, since 1992. Three years before I received any contact from the church, God placed in my heart a clear call to lead a church into becoming a multiracial congregation. The impetus of this transformational movement in my heart was my training in biblical studies. During the early years of my theological training, I wanted to serve as a pastor of a growing white suburban congregation. My doctoral studies redirected my focus in the multiracial direction. Throughout my intense pilgrimage of biblical studies, God ignited a passion within me to follow the pattern that the apostle Paul established in reaching out to diverse cultures while preaching the immutable gospel.[2]

In addition, God showed me how the variegated pieces of the puzzle of my own personal life formed a God-shaped pattern and vision. One of the subtle pieces of my puzzle was my own family heritage. My half-Chinese father served as a missionary to Hispanics, African-Americans, and Vietnamese in Port Arthur, Texas, during the 1960s and '70s. With his Chinese heritage, my father understood what it meant to live as a racial minority in a dominant white culture. For example, my parents could not legally get married in Virginia in 1948 due to his Asian descent. Consequently, my parents had to travel to the adjacent state of Maryland to get married. My wife, Sasha, also brings a diverse perspective into the ministry with her Hispanic heritage. Her mother, who grew up in Mexico, learned English while attending my father's inner-city ministry in our hometown. While involved in these literacy classes, my father encouraged her mother in her newfound faith in Christ. The multiracial connection between our families was established long before my wife and I met. In this divine orchestration of bringing our racially diverse families together, God taught me how important personal relationships are in crossing racial barrier.

In addition, my personal experience as a minority in all-African-American elementary and middle schools laid an early foundation for crossing cultural and racial barriers. Of my middle school's fifteen

---

[2] See my Ph.D. dissertation, "Paul's Contextual Approach for Evangelizing the Jews and the Gentiles against the Background of Acts 13:16–41 and Acts 17:22–31" (Fort Worth, TX: Southwestern Baptist Theological Seminary, 1992).

hundred students, only twenty were not African-American. I received a real-life racial lesson during my seventh grade gym class. The coach divided my class of 150 boys into groups of 50 and instructed the team captains to choose teams of 25. In my group, I was one of the two remaining boys yet to be selected. The team captains argued over who was going to be stuck with the "white boy." During their heated debate, I offered a critical bit of information that totally transformed their perspective of me. I told them that I was not white, but Chinese, and my last name was "Woo." Befuddled, one of the captains finally declared, "I want him on my team." At that time, they only knew they were to hate whites, but did not know exactly what to do with a Chinese student. God used this experience to teach me what it means to be a minority and how it feels to be treated differently based solely on skin color. In the same way the color of my skin dramatically determined and affected my personal relationships at school as a child, I now see similar effects on racial relationships within the local church.

God also instilled in me a call and desire for evangelism that mandates believers to reach all racial and ethnic groups with the gospel. One of my first experiences in this area occurred on Saturday mornings with my father as I accompanied him to the city jail to present the good news of Jesus Christ with inmates from all racial backgrounds. During this training period, God taught me to look beneath the skin color of the individual and to speak to the heart of the one behind bars. The shared prison experience across racial lines placed everyone at the same level, each person having one common vision: freedom. In reality, all of us are in an identical spiritual imprisonment that results from our rebellion against God (cp. John 8:34; Rom 3:23). Consequently all people groups, regardless of the color of their skin, share a common vision: spiritual freedom. Although all the inmates endured a similar experience, the black prisoners were separated from the white prisoners. I found it somewhat disturbing that I shared the same gospel from the same Bible twice, once to the blacks and the other time to the whites. I believe God placed it in my heart that one day in the future I would be able to share the same gospel from the same Bible simultaneously to blacks, whites, Asians, Hispanics, and all the nations.

As a result of these variegated puzzle pieces converging—biblical studies, personal experience, family heritage, and the heart for evangelism—God focused my vision to see the church as a place for the nations to come together as one body to bring glory to God and to accomplish His will. After this spiritual metamorphosis, I knew God called me to lead a multiracial congregation. Yet, I could not imagine how God would transform this vision into reality.

As these inner changes occurred, I was still serving as a pastor outside a small rural town in central Texas. Here, the whites literally lived on one side of the railroad tracks and the African-Americans on the other, while the overwhelming majority of Hispanics worked as illegal immigrant dairy farmers. For eight years, I could not completely understand why God called a pastor by the name of "Woo" and his Hispanic wife to an all-white rural congregation. Amazingly, during our eight years there, we saw God grow the church from an average of fifteen to over three hundred attending worship services. During my last two years there, I earnestly attempted to incorporate several nonwhites into the fabric of the church body. No matter how thoroughly I preached on reaching all of God's people and personally modeled a multiracial mind-set, the transition was superficial and short-lived. The initial resistance to the multiracial vision in that rural setting created a sense of unrest within me, which eventually drove me to the Word of God to search for answers. What does Scripture say about races coming together in one local church?

GOD'S BEGINNING

The biblical account opens with God's creation of unified humanity and concludes with all the different nations reuniting to worship the one true God. Genesis 1 and Revelation 7 are the two racial bookends of the Bible. What lies between is the journey of fallen humanity characterized by the rift between God and one another. One manifestation of this sinful separation is evident by the strife among the different races. This pilgrimage of fragmented people groups is traced from Genesis to Revelation. The biblical story tells of the sustained distance between races at the time of Babel and the ultimate racial reunion, first beginning at Pentecost and perfected around the throne of God.

This journey will guide you through the biblical foundation and pattern for the reconciliation among races, cultures, and people groups. This work has an ongoing parallel focus and interaction between the biblical account and a contemporary church that intentionally embraces and pursues the reconciliation process. The biblical account provides not only the basis but also the motivation to see the first fruits of Rev 7 here on this earth within the body of Christ. Many of these biblical truths become tangible to us as Wilcrest makes its journey toward the racial reunion around the throne of God. The contemporary church that served as the testing ground for this study is Wilcrest Baptist Church in Houston, Texas. This church is composed of believers who have struggled with multiple racial and cultural issues through a meticulous transformation process, evolving from a homogeneous church to a multiracial congregation. Consequently, the biblical model continually interacts with the Wilcrest model. I use the term *model* specifically in reference to Wilcrest not as something to be reproduced or copied, but as one church's experience that proclaims to the entire world that reconciliation among races is possible with the power of God.

Wilcrest is neither at the beginning ideal depicted in Gen 1 nor at the final convergence portrayed in Rev 7, but somewhere in the midst of a journey that is preparing them for that ultimate reunion around the throne of God. This chapter presents the biblical groundwork for what happened at Wilcrest and also serves as a guide to the future vision God has given the church. My prayer is that you will learn from the multitude of mistakes and failures that Wilcrest has experienced, while simultaneously learning the biblical principles that provide the motivation and the guidance to become what God envisions for His church.

During this journey, I have personally struggled with whether it is God's will for all churches to become multiracial churches and to what extent local churches should deal with racial reconciliation. My contention is that it is God's will that all churches move toward reaching across whatever racial and ethnic lines that have been established in their immediate community. At the bare minimum, the local church should reflect the racial make-up of the neighborhood and do whatever it takes to embrace and integrate all the nations.[3] Many churches have done well in going to all the nations, but the increasing dilemma occurs when the nations come to us.

THE BEGINNING—GENESIS 1

Let us begin our exciting journey with the first recorded Word from God to us: "In the beginning God . . ." (Gen 1:1). Anything and everything that we might say or do must come only after God has already spoken. God exclusively determined the design, direction, and pace of all of His created beings. In wisdom He orchestrated all things to reveal Himself in creation. I begin this study where God began His communication with us, with Himself as the source and center of all creation. What God says about how we are designed and how we relate to one another matters since He is the one who created us and knows us better than we know ourselves.

In Gen 1:26–27 there is a divine dialogue among God the Father, God the Son, and God the Holy Spirit concerning the creation of humanity. Subsequently, there is a purposeful progression in the flow of creation. God begins His creative work with foundational elements of light, sky, air, and water (Gen 1:3–8). Subsequently, God builds upon this foundation of His creation with dry land that yields vegetation (Gen 1:9–11). It is evident that dry land and soil with all of their minerals are more complicated than water; and vegetation that yields seeds that are deposited into the ground producing more vegetation is more complex than a rock. God continues to increase steadily creation's arrangement, design, and detail as living animals now fill the water and the dry land. Then in one masterful stroke, God brings His creation to its climax as He creates man and woman in His image. The grand finale of God's perfect creation was a perfect humanity made in His very image.[4] The difference between the creation of humanity and the prior elements of creation is that, as the pinnacle

---

[3] I will deal more thoroughly with the scenario of an individual or church located in a uniracial area and some practical steps to take in order to reach across racial lines in chapter 13.

[4] On this flow of thought, I am indebted to Josh Westbury, my former coworker. In the creation story, there are both unity and diversity; and God loves and values both. Stephen A. Rhodes depicts this truth in this way, "God created *both* the heavens *and* the earth; God created *both* the sun to rule the day *and* the stars to rule by night; God created *both* the sky above our heads *and* earth beneath our feet.... God created humankind in God's own image—*both* male *and* female God created us. You see, our God is not an either-or God;

and the crown of God's creation, humanity stand alone as the only created beings made in the "image of God."

The "image of God" is further described in Gen 2:7. This verse tells us that God breathed the breath of life into Adam, and thus man became a living soul. However, there has been much debate on what exactly the phrase "in His image" may mean. Whether this may include physical, emotional, mental, spiritual, or moral qualities or a combination of these qualities is still an open question.[5] However, in each of us, we bear a divine resemblance. Whatever Adam received, we all received. We may not know exactly what it means to reflect the "image of God" inside us, but we share that image equally. The fact that as humans we all equally possess a divine image necessitates that we perceive and treat each other with a dignity commensurate with this truth. To interact with someone who has been created in His image, regardless of skin color, affords us the opportunity to see the face of God as we gaze into the face of another created being.[6]

Whether the line of demarcation is race or status, how we treat another created being reflects how we treat our Creator. In fact, the writer of Proverbs contended, "The one who oppresses the poor insults their Maker" (Prov 14:31) and later, "The one who mocks the poor insults his Maker" (Prov 17:5). If you oppress or mock the poor or any of God's creation, that becomes an affront to God.[7] This sounds like an attainable goal, yet when we encounter people of different ethnic and cultural backgrounds and expressions, we often immediately detect the differences rather than the similarities. When you see someone who is different than you are racially, culturally, or ethnically, do you initially focus on what you have in common with that person or what the differences are? Our society programs us to

---

rather, our God is a both-and God." *Where the Nations Meet: The Church in a Multicultural World* (Downers Grove, IL: InterVarsity, 1998), 20.

[5] G. L. Wenham summarizes the five main proposals of what the "image of God" is: (1) Image and likeness are distinct, with the image referring to natural qualities such as reason and personality and likeness referring to the supernatural graces that make the redeemed godlike; (2) the mental and spiritual faculties that people share with the Creator; (3) physical resemblance; (4) the appointment of humankind as God's representatives on earth; and (5) the capacity to relate to God. *Genesis 1–15*, WBC (Waco, TX: Word, 1987), 29–32.

[6] Duane Elmer, *Cross-Cultural Conflict: Building Relationships for Effective Ministry* (Downers Grove, IL: InterVarsity 1993), 15. Elmer adds that as we submit ourselves to learning from other cultures, we catch glimpses of God's grace that would be unavailable in our own culture.

[7] J. David Hays, *From Every People and Nation: A Biblical Theology of Race* (Downers Grove, IL: InterVarsity, 2003), 50.

some extent to focus initially on the differences. However, with some spiritual deprogramming, we can learn to see our common created image and the potential connection that we have with one another in Jesus Christ and embrace, celebrate, and enjoy rather than ignore our differences.[8]

Since God created us in His image, it means that God thought enough of us to deposit some of Himself inside of us. In fact, because of His love toward us, God made us to be like Him. Since God created each human being, the one dominant characteristic that we all share is the image of God. Gary Deddo adds that "human identity cannot be grounded ultimately in race. The human being is essentially constituted by its relationship to God as the creature, reconciled sinner and glorified child of God."[9] The image of God in us should completely dismantle any concept that one race is either superior or inferior to another race. As human beings created in the image of God, regardless of the color of skin, we are designed to glorify Him. In fact His triune nature indicates that diversity is part of His design for revealing Himself in creation.

The divine dialogue that occurs among the different persons of the Trinity in Gen 1:26 provides a theological foundation for why diversity coexisting with unity in personal relationships glorifies God. When the writer records, "Let Us make man in Our image, according to Our likeness," it indicates that humanity was created to reflect God's triune nature and that all three persons of the Trinity were involved in the creation process. Scripture clearly teaches that each person of the Trinity is fully and completely God. There is not a distinction concerning "being." However, diversity does exist within the Trinity, namely, how each person of the Trinity relates to the others and the world.[10] In sum, "God is one, He is three, He is diversity and yet He is unity."[11] Consequently, the Godhead reveals why God desires to have a diverse humanity live in deep relational unity together. It allows us to reflect something of the diversity and unity of His triune

---

[8] It is not necessarily a negative to immediately detect differences in other races. However, what damages race relations is how one esteems others based on these differences.

[9] Gary Deddo, "Persons in Racial Reconciliation: The Contributions of a Trinitarian Theological Anthropology," in D. L. Okholm, ed., *The Gospel in Black and White* (Downers Grove, IL: InterVarsity, 1997).

[10] Wayne Grudem, *Systematic Theology* (Grand Rapids: Zondervan, 1994), 254.

[11] Stanley J. Grenz, *Theology for the Community of God* (Grand Rapids: William B. Eerdmans, 1994), 66.

being. Furthermore, the Trinity serves as a standard and model of how relationships among God's diverse created beings should function in unity. Michael Pocock, a professor at Dallas Theological Seminary, affirms this truth concerning gender: "When men and women make arrangements to live in community, they are also reflecting the inter-relatedness of God himself who exists in a Trinity."[12] Thus, the divine image is a corporate reality and only fully revealed in a diverse yet unified community. As human beings, we share the image of God equally, yet we are uniquely created with a divine connection to God and to each other.

Tragically, history teaches us that our differences drive a wedge between us in the manner in which we worship the one true God. Have you ever heard some of these statements? "They have their own style of music." "They are more comfortable with their own type of people." "We express ourselves differently than they express them-selves." "I like being around my own kind." "We do not have any thing in common with people from that race." All of these comments seem justified in homogeneous congregations, but are these words in line with the biblical standard? If we have been created in God's image, what is the biblical response to others who share this divine imprint on their lives? The Bible teaches us that we have been recon-ciled as one new person in the place of two and calls us to live out this reality (see Eph 2:14–16).

Following the creation story, Gen 3 then narrates the story of the fall of humanity into sin, thus marring the sinless image of God. Sev-eral questions emerge concerning the image of God within humanity subsequent to our contamination with sin. How much of that image has been damaged by the initial fall of Adam into sin? Do we today retain all, some, or none of the original image of God given to Adam? What we can conclude is that whatever we have remaining of the image of God, all of sinful humanity equally shares the same resi-due. Consequently, no one is better than anybody else, nor is anyone worse than anyone else. We all equally share the image of God, no matter how damaged that image may now be. Furthermore, God is

---

[12] Michael Pocock, "The Compass for the Journey," in *Cultural Change and Your Church: Helping Your Church Thrive in a Diverse Society* (Grand Rapids: Baker, 2002), 84. Pocock adds that the social nature of people flows from the nature of God in whose image we have been created.

reconciling a new humanity to Himself and to one another. By the church displaying unity in diversity, God reveals something of His own excellence, causing people in our generation to marvel.

YOUR BEGINNING

Before we move to the next segment, let me challenge you in the area of "beginnings." The beginning of a new stage or chapter in your life opens the possibility of advancement and growth, but it also entails the inevitability of facing the unknown. This fear factor often causes individuals and groups to become hesitant or even suffer paralysis, and they fail to move forward. When God offered the people of Israel the opportunity to leave Egypt after 400 years of slavery, they questioned the realistic possibility of moving across such an insurmountable barrier. Forty years later, the next generation of Israelites had to leave the chapters of their lives in Egypt and in the wilderness, in order to open the new chapter of the conquest of the promised land. The beginning required that they also cross another barrier, the Jordan River, to enter into occupied territory.

Every beginning mandates changes and adjustments but will also be accompanied with adversity and obstacles. The very fact that you are reading this material implies that God has afforded you an opportunity to experience a "beginning" in the area of racial reconciliation. I am reminded of the words of Jesus, who challenges us, "If anyone has ears to hear, he should listen!" (Mark 4:23). These words convey that if you are listening to God's call to racial reconciliation with your spiritual ears, then it is not too late. God graciously gives you an opening that you cannot afford to bypass or ignore.

If you could make a new start in the area of racial reconciliation, where would this new beginning be? Perhaps it would be in the area of increasing your awareness of the different races around you or the racial tensions and struggles in your immediate area. God may be moving you to interact intentionally with individuals from a different people group at your school, your work, and your neighborhood. I believe that many people are completely oblivious to what is happening around them racially and culturally. Perhaps God is working with your church to begin targeting different people groups in evangelism and in ministry.

THE END—THE HEAVENLY TRIBE

We will now leave the initial creation scene and go to the final redemption scene, in which all redeemed humanity stands before the throne of the Lamb of God (Rev 7). In the immediate context of this particular chapter, the apostle John witnesses the 12 tribes of Israel on earth receiving their mark of protection and identification during the time of the tribulation and the end times. Then God gives John bifocal lenses to see heaven and earth simultaneously. While the 12 tribes of Israel endure a time of persecution, there is a concurrent praise gathering of the saints who have already died and are now enjoying the presence of God without any barriers between them.

One Voice

The apostle John clearly identifies the heavenly choir of the redeemed in the following terms: "every nation, tribe, people, and language" all standing before the throne and before the Lamb. What is surprising is that the believers who are already present in heaven are distinguished by their race, culture, ethnicity, and language. Yet all the people groups sing in harmony the unifying song, "Salvation belongs to our God, who is seated on the throne, and to the Lamb!" (Rev 7:10). It is not the differences among the believers that are the primary emphasis, but the salvation that all of them share in Jesus Christ that brings them together. Although the Rev 7 scene is a very moving and powerful picture of heaven, it is possible to start earlier here on earth instead of waiting for heaven to enjoy all the nations around the same throne singing the same song at the same time.

According to the most recent studies, more than 93 percent of all congregations in the United States are not multiracial in their composition. There are more than 300,000 churches or religious congregations in the United States. The definition of a "multiracial congregation," according to Michael Emerson, is a congregation in which "no one racial group is 80 percent or more of the congregation."[13] This is a somewhat arbitrary definition, but studies have demonstrated that the dynamics of the entire group change when there is the presence of 20 percent or more of a minority group. What this statistic does not tell

---

[13] Curtis DeYoung, Michael O. Emerson, George Yancey, and Karen Chai Kim, *United by Faith: The Multiracial Congregation as an Answer to the Problem of Race* (Oxford: Oxford University Press, 2003), 2.

you initially is that this includes all types of churches and congregations. In fact, if you narrow the scope of data to include only evangelical churches, the percentage drops sharply to approximately five and a half percent of all evangelical congregations that fit into this definition of multiracial congregations.[14] Although the multiracial congregation defined by demographics is a beginning, my definition seeks to go beyond those parameters: *The multiracial congregation is composed of racially diverse believers united by their faith in Christ, who make disciples of all the nations in anticipation of the ultimate racial reunion around the throne.*

READY OR NOT?

At Wilcrest, we constantly project the Rev 7 picture to motivate and model our preparation for the final time. The sense of being prepared for Christ's second coming is common in both the teachings of Jesus and the apostle Paul.[15] In Rev 19:7–9, the primary responsibility of the bride or the body of Christ for the final marriage supper of the Lamb is to be ready. The apostle Paul in his letter to the Ephesians depicts this same sense of preparation. In Eph 5:25–27, Paul challenges the church to offer the ultimate gift to present to our groom, Christ, from the prepared bride. In both Rev 19:7–9 and Eph 5:25–27, practicing purity and holiness is one of the ways that believers prepare themselves for the final day. Consequently, preparation during our stay on earth is paramount as we approach the day when we will see Jesus face to face. On that final day, Rev 7 depicts the ultimate worship service composed of all people groups together around the same throne. In anticipation of the racial reunion, God calls His church to prepare for the coming of the Lord, which will usher us into heaven. In light of this truth, every worship service at Wilcrest is our essential groundwork and model for the final convergence of every nation and tribe. We understand our worship services to be "choir rehearsals" in preparation for the ultimate worship experience.

---

[14] Figures were obtained from Emerson's research group using the 1998 National Congregations Study directed by Mark Chaves.
[15] See Matt 24:42–44; 25:13; Luke 12:35–40; 1 Thess 5:1–7.

A LITTLE SLICE OF HEAVEN

Back in 2003, Wilcrest finally reached what I believe to be the critical mass of a multiracial congregation. We finally reached a point where there was not one majority group in the body of Christ: 42 percent white; 30 percent Hispanic; 23 percent African-American, African, Caribbean; 4 percent Asian; and 1 percent other. In addition, 44 different nations are now represented within our church family (see appendix 4). If you can imagine, at least 44 united nations are represented by spiritual ambassadors worshiping one God in one place. This has been a very long and difficult road for Wilcrest. At times, it has been only the Rev 7 vision of all the nations gathered around God's throne that has kept us on track and moving toward becoming what God called us to be. In our seasons of discouragement or disgruntlement, the apostle Paul continues to urge us to set our minds "on what is above, not on what is on the earth" (Col 3:2). If we set our minds on the unity that we will be able to experience in heaven around the throne of the Lamb of God, then we will worship together here on earth. However, if our minds remain on the earthly models of segregated worship, we will miss heaven on earth.

AND EVERYTHING IN BETWEEN

The question emerges from our study of the beginning of creation and the end around the throne of God: What do we do while we are in the parenthetical period between Gen 1 and Rev 7? In the beginning, we share God's image as part of His creation, while at the end, we share God's salvation with those who have placed their belief in Christ. If every believer has so much in common with God, why is the most segregated hour in the United States on Sunday morning in our churches? We work together, go to school together, play together, drive on the same roads together, and share the same sunrise and sunset, yet we worship separately. What has racially divided us?

Sin Separates Us

According to the prophet Isaiah, sin separates us from experiencing intimacy with God (see Isa 59:1–2). As sin drives a wedge between the creation and the Creator, sin simultaneously separates us from one another. One of the reasons this occurs is described in

Isa 53:6: "We all have turned to our own way." In our sin, we become self-centered, thus making it very difficult to connect with God or with others. If we are left alone, we will plunge toward isolation and self-destruction. It is impossible to avoid the ravaging effects of being pulled away from a loving God and the rest of His creation when we intentionally rebel against our Creator.

Christ Unites Us

Yet for the believer, there is a divine reversal in the direction in which we were formerly going. According to Paul, the sinner is no longer driven further from God; for now we are "brought near by the blood of the Messiah" (Eph 2:13). Through the blood sacrifice of Jesus Christ, the outsider (the Gentile) now experiences a transformation of spiritual status and identity. The vivid image of the Gentile brought near to God was completely foreign to Jewish thinking. It was already difficult enough for a Gentile to be brought into the covenant community of Israel. However, this was God's plan from the very beginning (see Isa 52:10; 56:7; 60:3; 66:18.). The great gulf is now bridged by the death and sacrifice of Christ. The spiritual result of the death of Christ is that we can experience intimacy with our Creator.

Peace Defines Us

When the believer comes into personal relationship with Jesus Christ, not only is the believer brought near to God, but also to each other. Paul adds in Eph 2:14 that Christ is now "our peace, who made both groups one." In addition to Christ bringing us peace between us (see John 14:27), He is also our personal peace. This divine peace is not confined to sinners and their relationship with God, but also is available to sinners in their relationship with one another. In God's plan of redemption of fallen humanity through the blood of Christ, there are now no more distinctions among individuals or among racial groups. Paul concludes by saying that Christ's death "tore down the dividing wall of hostility" (Eph 2:14). All believers, regardless of race, culture, or ethnicity, are now made into one new group. When Paul conveyed this powerful picture of the demolition of the dividing wall, there was a literal wall in the temple in Jerusalem that separated the Gentiles from the Jewish inner courts. For the readers of the first century, this dividing wall provided a perfect illustration of what it meant to be separated into different racial groups as the worshiper attempted to approach God. This inner court was exclusively the domain of the Jews alone. The Gentiles were allowed into the "Court of the Gentiles," but at the entrance to the next section specifically reserved for the Jews was a sign, which read, "Let no one of any nation come within the fence and barrier around the Holy Place. Whosoever will be taken doing so will himself be responsible for the fact that his death will ensue."[16] This sign kept the outsiders out and the insiders in. This dividing wall was firmly entrenched within the mind-set of both Jew and Gentile, and if the wall were ever to come down, it would require a divine intervention.

In the Jewish temple, there were clear lines of demarcation between Jews and Gentiles; however, even among the Jews in the inner courts, not all enjoyed complete access to every area. When Jewish worshipers exited the "Court of the Gentiles," they entered the "Court of Women." All Jews could enter into this area, but only the men could go further into the "Court of Israel." Even deeper in the temple area, there was a "Court of Priests" that separated the Jewish laymen and the Jewish priests. Within the "Court of Priests," there was the "Holy Place" and the "Holy of Holies." Within this section, there was a barrier between the priests and the high priest. Only the high priest could enter into the Holy of Holies on the Day of Atonement to offer up sacrifices for the forgiveness of the sins of the entire nation of Israel. Even in the Old Testament center of Jewish worship there were lines between Jew and Gentile, between men and women, between priest and layman, and between high priest and priest.

LET THE WALLS FALL DOWN

All of these barriers were rigidly defined and deeply etched in the minds and hearts of Jewish and Gentile worshipers. However, all of these racial, gender, and religious barriers were brought down with the death of Christ. As He died, the veil that separated the Holy of Holies from all courts was torn from the top to the bottom (Matt 27:51). The symbolism of the veil torn from the top signified that

---

[16] William Barclay, *The Letters to the Galatians and Ephesians,* rev. ed. (Philadelphia: Westminster, 1976), 112.

God is the one who provides intimate access in the Holy of Holies for all those who have placed their trust in Christ. Only in Christ are all of these barriers shattered.

In the early days of our country, the African-Americans worshiped in the balcony while the whites were seated on the main floor of the same church. The African-Americans used separate doors to enter the church, sat in different pews, but still worshiped in the same church building in the same worship service. Following major advances such as the abolition of slavery and the Civil Rights Movement, Christians went from worshiping in separate pews to worshiping in separate churches.[17] Now we have white churches, black churches, Hispanic churches, Asian churches, and a host of other uniracial congregations. Rarely do we see the removal of the dividing wall within the family of God. Jesus instructed His disciples on the night before He died for the sins of all races, "By this all people will know that you are My disciples, if you have love for one another" (John 13:35). There is no greater testimony of our commitment to follow our master than our love for one another regardless of race. The racially divided church does not communicate the love of God to a world in which their institutions are slowly transitioning from segregation to integration while the church is still firmly settled in segregation.[18]

NO FEAR—FREEDOM IS NEAR

All throughout His earthly ministry Jesus consistently crossed barriers. For example, Jesus touched lepers (Mark 1:41); invited the half-breed Samaritans[19] into the believing community (John 4:39–42); ate meals with tax collectors and sinners (Luke 5:27–32); exalted a poor widow as a model of sacrificial giving (Mark 12:41–44); claimed that no one could enter into God's kingdom who did not first become as a

---

[17] See Michael Emerson and Christian Smith, *Divided by Faith* (Oxford: Oxford University Press, 2000), 21–49. Emerson deals with this issue in his second chapter titled, "From Separate Pews to Separate Churches: Evangelical Racial Thought and Practice, 1700–1964."

[18] The best example of the most racially diverse institution is the United States Army. This was accomplished by increasing the supply of qualified minority candidates for officer positions and then aggressively promoting them. The improved racial relations among the military personnel were the necessary means to reach the overarching goal of defending the nation. See Michael O. Emerson with Rodney Woo, *People of the Dream: Multiracial Congregations in the United States* (Princeton: Princeton University Press, 2006), 112–13.

[19] The Samaritan group was the result of the intermarriage of the conquering Assyrians and the defeated northern ten tribes of Israel in 722 BC.

child (Matt 18:1–5); and included women as His key supporters (Luke 8:1–3). Jesus was free from fear and shame when He approached apparent obstacles perceived by sinful humanity. What Jesus started with His life, He finished with His death. When the blood of Christ broke down the dividing wall between the Jews and the Gentiles (Eph 2:13–14), religious, ethnic, cultural, social, economic, gender, and age barriers were also annihilated. The apostle Paul's passion for crossing the same barriers with the gospel is clearly conveyed in Rom 1:16: "For I am not ashamed of the gospel, because it is God's power for salvation to everyone who believes, first to the Jew, and also to the Greek." Fear and shame have no place for those courageous hearts who want to follow Christ in boldly crossing barriers. Once these dividing walls are destroyed, all humanity will then know what it means to be free. We can join in with Dr. Martin Luther King Jr.'s words, "Free at last, free at last. Thank God Almighty, we're free at last."

SUMMARY

You have just completed your first step of a lifelong journey toward racial reconciliation and the preparation for the ultimate worship service vividly portrayed in Rev 7. From this chapter, you now understand that from the very beginning God created each race in His own image (Gen 1:26–27). As a result of sharing the same divine image, we can eagerly anticipate sharing God's salvation (Rev 7). With these two racial bookends, we now know both our origin and destination. The challenge that we presently face is what to do in the interim period while we wait for our final destination. This chapter unveiled both God's ideal and our present reality. There will always be a tension between where we are and where we need to be going. My prayer is that this initial chapter led you to conclude that God's creation is intimately connected to God and to each other. This was God's design from the beginning and God's purpose for the future, but the question continues to emerge as to whether we are going in the same direction as God is leading right now. Wherever you are, my hope is that this journey will take you one step further down the road toward racial reconciliation.

DISCUSSION

1. Reflect on your own history and describe any event, person, church, class, biblical passage, conversation, or set of circumstances that God has used to begin this process of racial reconciliation. In what way has that pivotal point moved you closer to the Rev 7 model? Have you experienced any setbacks or opposition in your journey? If so, describe them.

2. If you could personally begin with one step toward racial reconciliation, where would it be? Would it be to cross the race barrier in an interpersonal relationship? Would it be in the area of a ministry that would bridge the gap between races?

3. If the Rev 7 picture is accurate, how much have you or your church prepared for the final gathering of all nations, tribes, peoples, and tongues around the throne in order to worship the Lamb of God who was slain for the sins of the whole world? Perhaps a better question would be if any preparation was possible, what would be involved in that preparation?

4. After reading Eph 2:13–14, what are some of the walls that need to come down among races? What are you doing to help to bridge the gaps among races? Are there any specific steps you can take to help the reconciliation process along? In what ways is your church or your ministry helping to build walls or tear them down?

5. Read Gen 1:26–27, which describes our original design. Now read 1 John 3:2, which tells us we will be like Jesus when we see Him face to face. As you understand how God originally designed us to be and what is awaiting us in the final day, what part of you truly reflects the image of God? What part in you needs to be discarded and replaced with God's design?

C H A P T E R   2

DARE TO DREAM IN COLOR

"Without revelation people run wild...."(Prov 29:18).

W hen Dr. Martin Luther King Jr. gave his famous "I Have a Dream" speech, he envisioned a time when all people regardless of color or race would integrate into one beloved community of believers. During that racially divisive period of our country's history, his dream was just a dream. A few decades earlier, the Church for the Fellowship of All Peoples, which had been established by Howard Thurman in the early 1940s in San Francisco, had made some headway in the pursuit of this impossible dream.[1] The rest of the country looked at that church as well as other similar attempts and perceived the effort to establish multiracial congregations as a novelty that would simply go away in time. With the beginning of a new millennium, the question persists: Is the multiracial congregation just a dream or can it become an expression of heaven on earth? If this multiracial church movement is from God, then no matter how slow or invisible it may be, God will bring it to fruition. Based on what I have seen and heard (cp. Acts 4:20), I believe the multiracial congregation is the most powerful expression of God's heart for the nations.

---

[1] *United by Faith,* 62–65. In his evaluation of this church, Alton B. Pollard III contended, "The degree of cooperation realized within the congregation caused it to be singled out as an unusual, unique and even 'peculiar' church. And yet this was precisely what caused Thurman so much anguish, because in his estimation it was not Fellowship Church but American Christianity which was the 'peculiar institution'." Alton B. Pollard III, *Mysticism and Social Change: The Social Witness of Howard Thurman* (New York: Peter Lang, 1992), 24. As a multiracial pastor, I consistently receive invitations from African-American pastors' fellowships, Asian pastors' fellowships, and Hispanic pastors' fellowships. At times, the Christian community does not know exactly where a multiracial congregation or pastor fits in the sea of homogeneous churches.

SMALL BEGINNINGS

All throughout Scripture, when God began a new nation or a new movement, He began small, and then it gained momentum over an extended period of time. When God formed the nation of Israel, He started with one individual, Abraham, and then more than 400 years later, Israel emerged from Egypt as a nation. The inception of Christianity began with one Jewish carpenter, and by the time of the Roman emperor Constantine (AD 313), Christianity had become the religion of the entire Roman Empire.

Whenever God makes a seismic spiritual shift in the landscape of humanity, He begins with a small seed. Even the opponents of first-century Christianity admitted the inability of humanity to curtail or capsize a genuine movement of God. Gamaliel, a Jewish teacher of the law in the first century, contended, "I tell you, stay away from these men [apostles of Christ] and leave them alone. For if this plan or this work is of men, it will be overthrown; but if it is of God, you will not be able to overthrow them. You may even be found fighting against God" (Acts 5:38–39). In the same way, if the multiracial church movement is from God and grounded in His Word, there will be no power that can stifle or stop it.

In Jesus' twin parables of the mustard seed and the leaven in Matt 13:31–33, Jesus illustrates the truth of how God and His kingdom work. God always grows His kingdom from small to big, from insignificant to significant, and from invisible to visible. The mustard seed was the smallest known seed of the first century, approximately the size of ground pepper, and could easily be lost under a fingernail. Yet when it was full grown, the seed transforms into a large garden plant. Jesus draws a striking contrast between the smallness of the seed and the greatness of the plant.[2] In the kingdom of God, true spiritual growth often occurs in secrecy, in the darkness of the soil and hidden from the human eye, yet it still grows. In the parable of the leaven, the cook adds a small bit of leaven into a loaf of bread and then it spreads silently and pervasively throughout the entire loaf. God grows His kingdom from smaller to greater and from the inside out. Some of God's most powerful forces are silent, such as leaven, salt, and light.

---

[2] Craig L. Blomberg, *Matthew* (The New American Commentary; Nashville: Broadman, 1992), 220.

The emergence of multiracial congregations may have a small and silent beginning, but genuine movements of God have retained the same pattern established throughout history.

Although the multiracial vision is not entirely visible to the American church at this time, it does not mean that it is not in the process of developing into a movement of sizable proportions. The racial reconciliation within churches and society that Dr. King perceived to be a dream can only become a living reality with reliance upon the revelation that is God's Word. The importance of having a vision is evident from Jewish wisdom literature. The writer of Proverbs contended, "Without revelation people run wild" (Prov 29:18). Other translations of this verse include: "Where there is no vision, people will cast off restraint"[3] or "wander aimlessly" or "run wild or out of control."[4] Without relying upon the revelation that God has provided, the church will engage in much activity without going in any definitive direction, even to the point of running wild. The people of Israel demonstrated this running out of control during the time of the judges when "everyone did whatever he wanted" (Judg 21:25). Although the twenty-first-century church produces much religious activity, there is a question whether any progress is being made in the area of reaching all nations, people groups, tongues, and tribes. We are more segregated in our services now than we were prior to the abolition of slavery.[5] History teaches us that without the intervention of God, we do not get better over a period of time, but we return to our selfish ways doing what is right in our own eyes. God has given His people a precise vision of their identity. We are made in the image of God (Gen 1:26–27), and we will arrive at our ultimate destination, with all people groups coming around the same throne worshiping the same Christ (Rev 7:9–10). Come dream with us.

THE CALL TO WILCREST

As a result of God placing in my heart the need to become a pastor of a congregation that would reach all people groups, races, and

---

[3] William Wilson, *Wilson's Old Testament Word Studies* (McLean, VA: MacDonald, n.d.), 307–8.

[4] Ludwig Koehler and Walter Baumgartner, *The Hebrew and Aramaic Lexicon of the Old Testament,* ed. and trans. M. E. J. Richardson (Leiden, Netherlands: Koninklijke Brill NV, 2001), 2:970.

[5] *Divided by Faith,* 21–49.

cultures, I was convinced that a Southern Baptist multiracial congregation would call me as their pastor. When the Pastor Search Committee from Wilcrest Baptist Church contacted me, I was so excited because a church from an urban context would obviously be God's answer to my cry. I did the mandatory research into the spiritual dynamics of the church (the infamous Baptist "B's": baptisms, budget, and buildings). What I saw was a church that was smaller than the church where I was serving by approximately one hundred people in Sunday morning worship attendance. Furthermore, I discovered they baptized less than ten people the previous year, while the rural church where I was serving was averaging forty baptisms each year. I thought that was a sign from God not to respond to their inquiries. Yet God exposed my motives of pride, and I then opened myself to an initial interview with the church.

THE INITIAL INTERVIEW

On the weekend of the initial interview, Wilcrest graciously provided for my wife and two sons to come with me. As we drove to the church from the airport, we quickly understood that we were no longer in an all-white rural farming community. The street signs were in both Chinese and English as we passed several strip shopping centers. My heart was so excited that God heard my prayers to place our family in an extremely diverse multiracial setting. When we pulled into the church parking lot, we saw several Chinese people coming in and out of the church facility. However, I eventually discovered the relationship between the white believers of Wilcrest and the Chinese believers of the Wilcrest mission was nonexistent.

As my family and I returned home, an ominous shadow lurked over my decision for any additional dialogue with Wilcrest. In my mind, I made a commitment never to go to a church that forced the previous pastor to leave or to go to a church that demonstrated any form of prejudice against multiple races. From my perspective, Wilcrest possessed both of these undesirable traits. Incidentally, I desired to receive a confirmation similar to my former church's call to be their pastor. When I walked into the sanctuary of the rural church, I knew immediately that God had called me to that church. My wife and I desired to walk covertly into Wilcrest's sanctuary to sense a similar divine confirmation. However, as we walked into the sanctuary, we looked at each other and were immediately aware of the lack of confirmation. It did not help that on the way back to the Houston airport, our rental car did a complete turn on a slick and wet ramp. My wife screamed as I attempted to regain control of the car, while my three-year-old son quoted, "When I am afraid, I will put my trust in you" (Ps 56:3 NASB) in the back seat. We concluded that the combination of these circumstances was a certain signal from God that we needed to pursue other ministry opportunities.

As much as I wanted to close this door and move on to the next opportunity, there continued to be a spiritual struggle that drove my wife and me to a period of fasting concerning their invitation. Simultaneously, one of the members of the Pastor Search Committee fasted because her spirit also struggled with these developments. As we shared our struggles with one another, my heart became open to take the next step in the interview process. During their interim season between pastors, Wilcrest strongly desired to move in a new direction. I felt the necessity to share my heart and my vision with the entire congregation and not just with the eight members on the Pastor Search Committee. I also needed to hear the hearts of all of the members and see if they were willing to follow what God placed on my heart before any official church-wide vote. We mutually agreed to the coming together of the entire church family for a combined service, meal, and interview.

THE CHURCHWIDE INTERVIEW

On a Saturday in March of 1992, the Pastor Search Committee and my family sensed that God was at work in a definitive way. During the interview period, the church asked a plethora of questions ranging from my leadership style to the role of the pastor's wife. The critical moment came when I shared how I thought God wanted me to lead Wilcrest over the next several years. When I cast the multiracial vision, I gave a detailed description of the process of incorporating all people groups into the body of Christ. I reminded them that God strategically located their ministry right in the midst of one of the most diverse communities in the entire United States and that God wanted to lead them across racial lines and over cultural barriers. If the church as a whole did not want to pursue that direction, then I obviously was not the pastor for them. I will never forget the deep desire that I saw on their faces that reflected their hearts to see God do something that could only be credited to Him. It was as if in one moment, there was a radical transformation from hoping to survive "white flight"[6] to grasping the God of the impossible. The church called for a vote that day, and more than 90 percent of the members voted in favor of calling me as their pastor and pursuing this God-sized dream.

After the vote, one lady came up to me and confessed, "Pastor, I went ahead and voted for you, even though I am prejudiced." Another lady came up and told me that she really felt God called the church to pursue this path for a long time but never had anyone to lead them until now. Another individual was offended at my statement that God called me more to the diverse area around the church than to the church itself. I responded that I had a deep desire for the church within the walls to reflect the potential church outside the church walls.

One key measurement that is often used to determine the effectiveness of the church is whether that particular church reflects the neighborhood surrounding the church. However, I did not want the church merely to reflect the community surrounding the church, but I knew God wanted the church to set the pace and establish the pattern that projects God into the community. When Jesus said the words, "By this all people will know that you are My disciples, if you have love for one another" (John 13:35), I knew our expression of love for one another across racial and cultural lines would announce to the world that God is present and working. This movement would not only announce God's activity but would attract outside observers to come and participate in the converging of races and cultures.

---

[6] "White flight" is when there is an exodus of white people leaving an area due to racial, economical, social, and educational changes. Brad Christerson, Korie L. Edwards, and Michael O. Emerson, *Against All Odds: The Struggle for Racial Integration in Religious Organizations* (New York: New York University Press, 2005), 58–59. For a case study of white flight, see chap. 4, titled, "White Flight or White Flux?" in *Against All Odds,* 58–79.

THE VOICE OF ONE

Since serving as pastor of Wilcrest, an interesting story recently surfaced from the Pastor Search Committee that no one told me during my first ten years here. Initially, they agreed on the policy that the entire committee needed to be in total agreement before they would invite the prospective pastor to come before the church for a final vote. All of the committee actually agreed on another candidate except one member. For some reason she was convinced that the committee needed to go in another direction. The rest of the committee did not receive her conviction with great joy, but reluctantly moved away from that particular candidate and toward interviewing me. During this entire discovery process, God worked with both my family and the Wilcrest family for the upcoming decade of transformation. As the years have gone by, it still amazes me how God prepares so many intricate details in advance for key moments. It appears that God strategically places multiple "Esthers" in our body to speak at decisive moments (see Esth 4:14) in our church's pilgrimage toward becoming a multiracial congregation.

CONFLICT WITH THE NAME "WOO"

During the interview process, a member of the Pastor Search Committee relayed a comment from one of the members of the congregation about my name. He asked if I had ever thought about adding a "d" to my last name so that the church would accept me more readily. The name "Wood" would be much more palatable than the name "Woo." I know this comment came from only one member, but it reflected a hesitation concerning the calling of a Chinese-American pastor to a predominantly white congregation. The concern was great enough to voice the idea to one of the members of the Pastor Search Committee. Furthermore, another member questioned whether Wilcrest's possible calling of this Chinese pastor would result in a mass influx of Chinese people into the church family. He perceived that neither he nor the church would know what to do with all those "different kinds of people." Perhaps I was blessed to have some of this information kept from me initially, but as new information arises, my appreciation increases for what God has done in the body of Wilcrest. When I initially came to Wilcrest, I realized that the name "Woo" once rescued me from being ostracized in an all-black middle school by changing the students' perception of my race. However, now the same name ostracized me from white brothers and sisters in Christ in church.

THE FORMATION OF THE MISSION STATEMENT

The *Experiencing God* study by Henry Blackaby in the fall of 1993 was the spiritual impetus and foundation to seek this God-sized task of becoming a multiracial congregation. The *Experiencing God* study is a thirteen-week workbook that concentrates on knowing and experiencing God in a deep and intimate way.[7] Several key concepts from this study were foundational in moving us from a homogeneous church to a multiracial church. One of these concepts is that God has a right to interrupt you at any time because He is the sovereign God. In fact, it is spiritually impossible to utter the words, "No, Lord," in the same sentence because if God is truly Lord, then our answer is never "No." Blackaby urged the participants to discover where God is working and then join in with Him in this activity (cp. John 5:19–20). Wilcrest understood that God was bringing nations from all over the world and depositing them at our front door step. During our first year at Wilcrest, I discovered that in Alief Independent School District, which is in southwest Houston, there were more than 60 languages spoken at home aside from English. This school district had approximately 32,000 students in 1992–93. Yet in the midst of this enormous diversity, the church staunchly maintained its island of homogeneity. When Wilcrest interacted with the primary theme of the *Experiencing God* study, which encouraged believers to develop a continual love relationship with God, we quickly discovered that the more we fell in love with God, the more we loved the same things and the same people that He loved.

If God was ready to move Wilcrest forward as one people with one call to love the nations, then the entire church needed to capture the God-sized vision for them. Proverbs 29:18 was the rallying Word from God to the church body to join together and move in the same direction toward reaching and incorporating all people groups.

---

[7] Henry Blackaby and Claude V. King, *Experiencing God: Knowing and Doing the Will of God* (Nashville: The Sunday School Board of the Southern Baptist Convention, 1990).

For several years prior to this time, there was only one thing on the church's mind: survival. Several questions controlled the church's decision-making process: Would the church survive the white flight? If the church were forced to change, would the church be radically different than it was presently? What type of leadership was required to turn the church around in a new direction? Would there be so many changes that the church would lose its original identity? Were large-scale changes really necessary? Could the church keep pace with the changes that were occurring in the surrounding neighborhood? What would the worship services be like? Would our church be a white church with other races attending or would it be a minority-led church with whites attending? If other races were incorporated into Wilcrest, could there ever be true fellowship among believers who were so different from one another? If other races were incorporated and given equal standing, would they be able to carry their part of the financial load? These questions had been asked for so long and without any apparent answers; it would take a God-sized movement to change the direction of the church.

The church formed a task force to address the vision of the church with the assistance of the area Baptist association. Through a process of small work groups over a period of several months, the church began to reach a consensus of where God wanted to take this body of believers. A part of this discovery process included random interviews with individuals from our neighborhood near the church facilities. Some of the people from the neighborhood perceived Wilcrest to be a completely Chinese congregation because of the new pastor's name that was posted on the church sign. Many did not even know that there was a church in their neighborhood even though they lived just blocks from the site of the church. The most sobering truth was how different the church within the walls was from the very community the church claimed to reach. Wilcrest had taken great pride in the fact that they were a neighborhood church for predominantly white young couples who had moved out to Alief in the late '60s and '70s. Now the neighborhood was dramatically changed and the church remained the same. It would be extremely difficult to maintain a white church program in a multiracial neighborhood. Something had to change.

This process culminated in a weekend retreat with 51 of our key leaders and members to finalize a vision statement. We felt that many vital elements were nonnegotiable. Through a series of dialogues we strategically reduced the many to the three: (1) a personal relationship with Christ was foundational to everything else we did; (2) we had to be intentionally multiracial; and (3) God had called the church body to become missionaries. An influence on our vision statement's content was the last phrase of Willow Creek Community Church's statement: "to become fully mature followers of Christ." We were going in that direction, but several of our people kept reminding us that we were missionaries on a mission field in Alief. At the retreat, God showed us principles from His Word that became the church's pivotal spiritual marker and the last phrase of our vision statement: Wilcrest Baptist Church is God's multiethnic bridge that draws all people to Jesus Christ, who transforms them from unbelievers to missionaries.

All three of these components were essential in establishing our unique identity as a body of believers strategically located in the midst of a very diverse area while at the same time being connected to Christ. Although Wilcrest is a Southern Baptist church, the initial point of interest and attraction is not the fact that we are Baptist, especially since our area is saturated with individuals of Catholic background or of no religious background at all. Our primary emphasis is having a personal relationship with Christ, and this Christ is for all people groups. Since we have so many people groups in our immediate area, it was very difficult to agree on our common points of interest that would connect each individual to the whole, such as, education, race, culture, age, economic, denomination, and even our expression of worship. Consequently, the only unifying factor that we all had in common was the person of Jesus Christ. This central focus exponentially accelerated our spiritual growth and development as a true body of Christ. We looked at each other, and on the surface there was not much in common, yet on a spiritual level, we all shared one predominant connection, the person of Jesus Christ. Presently, when we look across our congregation with approximately 44 countries represented, there is still not much else we have in common aside from Christ. As the apostle Paul contends, "We who are many are one body in Christ, and individually members of one another" (Rom 12:5). Since our focus was an intimate love relationship with the person of Christ, then we had to model a personal and intimate relationship with one another. In this newly established context and multiracial culture, transparency and openness became our standard and our reality.

The second aspect of the vision statement was that God called us to become intentionally multiracial. We learned through observation and experience that people will gravitate toward those like them. In the same way that Jesus "had to travel through Samaria," Wilcrest had to cross cultural lines. The church felt like the words "had to" (John 4:4) carried a divine mandate and left us with no alternative if we were going to be completely obedient to Christ. It is extremely motivating to get such bold marching orders from our Commander-in-Chief. Consequently, we had two very powerful forces driving the body of Christ to reach out in our community across all racial and cultural lines: (1) *internal*—the call and example of Christ, who permanently resided within each believer; (2) *external*—the expansive spiritual needs in our community. God used both of these elements intermittently and congruently to keep us on the road toward becoming a multiethnic church. I am convinced that God placed a call on many of our people to be a part of a multiracial ministry and congregation. As Paul states, "God's gracious gifts and calling are irrevocable" (Rom 11:29), and God's call to a multiracial ministry is a unique and powerful force. Some of our members attest to the fact that when they now visit homogeneous churches, they feel very uncomfortable and question what is wrong with the church or why our church is so different. There is a profound change that often goes undetected until exposed or tested in a homogeneous church environment or context. To me, this is an accurate and measurable gauge of how much of the Wilcrest vision permeates the lives and hearts of our people.

The final aspect is the one that God added to our hearts and vision at the last possible moment. The task force was about to agree on the goal of our multiracial community as "fully developed followers of Christ," but God injected a slight variation. Throughout all of our dialogues, the passion for missions kept coming to the forefront. Initially, we perceived missions to be a natural overflow of following Christ in a multiracial congregation. However, the task force believed the intentional inclusion of "missions" in our vision statement would accurately express our intense desire to have Wilcrest serve as a home base to reach the world. We knew God would begin to send believers from all over the world to our church body, and these individuals possessed the potential to reach their home countries as missionaries. As these international connections developed over a period of time, our people would then envision the entire global community under one Christ. When we first adopted this vision as a community of believers, we knew that not many have traveled this path. Year after year, the declaration and the implementation of all of our members becoming missionaries accelerated the multiracial process exponentially. In 2001, more than one hundred of our people went on international mission trips, which represented approximately 25 percent of our average worship attendance. Over the last seven years, our church has sent out approximately 225 of our people on international mission trips.

As a result of the establishment of this global vision, an entirely new mind-set began to form in the hearts of our people. In the present context of evangelical churches, there is an extreme emphasis upon church growth and gathering as many members as possible in one location. From our American mind-set, success in church is almost always gauged by how many people a church can incorporate into their system. In sharp contrast, we gauge our success based on how many missionaries we send out from the church body. As believers leave our church because of job relocation, change in schools, purchase of a new home in another area, or even a desire for a different type of ministry, I am confident that the departing missionaries will take the spirit of Wilcrest with them. Many of our believers sense that God commissioned them to homogeneous churches in order to introduce and instill a multiracial heart in their new church context. Some of our transplanted missionaries are now multiracial catalysts by introducing written material, Web sites, testimonies, music, and other resources to spread the multiracial vision.

Our immediate mission field, Alief, is a racially transitional community with a large number of apartment complexes and rental property, so we have many members who only stay for a short time. At times, this mobile and transient nature of our people is frustrating, yet God reminds me of our unique call to keep sending them to other mission fields. My wife, Sasha, has often called Wilcrest the "Stop-and-Go Church" because of the constant turnover. There was a period at the beginning of my ministry at Wilcrest when the church had to grow from 75 to 100 new members each year just to remain the same size. I know our local context is unique from many other churches and ministries, which means that our expression of the call of God may look different. This does not mean that they are wrong and we are right, but we need to be faithful to the biblical call that God has entrusted to us. After 15 years of implementing this vision, I can see why God moved us in this direction. The elements of racial diversity and a transitional community caused many homogeneous churches either to move or to die, yet God used these identical factors as a source of strength and an expression of our unique identity.

SPREADING THE VISION

It is absolutely essential for a church to have a clear biblical vision if they dream this God-sized dream of all the nations coming together for the glory of God. The process of developing our multiracial vision at Wilcrest was painstakingly slow and meticulous, especially transitioning from an all-white congregation. As leaders we can cast a vision for the people, but until they make it their own, it will live or die with the leader. The two key steps that a leader needs to take to transfer the multiracial vision from God to the hearts of the people are: (1) consistently explaining what the Word of God mandates about reaching across racial and cultural lines; and (2) consistently exemplifying a life that has a heart for the nations. From the beginning, our goal was to have as many people as possible to catch the vision and begin to flesh out the details of what that would mean in the life of our congregation and also in their own personal lives. Our goal was to hear what the Samaritan villagers said after responding to the Samaritan woman's report of her encounter with Jesus: "We no longer believe because of what you [the Samaritan woman] said, for we have heard for ourselves and know that this really is the Savior of the world" (John 4:42). The villagers' belief was initially based on what the Samaritan woman had told them about Christ, but now their direct contact with Christ Himself moved them to a new level of belief. In the same way, the congregation can be introduced to the multiracial vision based on what the leader said, but until there is spiritual interaction with God's plan for the nations and it becomes their own, the vision will not spread.

SUMMARY

Throughout the development of the vision, the God-sized dream to embrace all people groups, all nations, all tongues, and all cultures began to become a living reality. When first-time visitors walk into our sanctuary for our worship services, they immediately are taken aback by the presence of so many different races worshiping God in the same place at the same time. Recently, a film group from a Baptist organization did a story on our church. One of the members of the film crew offered two insightful observations. The first one was his amazement at the fact that the different races actually sat together in the worship service. He heard about the multiracial expression of our church and initially assumed that racial groups would sit separately from one another. Secondly, he was shocked that individuals from different racial groups seemed to know and love each other. He noticed as individuals entered the worship service, they would greet and hug each other like family members. The leader of the film group, who was encouraged by the multiracial worship service and the people's interaction, was a white man who had grown up in a Baptist church all of his life. He left the service marveling at what his own eyes had seen. What this film crew observed that day started with a small beginning and a God-sized vision. God never promised us that the fruition of the vision would happen quickly. From the inception of God's design for Wilcrest, our prayer has been that whatever God does, He alone would receive the glory and honor for what happens. There is no other explanation for what we see at Wilcrest except a movement of God.

PRACTICAL APPLICATION

Here are a few guidelines that will help in the process of dreaming a God-sized vision.

1. *Patiently learn God's vision for the church*—Each time God took the initiative in Scripture to reveal Himself to His key leaders, the predominant response was a strong sense of availability and readiness. When the Lord appeared to Abraham in preparation for him to sacrifice his son, Isaac, Abraham responded "Here I

am" (Gen 22:1). When the young Samuel heard the voice of the Lord calling his name with the news of impending judgment to Eli's house and the nation of Israel, he responded with "Here I am" (1 Sam 3:4). Isaiah responded in the same manner when God called out for someone to preach to the rebellious and disobedient house of Israel (Isa 6:8). Although we may know that God has spoken to the church through His Word regarding a plan of action in our ministry situation, that does not necessarily mean that our timing is in sync with His. Given the context of our ministry circumstances, the implementation of God's Word in our church may require a period of waiting. Patience is often necessary. But during such periods it is absolutely imperative for believers to continue seeking the heart of God through the Word of God. For, when God speaks through His Word, we must be ready to transform what He has said into action. For example, when God called Abraham to sacrifice his son, Isaac, "Abraham rose early in the morning and saddled his donkey" (Gen 22:3 NASB).

2. *Act on God's vision as revealed in His Word* —When God speaks to us through His Word regarding a plan of action to implement in our church and community, He does not want us to think about it and get back to Him later. He wants us to take action right at that moment. In the same way, Esther acted right at the moment her uncle Mordecai challenged her with these words, "If you keep silent at this time, liberation and deliverance will come to the Jewish people from another place, but you and your father's house will be destroyed. Who knows, perhaps you have come to the kingdom for such a time as this" (Esth 4:14). God used Esther in the deliverance of the Jews from their enemies because of her immediate response to God's call. In the same way, God calls the church to respond immediately to the call to reach across racial lines in order that the world may see our love for one another and glorify God in heaven.

DISCUSSION

1. What is the vision or the dream for your church or congregation? You and your church may not have a published vision, but what do you believe God wants you to be and to do as an individual

or as a congregation? Does that vision include reaching different races, cultures, or people groups? If your church has already
adopted a vision statement, how can you incorporate reaching
diverse races into your current vision statement?

2. What does the Bible say about reaching beyond our own race?
   Read Matt 28:18–20; John 4:4; Acts 1:8; Rom 1:14–16. What is
   our personal responsibility to ensure that this dream becomes a
   living reality?

3. What are some possible barriers that would inhibit you or your
   church from reaching different people groups in your local
   neighborhood or globally? What are some obstacles that would
   hinder the incorporation of other races into your church? Some
   of these might include necessary leadership changes, changes in
   worship style, which group would control the church or make
   decisions, will we really get along with so little in common, will
   we be able to survive financially, and would we lose our original
   identity? If there are other barriers, list and explain what they
   are and how you might overcome them.

4. If you are a leader casting the multiracial vision to your congregation, what are the two most important steps you can take to
   transfer the vision to the people as a whole? Read John 4:39–42.
   What was the primary reason that the Samaritan villagers' belief
   moved from the Samaritan woman's testimony to their own? In
   assessing your congregation, is the multiracial vision based on
   the leader's belief or their own?

5. Write a personal vision statement for your ministry. This vision
   statement should be biblical, clear, concise, and measurable.
   One measure of success for Wilcrest is how many missionaries
   we send out from the church. As you write this vision statement,
   remember Prov 29:18. Without the revelation of God in His Word,
   you will wander aimlessly throughout your spiritual journey.

6. If you are not clear on what God's vision is for your ministry,
   take time now to meditate on God's Word and ask Him to show
   you. Do not stop until God makes it known to you. Meditate
   on Ps 32:8; Isa 6:8; 65:24; 66:18; Jer 33:3; Acts 10:34–35; Gal
   3:28; Eph 3:20.

C H A P T E R 3

THE BELIEF BEHIND THE BEHAVIOR: A THEOLOGY OF MULTIRACIAL CHURCHES

"There is one body and one Spirit, just as you were called to one hope at your calling; one Lord, one faith, one baptism, one God and Father of all, who is above all and through all and in all" (Eph 4:4–6).

When Wilcrest was transitioning from a homogeneous congregation to a multiracial congregation, several questions surfaced about the biblical theology of the transformation. Some of these included: Is there a difference between a theology of multiracial ministry and a theology of uniracial ministry? Are the biblical guidelines for ministry consistent regardless of race, culture, ethnic group, or nationality? How much of one's belief should affect the desire and commitment to reach across racial lines or incorporate different races into the body of Christ? Is the multiracial model a biblical model? Is the multiracial model just another model that would join the Willow Creek or the Saddleback model? Will this multiracial model just be one alongside the white, black, Asian, and Hispanic models of how to do church? These questions compel us to go back and search the Scriptures and see what God says concerning the theology behind how we minister across racial lines. Much of the multiracial theology that Wilcrest learned was not in a spiritual vacuum or solely in conceptual terms. God showed us His important truths though multiple experiences of trials, failures, adversity, and setbacks. Consequently, the church discovered that if they were to cross racial barriers in order to reach the nations for Christ, they needed a strong theology of multiracial ministry.

THE NEED FOR THEOLOGY

During my first year at Wilcrest, my primary focus was the development of the vision statement on a church-wide scale. At the time of my arrival at Wilcrest, God had already firmly planted the multiethnic vision in my heart. The first three years were spent implementing the vision, which included communicating it and making key changes along the way. While still in the early stages of implementation, I talked with a missionary from Kenya about what would be needed to realize this vision. We both came to the stark realization that all the effort and focus that our church invested in the two most visible aspects of the multiracial vision of worship and leadership could easily be perceived and implemented on a surface level. Initially, I thought that changes in worship and leadership would automatically signify that we were a multiethnic congregation. Hypothetically, within one week, our church could hire one or two nonwhite staff members and our worship leader could make some major adjustments in the songs, dramatic skits, or the reading of Scripture in the upcoming worship service that would project our racial diversity. Even with these superficial changes, however, it would not mean that we were a multiethnic congregation. God showed me that I would have to instruct the body of believers in the area of theology if lasting change was to occur.

I am a strong proponent of the idea that *your beliefs determine your behavior and your behavior reflects your beliefs.* Often when dealing with multiracial issues there are many words of support, interest, and excitement, but rarely is there any systemic transformation unless the change occurs in one's theology. Adjustments in methodology will only result in a superficial gloss of a heart issue and fail to transform our racism and prejudice into reconciliation and unity.

As Bible-believing Christians, we are "people of the Book," implying that we read, know, and practice what the Bible teaches. That same claim forces us to examine our actions and motives according to what the Bible says about reaching across racial lines and fully integrating different cultures into the local church. Most Christians have sought to justify a "separate but equal" practice among local churches in the United States as long as we keep sending missionaries to different countries. This practice allows us to announce and celebrate our support of missions and different cultures, but from a safe and remote distance. International missions served as the basis and heartbeat of Baptists from our inception, but it is inconsistent to reach across racial and ethnic barriers for Christ on the international soil but not in our own backyard. While we want to reach the ends of the earth, we must not fail to reach our Jerusalem.[1] A serious revisiting of Scripture must take place in order to discover and embrace the will of God concerning His heart for the nations. An intentional and accurate theology of multiracial ministry will have a transformational impact with eternal results. A cultural shock awaits many in heaven when all the homogeneous churches converge and notice that there is a multitude of nations who will be worshiping the same God around the same throne wearing the same robes singing the same song for all eternity. Consequently, multiethnic congregations will have a head start in practicing the throne scene of Revelation 7 before arriving in heaven.

THE THEOLOGY OF UNITY

In 1996, God placed on my heart the theme of "Unity in the Midst of Diversity" as the primary focus of everything we would do for that year. On the first Sunday of the year, I conveyed to the church body that over the previous three years we had spoken of multiethnic ministry in concept and principle, but now we could speak to some degree experientially. We had seen, felt, and agonized over this unique expression of ministry across racial lines. We readily saw the new diversity within the church family, but the real question was, "Is true spiritual unity possible, and how does it work?" I emphasized that our differences were becoming more apparent, but our primary connection was also becoming more powerful. Our shared relationship with Jesus Christ overshadowed, overruled, and overwhelmed all other differences. The key biblical passage for that year was Eph 4:1–7, which began with the unity we have in Christ while at the same time celebrating the diversity within the body. God began His creation on the underlying principle of unity and oneness. In Gen 1:26, God said, "Let Us make man in Our image." This one statement indicates that according to God's original plan, every single human being possesses a similar likeness to our Creator. There is only one Creator and one

---

[1] Acts 1:8 is the missionary mandate for all believers to reach all nations in our Jerusalem, Judea, Samaria, and to the rest of the world.

humanity.[2] As the people of Israel were formed to be a kingdom of mediators between a holy God and a fallen humanity, the key verse of the Mosaic covenant was, "The LORD our God, the LORD is One" (Deut 6:4). This was the first verse that all Hebrew children were to memorize in order to be a part of the covenant people. God instilled the truth that the unity of the Godhead could not be divided in the hearts of His people. In fact, the Israelites were distinctive with their strong belief of monotheism in the context of the surrounding nations who practiced polytheism. This foundational belief of oneness was also taught and demonstrated by Jesus and His relationship with the Father. In the Gospel of John, Jesus prayed to His Father, "I have given them the glory You have given Me. May they be one as We are one" (John 17:22). The unity between the Father and Son serves as a basis and a model for the unity that we are to have with the Father and with each other.

THE THEOLOGY OF DIVERSITY

In the midst of the unity of creation and the Godhead, there is also the coexistence of diversity. The diversity of creation adds beauty and cohesiveness to all creation. How beautiful is the rainbow with a multitude of colors rather than only one color! In the New Testament, the apostle Paul instructs his readers that in the midst of our diversity, our unity originates solely from Christ. In Eph 4:1–7, Paul deals with the tension between the unity believers share in Christ and the diversity believers celebrate as the body of Christ. This passage serves as a theological basis for multiracial ministry.

In Eph 4:1, Paul begins by highlighting what each believer has in common in relationship to Jesus Christ with the simple identification, "the prisoner in the Lord." Although each believer is unique and has different gifts, all believers share the same Master. It is important to remember that Paul wrote this epistle from prison with the chains still clinging to his wrists and ankles. Yet the imprisoned apostle called himself "the prisoner in the Lord," for he voluntarily attached himself to his new Master, Jesus Christ. As prisoners of Christ, we no longer belong to our own desires and comforts, but to Christ alone. As slaves of Christ, each believer shares the same Master and the same rela-

---

[2] For a detailed discussion of the unity in creation, see chapter 1.

tional status. We are connected to Christ as our Master and to each other as fellow slaves.

When the first European missionaries to West Africa packed for their voyage, they carried their possessions in coffins. The coffin was a necessary piece of equipment because the majority of the missionaries died within the first two years of their missionary service. Their lives demonstrated a relinquishing of total control to their new Master regardless of the cost, even their own lives. In the same way, regardless of the cost of racial reconciliation, our Master calls us to follow His command to make disciples of all the nations.

The next issue is in the area of obedience. As a result of God calling Paul as a prisoner of the Lord, he walked "worthy of the calling" (Eph 4:1) of his Master. Now the apostle appeals to his readers to follow that same voice of Christ. The term *walk* implies daily movement in response to the leading of our Master.[3] Two truths are revealed by the phrase "the calling you have received": (1) as believers, we have a calling; (2) God is the one who is calling us. Many members unite with our church body due solely to God's call to a multiracial ministry. Since our Master has called us to reach each person regardless of race, then we as His slaves have only one appropriate response: obedience.

PUTTING THEOLOGY INTO PRACTICE

This unity is only experienced through the process of yielding our wills and hearts to the power of another person, Jesus Christ. Apart from releasing ownership of our lives to our new master in total obedience, unity within the body of Christ, especially a multiracial one, would be impossible. Developing unity in a racially diverse context will not occur overnight, but requires time in the implementation. It takes practice. This process is depicted with the words *humility, gentleness, patience,* and *forbearance* (Eph 4:2). All of these words convey the sense of seeing ourselves in the light of Christ.

Humility begins this slow implementation by developing a deep consciousness of our unworthiness before a holy and righteous Christ. The Greeks never used this term favorably, but the life and death of

---

[3] *Exegetical Dictionary of the New Testament*, ed. Horst Balz and Gerhard Schneider (Grand Rapids: Eerdmans, 1990), 3:75.

Christ was clearly clothed with humility (Phil 2:5–8).[4] This attribute lays the essential groundwork in believers as they integrate fully into a multiracial congregation. On a weekly basis, decisions or expressions require each member to sacrifice his or her needs, desires, and agendas. Multiracial worship is one of the critical testing areas in regards to humility, for each culture strongly desires their own unique expressions in worship. Yet when our multiracial congregation gathers, each group is called to sacrifice some part of their culture for the good and well-being of the whole.

The word *gentleness* conveys a "state of powerlessness; inability to forward one's cause; and in every case God either is, does, will, may be expected to, or should come to the rescue."[5] Consequently, believers must acknowledge their powerlessness and yield to the Christ who lives inside of believers of a different race or culture. However, *gentleness* never meant weakness, but implied "the conscious exercise of self-control, exhibiting a conscious choice of gentleness as opposed to the use of power for the purpose of retaliation."[6] The multiracial expression of unity initially creates a difficult challenge for some of our white members, who are called to yield to the Christ in a person who speaks little or no English, who dresses differently, or who is at a different economic or social level. Many of our non-Anglo members are recent converts, and our white members are accustomed to being in the position of providing the help they so desperately need. However, as these new believers mature and are placed in key leadership positions, there is a series of transitions from a white base of power to a multiracial one. The control of the church is no longer in the hands of the white majority, but now permeates across racial lines. The expression of gentleness also implies a grace that accompanies this yielding to the needs of others. Simply yielding will not produce the desired unity, but this yielding must be accompanied by grace. Oftentimes, the yielding takes place because an individual or group was out voted or outnumbered and there remains resentment

---

[4] The word *humility* does not occur in the Greek language before New Testament times since the Greeks did not consider this a virtue. In fact, the Greek philosopher Epictetus listed *humility* as the first among qualities not to be commended. See Harold H. Hoehner, *Ephesians: An Exegetical Commentary* (Grand Rapids: Baker Academic, 2002), 505–06.

[5] John Nolland, *The NIGTC: The Gospel of Matthew* (Grand Rapids: Eerdmans, 2005), 201.

[6] Hoehner, 507.

or a sense of defeat, but God desires that grace be connected to our gentleness.

Patience "makes allowances for others' shortcomings and endures wrong rather than flying into a rage or desiring vengeance."[7] In addition, it embodies the spirit that suffers long without giving up or quitting even in the presence of adversity. Many times, I am tempted to quit and move to a homogeneous church, but God keeps reminding me that His work of reconciliation will take a lifetime. God has not called me or the church to be successful as much as He has called us to be faithful to His call (see 1 Cor 4:2). We are discovering that Wilcrest often attracts people from a variety of cultures and races, but few stay for the duration. The multiethnic congregation initially piques their interest and draws them into the fellowship of believers, but the cost and sacrifice are often too great for them to stay with us. For our people who remain committed throughout the transformation process, *patience* reminds them that this is a lifelong pilgrimage of change, adjustment, and sacrifice.

Finally, *forbearance* is not a "separate quality from *patience,* but an amplification of what patience means."[8] This trait gives other people, especially from a variety of races, permission for their differences and bears with their weaknesses. The body of Christ at Wilcrest gives me great latitude in attempting different methods or approaches in order to experience this God-given vision. Many times I come back to them and report that a new idea was totally ineffective, and their forbearing spirit receives me with grace and gives me permission to try again. This forbearing spirit is desperately needed as various cultures converge in one local body. One of the small items that irritate some of our people is the headsets that our Spanish-speaking members use to hear the translation of the worship services. At times, the listener has the volume turned up so loud that the persons sitting near the headset become distracted. In spite of this audio distraction, several of the Spanish-speaking individuals have responded to the gospel by receiving Christ at the front of the church with their headsets still

---

[7] Peter T. O'Brien, *The Letter to the Ephesians* (Grand Rapids: Eerdmans, 1999), 278. This word describes God's patience with His people, which mandates the manner believers should act with others.

[8] C. Leslie Mitton, *The New Century Bible Commentary: Ephesians* (Grand Rapids: Eerdmans, 1973), 138.

in their ears. Forbearance in a multiracial congregation reaps spiritual and eternal dividends.

In Eph 4:3, Paul reminds the readers of the real possibility of disunity within the Christian community. Ultimately, true spiritual unity comes only from the Holy Spirit. Yet as believers, we are responsible to strive earnestly to make visible this invisible unity we have in Christ. The first-century believers must have grown weary of constantly preserving the unity between Jewish and Gentile believers. In multiracial churches, it is difficult to maintain the unity when there are so many obvious differences and distinctions. *Diligence* requires that we maintain the discipline to continue to cross over cultural and racial barriers regardless of the inconvenience and discomfort. Paul's encouragement to be diligent also implies "that the unity of the Spirit is something that can be lost unless every effort is made to retain it."[9] There are many who start this multiracial journey, but few finish.

The apostle Paul then emphasized the reality of this unity with seven different phrases: *one body, one Spirit, one hope, one Lord, one faith, one baptism*, and *one God* (Eph 4:4–6). *One body* represents one living organism that shares the same energy and the same head, Jesus Christ.[10] When the body follows the head, there will be unity. Although each individual member of the body is different in appearance and function, we are related and dependent upon the others, but ultimately the church body has now become the hands, feet, eyes, and heart of Jesus. All believers possess the same Spirit, who is the agent of regeneration, making spiritual life available to each member.

Paul continues by reminding the congregation of the *one hope* of their calling, which has been extended to both the Jews and the Gentiles to join in the same salvation of God. The next three items express the reality of this unity of the body. The early church shared the same confession of *one Lord* or *Jesus Christ is Lord*. Our expressed allegiance to Jesus Christ outweighs any differences or distinctions among the believers. As followers of Christ, we also share in the same act of trust, *one faith* that has brought us into the body of Christ and connects us to the Lord. There is also the public expression of

---

[9] John Muddiman, *The Epistle to the Ephesians* (New York: Hendrickson, 2001), 180.
[10] *Exegetical Dictionary of the New Testament,* 3:324.

our confession and faith, *one baptism*. We share the same immersion and are baptized in the same name. Paul closes this list by naming the source of our unity, *one God*.

While this unity serves as a basis of our connection with Christ, there is freedom for the diversity of expressions, gifts, and backgrounds. In fact, our unity is enriched by our diversity. In Eph 4:7, Paul tells us that each one of us individually has received a measure of God's grace, thus implying that God's grace is made full as we connect to one another. No member is so perfect and complete without the help of other parts of the body to meet his or her needs. Consequently, we need each other no matter how different we are from one another.

A DIVINE CALLING TO WILCREST

Attached to this theology of unity in the midst of diversity, there is a strong sense that each person who comes to a multiracial congregation must have a call from God. Before any person joins our church from another church, I ask them if they sense God calling them to Wilcrest. The reason this calling is so important is that the connection with Wilcrest will demand a great deal of sacrifice and if this calling is not firm, it would be easy to waver or drop out. In our market-driven church culture that emphasizes the customized church to meet each person's individual needs, Wilcrest stands diametrically opposed to making sure one's "felt needs" are met. Much like Winston Churchill, all we offer our new members is "blood, sweat, and tears." If a person's attraction to Wilcrest is based on our programs or personalities, these items will inevitably change.[11] In addition, the needs a person feels that they presently have may not be the same needs years later. Consequently, only God knows what a person needs now and what a person needs in the future. If God calls a believer to Wilcrest, then God knows that the Wilcrest family and vision will be exactly what is needed.

---

[11] During these last 15 years, many of our key staff and lay leaders have moved. Our music constantly changes. Our ministry programs are continually being revamped or replaced. The racial composition of the congregation fluctuates each year. For example, in 2005, we had people join Wilcrest from 17 different countries.

FURTHER DEVELOPMENT OF THEOLOGY

After developing the theology of unity in the midst of diversity over several years, our church came to another crossroads theologically. As more people groups came into the body of Christ, there was a growing sense of celebrating the diversity of cultures and races while simultaneously experiencing the unity that can only be found in Christ. However, many of the people God sent to our church from across the world expressed their Christianity differently than those who grew up in the United States. At times, the difference was more than language or culture or contrasting worship styles; it seemed to strike right at the heart of those who were in Christ and the role of the church globally. Within American Christianity and some of our members at Wilcrest, there is an element that craves comfort which stands diametrically opposed to the global Christianity flowing into our church from the third world. For example, many of our international Christians have fled from countries that persecute believers for their faith in Christ. Consequently, the convergence of American and global Christianity at Wilcrest created an awkward discomfort.

THEOLOGY OF DISCOMFORT

In 2002, God clearly conveyed to me to call Wilcrest to the "Year of Discomfort." When I announced to the church the upcoming theme during my annual state of the church address, it was met with an overwhelming quietness and disbelief, almost as if to ask, "Why would God purposely call our entire church into a season of discomfort, pain, and suffering?" The focal biblical passage for that year was 2 Cor 12:7–10, when the apostle Paul prayed three times for the Lord to remove the "thorn" from his flesh. After the third petition, God responded with these words: "My grace is sufficient for you, for power is perfected in weakness" (2 Cor 12:9). In the apostle Paul's case, this thorn was not removed in order to instill humility and a sense of dependency upon God. Up until that time, Paul had been a successful and influential church planter and evangelist as the gospel began to spread across the Roman Empire. Yet in 2 Cor, Paul suffered severe attacks on his character while his apostolic leadership was undermined and his love for the believers was called into question. Furthermore, 2 Cor 11 chronicled Paul's multiple discomforts and hardships that he experienced as a result of his ministry and reaching across racial barriers.

Throughout the "Year of Discomfort," God brought to light the necessity of experiencing suffering and hardship if we were going to move to the next dimension of becoming a fully integrated multiracial congregation. The life of Jesus served as the supreme example of living a life of discomfort. The writer of Hebrews reminded us, "Though a Son, He learned obedience from what He suffered" (Heb 5:8). If the perfect Son of God had to learn obedience through suffering, how much more necessary should it be for believers also to experience suffering in order to instill a heart of obedience? All throughout Scripture, the great men and women of God had to endure suffering in fulfilling the call of God on their lives. For example, Joseph spent many years in slavery and in prison before being exalted to second in command to Pharaoh. Furthermore, Moses entered the wilderness as an arrogant murderer, but exited the wilderness 40 years later as a "very humble man, more so than any man on the face of the earth" (Num 12:3).

Throughout this pivotal year God stretched our people in the area of discomfort while at the same time using our influence to make an impact on the nations living right next to us. That year, our choir and drama team presented an Easter pageant. Surprisingly, as a result of this performance, an Afghan family not only saw the performance but went to search for a Bible. They first walked to an area pharmacy but did not find a Bible there. They returned to the church later that afternoon and asked if they could purchase a Bible from the church. In addition, they insisted that the Bible could not have the title "Bible" or "Holy Bible" on the cover for fear that one of their family members might see it. The wife of our worship leader located a youth version of a Bible without any clear religious markings on it and gave it to them. The Afghan family insisted on paying her five dollars for the Bible. After talking with this family, she discovered that the husband and wife had opened their hearts up to Christ and prayed at the service that morning. When asked if someone from the church could visit their home, they quickly responded that if any of their family were to discover that they visited a church or had received a Bible, their lives would then be in danger. She then encouraged them by reminding them that they are now in the United States and they are free to worship whoever and wherever they wanted. Yet they contended that their lives would still be in danger.

Perhaps our perception of discomfort as American believers is really not discomfort in the global scope of Christianity. As God continues to call the church body to embrace and live a life of discomfort, these testimonies serve as a reminder and a motivator to get out of our comfort zone with the gospel of Jesus Christ. To move out of our comfort zone requires intentionality, along with strong encouragement and helpful guidelines. It is difficult to move out of our comfort zone in every area of our lives all at once, so it may prove wise to move out in one area at a time. For example, at the Riverside Church in New York City, Pastor James Forbes espoused the "seventy-five percent" philosophy specifically in the area of the worship service that gives a sense that discomfort should be the norm for every aspect of Christianity. Forbes states:

> A truly diverse congregation where anybody enjoys more than seventy-five percent of what's going on is not thoroughly integrated. So if you're going to be an integrated church you have to be prepared to think, "Hey this is great, I enjoyed at least seventy-five percent of it," because twenty-five percent you should grant for somebody's precious liturgical expression that is probably odious to you; otherwise it's not integrating. So an integrating church is characterized by the need to be content with less than total satisfaction with everything. You have to factor in a willingness to absorb some things that are not dear to you but may be precious to some of those coming in.[12]

If Forbes calls his church to strive for at least a twenty-five-percent discomfort level in a worship service, how much more should the multiracial congregation be ready to experience discomfort in multiple areas. In a recent church advertisement in the Houston area, the flyer encouraged people to come to their church in "comfy shoes" and experience a comfortable church service with a promise that you will relax and enjoy yourself. This typical appeal to attract the religious consumer is where American Christianity has perverted the theology and practice of biblical Christianity. The predominant

---

[12] *United by Faith*, 82.

belief is that a church should meet a person's needs, implement programs that fit the person's schedule and tendencies, and offer a setting that is comfortable and convenient, or else the religious consumer will shop elsewhere. Biblical Christianity reminds us that following Christ and adhering to His words will constantly put us in uncomfortable positions in the midst of this world. Jesus soberly reminded His disciples and us on the night before His crucifixion with His prayer to the Father, "I have given them Your word. The world hated them because they are not of the world, as I am not of the world. I am not praying that You take them out of the world but that You protect them from the evil one" (John 17:14–15). Believers are passing through and this world is not our permanent and eternal home, so we should not become too comfortable with this world and its ways. In the same way, Christ called His disciples to deny themselves, pick up their cross daily, and follow Him (Luke 9:23). Interestingly, Luke recorded that Jesus spoke "to [them] all," indicating that Jesus defined discipleship for all believers at all times. The standard for following Christ has not changed. Striving for comfort while simultaneously attempting to become a multiracial congregation is a contradiction of what a biblical congregation should look like. A multiracial congregation is by nature and definition a place of contrast; this moves us out of our comfort zone and forces us to trust in the God of all peoples.

IMAGES OF MULTIRACIAL CONGREGATIONS

Finally, several pertinent images communicate a clear picture of what a multiracial congregation should look like from a biblical perspective. The first image is *one church*. The Greek word for "church" is *ekklêsia*, which literally means "called out ones."[13] This word gives believers a sense of mission and purpose that aligns with the purpose of God. When the apostle Paul addressed the church at Corinth in 1 Cor 1:2, he perceived them to be one assembly as he called them "God's church at Corinth." Yet, in his depiction of the Corinthian church as "foolish, weak, base, despised," Paul gave the impression of multiple fragments making up the composition of the church. However, as the people of God are gathered together, they are no longer defined by the demarcations of society or arbitrary walls erected by human

---

[13] *Exegetical Dictionary of the New Testament,* 1:411.

leaders, but rather they become a people called out of the world by God. Although our church is made up of believers who are called out of 44 different countries, we are now all called by the same God for a common purpose: becoming missionaries to reach all nations for Jesus Christ in our Jerusalem and beyond. In order to join Wilcrest, it is so vital that each believer understand that there is a calling from God to connect with a multiracial congregation. The church should not look or act or think like the world. The world naturally gravitates toward homogeneous groupings, but God places a call that disrupts and confronts that comfort mentality. To proclaim that we are "one church" and say that we have a black congregation, a Chinese congregation, a Korean congregation, and a Hispanic congregation seem to undermine the biblical understanding of "one church." Either we are or we are not. The Word of God alone determines the guidelines of defining exactly what "one church" means.

The second image is the *body of Christ* (see 1 Cor 12:12–27). The apostle Paul now portrays the believers as different members of the same body. Each member possesses a specific function, but all the members are under the authority and control of one head, Jesus Christ. This is a remarkable contrast that counteracts the world's manner of separating humanity into competing fragments. In a multiracial congregation, this one body manifests itself in a unique unified expression. As a result of becoming a multiracial congregation, we attract many biracial marriages. The biracial marriages serve as a perfect analogy of how the bride of Christ relates to one another and to Christ. On the surface, it would appear that there would be a great disparity between a white and an African-American or between an Asian and a Hispanic. However, the commitment to oneness overrides all the differences. In the same way, the common commitment to Christ by believers from different ethnic groups outweighs any potential racial and ethnic difference that may be present. On a larger scale, I do not believe it projects to the world that the body of Christ is one when each race predominantly worships separately. If one of the parts of the physical body is detached from the other parts, the natural result would be the slow deterioration and ultimately the loss of use of the body part. If the different races persist in the segregation of churches, it would also lead to the deterioration of the body of

Christ or even the loss of that particular part's usefulness to the body as a whole.

The third image is *one family* or "God's household" (see 1 Pet 4:17; Gal 6:10; Eph 2:19–22). The familial terms *brother*, *sister*, *mother*, *father*, *friend*, and *neighbor* are now reinterpreted and redefined by Jesus. As a result of the blood of Christ, all believers are transformed into a new household of reconciliation and solidarity. The community of Christ is the conduit of convergence for the great rivers of humanity. This new relationship to the body of Christ now takes priority over all other human relationships, such as family, race, culture, gender, and nation. Vincent Harding accurately depicts the struggle that nonwhites have experienced in trying to integrate into the white majority by contending:

> For years white America was busy building this house, and then had people from different cultural groups living in yards or shanties around the house. The liberal contribution since the civil rights activity of the 60s has been to say, "We have to open our house and invite these people to come in and stay." But the problem . . . is (it's) still their house. We're still guests.[14]

Wilcrest originally established ethnic mission churches in the early 1980s in order to separate the African-Americans and the Chinese from the primary white congregation. Many reasons were given for this particular strategy of remaining separate but sharing the same facilities. One predominant reason given by our white members was the fact that there were language and culture barriers that were insurmountable. The contention was that the African-Americans and the Chinese would be more comfortable with their own people and style of worship. Furthermore, our white members contended that these distinctive people groups would like to maintain their own separate racial and cultural identity without having to sacrifice who they were by the integration process. However, Dietrich Bonhoeffer contended, "The more genuine and the deeper our community becomes the more will everything between us recede, the more clearly and purely

---

[14] Vincent Harding, "With Drums and Cup: White Myths and Indian Spirituality: An Interview with George Tinker," in *America's Original Sin* (Washington, D.C.: Sojourners, 1995), 133.

will Jesus and His work become the one and only thing that is vital between us."[15]

We discovered that many of our people who were born or grew up in another country now perceive Wilcrest to be their extended and intimate family. Many of our people who immigrated into the United States come from cultures that are family-oriented and until joining their spiritually adopted family at Wilcrest, there was no family connection. The call to be a part of a multiracial church family is a call that places our faith in Christ above any similarities or differences.

The final image is *fellowship* or *koinōnia* (see 1 John 1:3,6–7; Acts 2:44–47; 4:32–35). The word *koine* means "common,"[16] and this form of the Greek language was used by the common person of the first century and was accessible to everyone regardless of their education level. In the same way, the multiracial church encourages participation from every believer regardless of their diverse backgrounds. In the fellowship of a multiracial congregation, not only does each person have access to the same Christ but the multiracial vision calls for substantial and persistent sacrifice and sharing with one another. Among the Native Americans, *koinōnia* is most visibly expressed in a circle, which has no beginning or end and all in the circle are of equal value. One tributary of this image of *koinōnia* is table fellowship. The table of God's community is open to everyone. In fact, this openness was a charge that Jesus' enemies made against Him (Matt 11:19; Luke 7:34). In Jesus' parable of the great banquet, He illustrates the compassion of God and the inclusiveness of His table by inviting even the most unwanted guests (Luke 14:15–24).

Although the primary target of Jesus' earthly ministry was the Jews, Jesus intermittently reached out to the Gentiles at pivotal points in His ministry (see Mark 7:24–30; Luke 7:1–10; John 4; 12:20–26).[17] Jesus' parable of the great banquet reiterated Isaiah's prophecy that the Messiah "will prepare a feast for all the peoples" (Isa 25:6), which stood in sharp contrast to the popular rabbinic understanding of this promised Messianic banquet. For example, the Qumran community contended that all Gentiles and imperfect Jews would be excluded

---

[15] Dietrich Bonhoeffer, *Life Together* (New York: Harper & Row, 1954), 26.
[16] *Exegetical Dictionary of the New Testament*, 2:303.
[17] See Mark 7:24–30; Luke 7:1–10; John 4; 12:20–26.

from this meal.[18] Furthermore, the Jewish *Targum* paraphrased Isaiah's prophecy in the following way:

> Yahweh of hosts will make for all the peoples in this mountain a meal; and though they suppose it an honor, it will be a shame for them, and great plagues, plagues from which they will be unable to escape, plagues whereby they will come to their end.[19]

Yet Jesus rejected the first-century Jewish view of the exclusion of the Gentiles from this final banquet, and reaffirmed Isaiah's prophecy that included all people around His table. In fact, Jesus not only granted the Gentiles a place of honor, but He excluded in shame any Jew who would reject Jesus (see Luke 14:24).

This issue of table fellowship is also depicted in Peter's withdrawal from eating with the Gentiles and Paul's subsequent confrontation of Peter (see Gal 2:11–14). Peter's refusal to eat with the Gentiles was a claim that the new Gentile believers were second class citizens of the kingdom of God. Yet, God's table has no such lines of demarcation, for all have become a part of the family of God through the same faith in Christ.

All of these images originate from the biblical text but also clearly depict how a contemporary multiracial congregation should look and function. These same biblical images often are used to strengthen believers within homogeneous congregations. The belief that we are members of the same body of Christ or that we are members of the same family emphasizes the visible common characteristics of each race. In many instances, people automatically assume that if a black person is searching for a church home then he or she would be directed toward a black church. When a white person is looking for a place to worship, we assume that seeker would feel most comfortable in a white church setting. From the homogeneous perspective, the *koinônia* then becomes what is the common color of skin, the

---

[18] 1QSa 2:11–22 "The Messianic Rule." Isaiah's vision of all nations gathering around the Messiah's banquet table is eliminated. First Enoch 62:1–16 also contends that the Gentiles will be excluded from this great banquet. See *The Old Testament: Pseudepigrapha,* ed. James H. Charlesworth (New York: Doubleday, 1983).

[19] Kenneth E. Bailey, *Poet and Peasant and through Peasant Eyes: A Literary-Cultural Approach to the Parables in Luke* (Grand Rapids: Eerdmans, 1976), 90. The Jewish *Targum* is the Aramaic translation of the Old Testament with commentary on the biblical passages.

common culture, or the common worship style. However, in the biblical context, all of these images emphasize the unity we have in Christ and the diversity that we should celebrate in the unique individual parts of the body of Christ.

SUMMARY

Belief matters! What one believes will ultimately determine how an individual will act and relate to other races. The belief that the church can experience spiritual unity in the midst of racial diversity is foundational to everything a multiracial church does. The common faith in Christ connects all races to the same head of the body, while the diversity within the body reminds each individual part of the unique value of the different members of the body of Christ. As the Godhead is unified, so the body needs to be unified. Yet in the same way that God's creation displays beauty through its striking contrasts, the diversity within the body of Christ emanates the divine splendor of the majesty of God.

Another key element of the theology of multiracial ministry is the role and result of suffering. God uses discomfort to help shape His diverse church into the image of his Son (Rom 8:26–29). There may be different expressions of diversity within a homogeneous congregation, but in a multiracial congregation, the racial diversity is a visible challenge and call to remind us that we are not to be content with a life of comfort. Finally, the Bible offers several images that convey what a multiracial congregation should look like. These include: one church, the body of Christ, one family, and *koinônia*. One's actions spring from belief, while belief is clearly reinforced through one's actions.

DISCUSSION

1. Read Eph 4:1. What are the two key elements that lay the groundwork for developing a theology of unity in the midst of diversity? Which characteristic comes first? Why is the order significant? Of these elements, which is the most challenging for you and why?

2. Read Eph 4:2–3. What are the four traits that Paul urges the believer to practice in order to develop the unity in the body of Christ? Which one of these traits is your strongest and which your weakest? Explain.

3. Read Eph 4:4–6. What are the seven unifying terms that Paul used to depict the "oneness" that we have in Christ? Of these seven, which one best describes your connection to other believers and to Christ? Which one do you think needs further development and why?

4. Read 2 Cor 12:7–10. What level of comfort or discomfort should you feel in your worship experience, in your ministry, in your interaction with other believers? What steps can you take as a believer to ensure that you are in the best position to experience a place of racial discomfort?

5. Which of the four images of multiracial congregations do you most readily identify with and why (one church, body of Christ, one family, fellowship)? Which one of these images creates the greatest challenge to you and your church in becoming a multiracial congregation?

CHAPTER 4

THE BIBLICAL MODEL OF
REPENTANCE FROM RACISM

---

*"...that they should repent and turn to God,
and do works worthy of repentance"(Acts 26:20).*

P roviding the biblical basis for the mandate to reach all nations
without addressing the issue of prejudice and racism would
leave a gaping hole in our spiritual foundation. The overwhelming number of segregated churches in the United States provides ample evidence that American churches have relegated biblical
repentance from racism as nonessential. Because there is such a wide
variety of views on the racial divide, it is necessary to understand that
one's racial background will often determine how the racial problem
is perceived. According to Emerson, many white Americans believe
that "it must be blacks themselves who are to blame. Whether because
they cannot forget the past, are overly sensitive, or incited by black
leaders, blacks exaggerate the problem."[1] However, to ignore that racism is real or to blame the perceived problem on the media or the
minorities allows believers to avoid personal and corporate responsibility for the problem and solution to racism. The first step toward
a solution is to acknowledge there is a racial problem in the United
States and then take the appropriate biblical steps in repentance on
both the individual and the corporate levels.

In the history of evangelical churches in the United States, there
was a painful period of racial schism that needs to be both addressed
and confessed. Any church that envisions becoming a multiracial
congregation must deal with the sin of racism at all levels. I am a
member of the Southern Baptist Convention, which originated from

---

[1] *Divided by Faith*, 82

a group of Baptists in 1845 primarily in defense of slavery. Southern Baptists have struggled with this pivotal and volatile issue of racism. Even though I am a member of a denomination that once advocated racism, as a Southern Baptist pastor, I want to be a part of bridging the gulf between races, healing the impact of racism, and moving to a full integration of all believers regardless of race or culture.

RACIALLY SEPARATED

When I came to Wilcrest, I knew I would be ministering in Alief, a multiracial community. However, this community had not always been multiracial; in fact, the area had taken pride in the fact that it was predominantly white middle and upper class during the late sixties to the mid-eighties. This spirit of separation and racism also filtered into the church. At my initial interview, I made it extremely clear that God gave me a heart and passion to lead a church to become a multiracial congregation, something that church had never seen. A key part of this monumental process of transformation from a homogeneous congregation to a multiracial church would be to repent from the sin of prejudice and racism. Many members in our church family had a love for all the races and cultures and even a desire to reach them for Christ, but the church had not integrated any other races into the body as a whole. In fact, Wilcrest established an African-American mission and a Chinese mission to reach the two most predominant nonwhite racial groups in our immediate area with the gospel. At this time, this was the most common and popular model for one church to reach across racial lines and include different people groups.[2] Although this methodology of church planting possesses strengths, it does raise the question of what exactly the motive is for the establishment of separate racial missions. The predominant answers from Wilcrest members included the issues of language barriers, dramatically different worship styles, and historically different traditions. Many of the members contended that "those people" want to worship with "their own people" in "their own way." If any individual seeks meaning and

---

[2] This approach is known at the "Homogeneous Unit Principle," which advocates the formation of churches and reaching different people by what people have in common. This view contends that the more people have in common, the easier it will be to reach them with the gospel. See C. Peter Wagner, *Our Kind of People: The Ethical Dimensions of Church Growth in America* (Atlanta: John Knox Press, 1979).

belonging, it is more likely they will fill this need in a racially homogeneous congregation. In contrast, the heterogeneous congregations will be far more challenging and less satisfying. Yet, if a congregation is established based on one's level of comfort, there is a strong contradiction to the teachings of Jesus and the practice of the early church.[3] Although, the contemporary church may give lip service to the effect that churches are open to all races, the truth remains that the overwhelming majority of evangelical churches persist in their racially segregated services. Arguably, at the heart of segregation in the United States is racism. Since our church was racially segregated while at the same time located in the racial sea of diversity, we needed to deal with our heart of prejudice with a sense of urgency.

ROAD TO REPENTANCE

The key passage that deals extensively with the issue of repentance is 2 Cor 7:8–11. In the context of 2 Cor, the apostle Paul made a painful visit to the city of Corinth and was publicly insulted by some of the leaders who were calling his apostleship and authority into question. Paul then confronted his opponents, but the church at Corinth did nothing to support the apostle. As a result, Paul sent a harsh letter containing a stern rebuke (2 Cor 7:8) with his representative Titus. Paul felt so uneasy about the turn of events that he set out looking for Titus in order to receive a more rapid response from the church at Corinth. In this encounter, Paul dealt thoroughly with the issues of sorrow and repentance. The church at Corinth was aggressive in ministry, knowledgeable in the Scriptures, confident, but utterly passive in regard to sin. It is apparent that a church like Corinth can have multiple ministries and experience numerical growth but neglect the area of heart repentance. In our contemporary context, churches are growing exponentially and have extensive ministries locally and globally, yet remain predominantly homogeneous in their composition. Because my own denomination was established based primarily on a racial issue, we can no longer allow the historical and religious precedents to set our future course. God's Word calls us to look inwardly.

---

[3] See chapter 3 in the section titled "Theology of Discomfort."

WORLDLY SORROW VERSUS GODLY SORROW

In 2 Cor 7:9–10, Paul contends that sin yields two types of sorrow: (1) worldly sorrow and (2) godly sorrow. Worldly sorrow fashions itself around the guidelines and the pressures of the world, always centered on self. At times, this sorrow expresses itself in tears. For example, in the life of Esau, he desired to inherit the blessing from his father Isaac after selling his birthright for a single meal to his brother Jacob. However, Esau "was rejected because he didn't find any opportunity for repentance, though he sought it with tears" (Heb 12:17). One can outwardly express grief and sorrow with an abundance of tears, but this is not how God gauges sorrow that ultimately leads to repentance. In worldly sorrow, self is the central point. The sorrow does not come as a result of shame and hurt for one's sin or the fact that the sin has grieved God, but because of the painful and unwelcome consequences of sin. When I go to the jails to visit the prisoners, I often find that they have deep sorrow and grief not over their actual offenses or crimes, but more over the fact that they were caught. The person under worldly sorrow feels the failure and consequence of the sin, but not the sin itself. One of the test points would involve responding to this question: "If you were given the chance to do the sin again minus the consequences, would you?"

In the Corinthian passage, Paul clearly states that the sorrow of the world ultimately leads to death. This worldly sorrow produces self-destruction, for the resentment and bitterness will cause internal erosion that will not stop until the person is completely destroyed. Judas is an example of someone who felt remorse for his betrayal of Jesus that led him to his self-destruction, hanging himself in sorrow (see Matt 27:3–5). Many believers cannot distinguish between these types of sorrow because with both of them there is a sense of deep sorrow, but God's Word makes a sharp distinction. On the surface, it may appear that the sorrow that is accompanied with tears and grief would be sufficient, but the examples of Esau and Judas remind us that there is more required than just feeling remorse for what was done. Both of these individuals were in close proximity to God's blessing and presence, yet their external attachment to God's people or to Christ did not produce a godly sorrow. It is not enough

for church leaders to cry out in worldly sorrow over their own personal racism or even the church's racism. This alone will not bring
reconciliation and restoration between divided parts of the body of
Christ.

Godly sorrow stands in sharp contrast to worldly sorrow, because
it centers the entire sinner's attention on the holy God.[4] The phrase
"the sorrow that is according *to the will* of God" (2 Cor 7:10a NASB)
establishes the parameters of this sorrow. In this sorrow, the person
sees himself through the eyes of God, just as the repentant King
David did in his prayer of confession, "Against You—You alone—I
have sinned" (Ps 51:4). Godly sorrow will ultimately lead to salvation away from oneself and into the rescuing hands of God. A good
analogy to help understand the difference between worldly sorrow
and godly sorrow is the situation in which two people are having cof-
fee and one accidentally spills the cup on the other person. Worldly
sorrow will say, "I am sorry. I am so clumsy. I cannot believe I did
this! I am an awful person!" On the other hand, godly sorrow will
say, "Here are some napkins. I will get the table cleaned up, and
please let me pay the cleaning bill." One sorrow focuses on self and
will berate self, but godly sorrow will focus on the pain caused to
the other and will take steps to make the situation right in God's eyes
and the person who was hurt. The sin of racism is not targeted exclusively at different races, but the God who made all races in His own
image. It is ultimately against the Christ who ". . . is our peace, who
made both groups [Jews and Gentiles] one and tore down the dividing wall of hostility" (Eph 2:14). Christ adds, "Truly I say to you, to
the extent that you did it to one of these brothers of Mine, *even* the
least *of them*, you did it to Me" (Matt 25:40 NASB). Racism goes
against God's perfect plan for all the nations to gather at His throne
and offer up praises simultaneously toward the Lamb who provided
salvation to all people groups (Rev 7:9–17). When we realize that
we break the heart of God with our racism and prejudice, then we
are in position to repent and be restored to fellowship with God and
the body of Christ.

---

[4] Scott J. Hafemann describes "godly sorrow" as missing out on God. See *2 Corinthians,* The NIV Application Commentary (Grand Rapids: Zondervan, 2000), 312.

REPENTANCE WITH REGRET VERSUS
REPENTANCE WITHOUT REGRET

In the same way that sin yields two types of sorrow, worldly sorrow and godly sorrow, godly sorrow yields two types of repentance, *repentance with regret* and *repentance without regret*. The *repentance with regret* is most clearly seen in the life of King Saul after the battle with the Amalekites in which he failed to follow the instructions of the Lord completely. After being confronted by the prophet Samuel, Saul said, "I have sinned. Please honor me now before the elders of my people and before Israel" (1 Sam 15:30). He knew he had sinned, yet he attempted to save face before the people whom he served as their leader. Saul went partially down the road of repentance, but there was not a complete turning toward God. It is as if he repented, but there was a hesitation or a condition that was attached with his repentance. Saul still longed for human honor. At Wilcrest, we have people who have verbally confessed their sin of prejudice and racism, yet it does not carry over into every aspect of their lives. They may worship at a multiracial congregation, but they refuse to enlarge their circle of friends beyond their own race or they are alarmed when their child begins to date another believer from a different race. They are moving in the multiracial direction, but they are intermittently distracted or drawn back to a uniracial mind-set.

Repentance without regret means there is no looking back or change of mind or any regrets once an individual repents.[5] The same phrase, "without regret," is used in Rom 11:29 in reference to the gifts and the calling of God that cannot be changed or altered once they have been issued. Both King David and the apostle Peter demonstrated this type of repentance and proved it with their subsequent actions. King David willingly accepted the punishment that God gave him while Peter moved from his cowardly denials to his courageous public alignment with Christ on the day of Pentecost. Repentance without regret involves hating what once was loved and cherished and consistently moving in a new direction. In the area of racism, this means that once you move in the direction of reconciliation, there can be no turning back. The words of Jesus ring true: "No one who puts

---

[5] Paul Barnett, *The Second Epistle to the Corinthians* (Grand Rapids: Eerdmans, 1997), 376.

his hand to the plow and looks back is fit for the kingdom of God"
(Luke 9:62). May this also ring true for racial reconciliation.

The apostle Paul then depicts the seven marks of true biblical
repentance in 2 Cor 7:11. Yet before the marks can be understood, the
word *repentance* must be defined. There are two facets of repentance:
(1) the negative element involves a turning away from sin and fleeing
in the opposite direction, and (2) the positive element involves turning to God and yielding to His rule and reign in every area, but specifically the area in which the sin was committed. Repentance involves
a choice on the believer's part that is in response to God's work.[6] God
will do His part; therefore, we must do ours.

Why such an enormous emphasis and priority on repentance?
When the pages of the Old Testament closed with the writing of the
book of Malachi in approximately 460–430 BC, there was not a fresh
word from God until the arrival of John the Baptist. In Matt 3:2, the
first words that come from John the Baptist, the forerunner of Jesus,
are "Repent, because the kingdom of heaven has come near!" The
first sermon of Jesus recorded by Mark's Gospel also reflects the high
priority on repentance: "The time is fulfilled, and the kingdom of God
has come near. Repent and believe in the good news!" (Mark 1:15).
As the apostle John depicts the end times in the book of Revelation,
a continual issue is the people's failure to repent. In Rev 16:9, after
God had poured out the fourth bowl of His judgment, John records,
"and they did not repent and give Him glory." Then after the pouring
out of the fifth bowl of God's judgment, John writes, "yet they did
not repent of their actions" (Rev 16:10). If "repent" was the first word
of both Jesus and John the Baptist and the last one issued during the
days of God's final judgment, then it demands a high priority on all
believers between the first and second coming of Jesus.

THE ATMOSPHERE OF REPENTANCE

Repentance usually occurs most effectively in an atmosphere
and proximity of judgment. If circumstances are going well, sinful
individuals usually do not repent. This has been the primary factor
concerning why churches do nothing about the reconciliation process

---

[6] Paul teaches that God is the one who grants repentance when he says, "Perhaps God
will grant them repentance to know the truth" (2 Tim 2:25).

between different races and cultures. In their own separate churches and people groups, believers feel that they have everything they need spiritually such as preaching, worship, fellowship, ordinances, networking, counseling, programs for every age group, yet they fail to see the body of Christ through the eyes of the heavenly Father. As the apostle Paul asked the church at Corinth, "Is Christ divided?" (1 Cor 1:13), might we also ask, "Is Christ divided by race in the American church?" The fact that our churches are functioning and growing numerically does not mean that we are living according to God's design. We often attempt to justify our failure to experience racial and cultural reconciliation by showing our growth and diverse ministries, programs, mission trips, giving, buildings, staffing, community involvement, and doctrinal integrity.

The racial divide in the United States is such a painful and neglected issue that for the homogeneous church to remain silent would invoke God's judgment.[7] Yet if the churches truly repent by the biblical standard, then there must be a turning away from our racism and prejudice and a decisive turning toward God in complete humility and obedience. The church would look extremely different from what it does now. Interestingly, the Hebrew word for repentance is *shuv*, which means "to return."[8] This term mandates a call to return to the Edenic state, where humanity truly reflected the image of God as intended. The rabbis and Jesus understood repentance as becoming more of who God originally purposed humanity and the church to be. Consequently, as the church follows biblical repentance, the body of Christ on this earth would look more and more like the church that is gathered around the throne in Rev 7, where every nation, every tribe, every tongue, and every people are worshiping the same Lord, singing the same song, wearing the same white robe at the same time.

---

[7] The prophet Amos delivered God's message of judgment to Israel concerning a multiplicity of social injustices, e.g., slave trading, cruelty to prisoners of war (Amos 1). The prophet Jeremiah claimed that if he did not speak of God's judgment against Judah for their injustices and acts of disobedience, then "His message becomes a fire burning in my heart, shut up in my bones. I become tired of holding it in, and I cannot prevail" (Jer 20:9). God does not sit passively while social injustice occurs; He calls His people to action. Since God judged His people for their injustices and cruelty against other nations, God's judgment will certainly come against the church that separates His body based on the color of their skin.

[8] Wilson, 350.

SEVEN MARKS OF REPENTANCE

After Paul establishes the prerequisites for repentance, he then enumerates seven distinguishing marks of repentance: "For behold what *earnestness* this very thing, this godly sorrow, has produced in you: what *vindication* of yourselves, what *indignation*, what *fear*, what *longing*, what *zeal*, what *avenging of wrong!*" (2 Cor 7:11 NASB).[9] I want to challenge you to ask the following two questions after you complete the reading of each individual mark: Do I understand the meaning of this mark? Does this mark characterize my repentance? Examine your heart of repentance through this biblical passage.

Earnestness

The first mark of repentance is *earnestness*, which is a zealous and eager pursuit and serious diligence of taking great care to every minute detail of the sin.[10] The antithesis of this mark is a sense of carelessness or indifference to what damage the sin might cause or the agonizing separation that occurs between sinful believer and holy God.[11] When believers are not earnest in repentance, sin still blinds their eyes so they cannot see that God has hidden His face from those who refuse to repent (see Isa 59:1–2). This casual indifference is often evident in our prayers when we superficially and casually ask God to forgive us of all of our sins and assume we will receive immediate forgiveness. Many Christians attach this magical phrase at the conclusion of their prayers in order to ensure that if they have forgotten something or overlooked a sin that they will be covered with this blanket of God's forgiveness. It is best to deal with each sin on an individual basis as a safeguard against overlooking or neglecting integral steps of the repentance process. The most graphic illustration of the failure to repent earnestly of sin is in the church of Corinth itself. Apparently, the church allowed one of its members to have an immoral affair with his stepmother and refused to deal with this situation (1 Cor 5). There was no confrontation, no concern for detail, and no seriousness in regard to the sin that had been committed. Just as the apostle Paul confronted the church in their failure to deal with

---

[9] Italicized words are the author's emphasis.

[10] *Exegetical Dictionary of the New Testament*, 3:267.

[11] Philip E. Hughes, *The Second Epistle to the Corinthians,* NICNT (Grand Rapids: Eerdmans, 1962), 274.

every detail of the sin of immorality within the congregation, God now calls the American church to cover every detail of the sin of racism. Some of these details may include past actions done by churches or denominations corporately, past and persistent attitudes that have divided the races within Christianity, and failure to see the pain that has been inflicted on other believers who are not of the same race.

Vindication

The second mark is *vindication*. This is a translation of the Greek *apologia,* from which we get our English word "apology" or "defense." In this particular scenario, we make our defense not in the context of innocence but in the admission of guilt. Now the repentant one is eager to clear the record and never be accused or charged with the same crime again, thus vindicating or proving their repentance.[12] This action will explain and prove the legitimacy of this repentance that from this moment on, the charge will never be made against the person. As a point of application, how many believers are repeat offenders in the area of one particular sin? Or another question is, "Do you find yourself asking for forgiveness for the same sin repeatedly?" We may call these sins "pet sins." According to this definition, if you continue to do the same sin repeatedly, then true repentance has not occurred. Specifically, the way in which we will vindicate ourselves of racism and prejudice is to act and speak in a manner that we will never be charged with the sin of racism again. One woman at Wilcrest was a major part of the transformation process, yet she admitted that she still struggles on a regular basis with prejudicial thoughts. She admitted that some stereotypical attitudes toward certain people groups still emerge from her past. Yet when the thoughts come now, there is a guard or filter of vindication that will not permit the sin of prejudice to enter undetected or unchallenged. Most of our people still struggle to a certain extent with racial prejudices due to the fact that we are exposed to so many different groups at such an intimate level, but these thoughts now must be confronted with the heart of vindication.

---

[12] Hughes, 274. C. K. Barrett argues that the Corinthians' attempt at clearing themselves of a charge is indicative of their innocence. See Barrett, *The Second Epistle to the Corinthians* (London: Hendrickson, 1973), 212.

Indignation

After believers take every detail of their sin seriously and seek to vindicate themselves by never being charged with that sin again, their perception of sin dramatically changes. This new perspective is evident in the third mark of repentance, *indignation*, which expresses itself as a deep vexation and uneasiness of spirit or a profound displeasure at sin.[13] The truly repentant heart becomes disgusted at the sight or thought of that particular sin. As one sets his heart completely on Christ, the believer loathes the sin that separated him from Christ initially. This same word is used to describe Jesus when the disciples were pushing the children away from Jesus and He became *indignant* with them (Mark 10:14). The key question on this mark would be, "Do you repent from sin and invite it back, or do you repel the sin?" "Do you find your heart wishing or longing for the sin, or is there a feeling of disgust at the memory of the sin?" Righteous anger would be a manifestation of this trait as our hearts become like the heart of Christ, seeing sin the way Christ sees sin. All throughout the ministry of Jesus, the Gospel writers repeatedly record the anger of Jesus at the religious leaders for their hypocrisy or their evil motives in their hearts (cp. Mark 3:5; 11:15).

This same righteous anger erupts when there is a trace of prejudice or racism exhibited by any follower of Christ. Instead of laughing when a racist joke is passed along, our spirit should grieve. Our indignation toward racism should be so strong that we would be willing to stand up and say something instead of responding in silence. Many of the members of Wilcrest who have aligned themselves with the vision and heart of the multiracial ministry are now deeply offended when anyone says anything about another people group in a derogatory manner. One of our women formerly referred to a certain race as "those people," but after several years of experiencing a multiethnic church, she confesses that she cannot do that anymore because she now has friends in that people group. She adds that when she sees or meets anyone in that race for the first time, she wants to know them by name. She has vindicated herself from being guilty of grouping every person in a certain race under the category of "those people," to seeking and knowing individuals by name. Now when she hears

---

[13] Linda L. Belleville, *2 Corinthians* (Downers Grove, IL: InterVarsity, 1996), 197.

others do the same thing that she used to do, she becomes angry with a righteous indignation.

Fear

The heart of repentance alters not only our perspective of sin but also of God. This new spiritual sight is characterized by the fourth mark, *fear*.[14] The object of this fear is primarily God and His judgment, since repentance so often occurs in the atmosphere of judgment. The holy fear of God then is transformed into the fear of sin, disloyalty to Christ, grieving the Holy Spirit, and giving the enemy the advantage. The Reformer, John Knox, was known not to fear death or bodily torture, but he was terrified at the prospect of sin. The repentant heart does not act casually in the presence of holy God, but experiences and expresses itself in a profound sense of reverence and a holy awe.[15] This sin finds a safe place to express itself when the "fear of God" factor is removed and replaced by the receptive audience of like-minded individuals. A key issue would be Paul's question: "For am I now trying to win the favor of people, or God? Or am I striving to please people? If I were still trying to please people, I would not be a slave of Christ" (Gal 1:10). Ultimately, each believer will appear before the judgment seat of Christ to give an account for what he has done, good or bad (2 Cor 5:10). Jesus adds that we should not fear the one who is able to kill our body, but "fear Him who has authority to throw people into hell after death" (Luke 12:5). Until one comes face to face with the fear of God, it is difficult to jolt him out of his comfortable sin zone.

Additionally, when God manifests Himself in this way, it is impossible to remain the same. For example, one Sunday morning in 1995, I got up to preach and God would not permit me to open my mouth until I confessed my sin of unbelief and pride. I had my sermon notes in front of me ready to start, and then suddenly the Holy Spirit gripped me in such a way that I felt that if I said one word other than what God wanted me to say, I would not be able to take one more breath. After I stood behind the pulpit for several minutes without

---

[14] We derive our English word *phobia* from this Greek word in 2 Cor 7:11.

[15] Paul uses this term five times in 2 Cor, each time conveying a sense of reverence or respect for God or the apostle Paul (2 Cor 5:11; 7:1,5,11,15). Simon J. Kistemaker, *2 Corinthians* (Grand Rapids: Baker, 1997), 257.

saying a word, I shared with the congregation that I had sinned by not believing that God could make this church what He wanted to be. At that time, there was some resistance to the overall vision and some unrest concerning the rate and methods of change of how we were expressing the vision. For a long time, I had tuned my spiritual acoustics to the voices of men and I had taken my eyes off the power of God. The church graciously forgave me for my sin. Amazingly, right after my confession, several people lined up in the front of the congregation and boldly confessed their sins as well. In that service, there was an unusual sense of the holy presence of God.

Longing

Each of these marks builds on the previous one. Believers must first take their sin seriously to the point of vindicating themselves, then their perspective on sin and the holy God changes. As the believers are turning away from sin and towards God, they begin to understand the intimacy with God that sin severed. As a result, the new heart experiences a *longing*, which is the fifth mark of repentance. The word here does not have an object, but the other two places where the apostle Paul uses this term convey the sense of longing for someone whom he has not seen for a while (cp. Rom 15:23; Phil 4:1). When I was dating my wife during college, we were separated by more than 200 miles. One night after speaking at a church on a Friday night in the area around the college, I decided to try to make it home to see her. Approximately 45 minutes into my journey home to see the love of my life, it started to pour down rain and my windshield wipers did not work. The sane and responsible thing to do was either turn around or pull off the road until it stopped raining. However, I had not seen my fiancée for over two months and there was no obstacle, neither rain nor distance, that would be able to keep me from seeing her face. Consequently, I kept driving with the window down, using my hand as a windshield wiper. In the same way, the repentant heart longs to see the face of Christ, since sin separated us from our first love, thus losing both intimacy and power.[16]

---

[16] This longing signals that the Corinthians want the relationship fully restored. See David Garland, *2 Corinthians* (New American Commentary; Nashville: Broadman, 1999), 357.

The prophet Isaiah described this separation in this way: "But your iniquities have built barriers between you and your God, and your sins have made Him hide His face from you so that He does not listen" (Isa 59:2). After Lot's wife left Sodom and Gomorrah because of an angelic appearance and family pressure, her heart still yearned and longed for her old life. As she turned her face to the place in which her heart was already aligned, God turned her into a pillar of salt. Sin cuts off the connection with God as the psalmist wrote: "If I regard wickedness in my heart, the Lord will not hear" (Ps 66:18 NASB). Consequently, when the intimacy with God has been severed, there is an absence of the joy and peace of God. Yet when one confesses sin and turns wholeheartedly to God, the cleansed sinner now can approach God face-to-face. Jesus states this truth clearly in his Sermon on the Mount: "Blessed are the pure in heart, because they will see God" (Matt 5:8). Seeing God involves seeing His face and enjoying His presence and favor.

When James Darby was called to Wilcrest as our minister to students, his initial vote was a little more than 75 percent in favor of him coming. Over the next several years, several of our members came up to him confessing their prejudice toward blacks and asked him to forgive them. With their repentant heart, now they were able to come face-to-face with James with a clean and pure heart. Prior to their confessions, many of them avoided talking to James, or when they did, they addressed him with anger, arrogance, or prejudice. This new longing produced by repentance will not be satisfied until the pure heart sees the face of Christ.

Zeal

After reconnecting with the person of Christ in intimacy, there is a renewed *zeal*, the sixth mark of repentance. This mark is a deep inward burning and great fervor in attaining purity in our relationship with God. The opposite is apathy and lethargy. After God forgave the sin of those who were present at Pentecost, they "were continually devoting themselves to the apostles' teaching and to fellowship, to the breaking of bread and to prayer" (Acts 2:42 NASB). This devotion is an attitude that persists, and continues steadfastly, allowing nothing to interfere with the completion of the task. Literally the word *devotion* means to "be strong toward,"[17] and that is what happens when authentic repentance occurs. The group at Pentecost heard Peter's call to repentance (Acts 2:38) which produced a zeal and devotion to do what God wanted them to do. In regard to being zealous in our repentance of racism and prejudice, this zealous spirit will provide the fuel to help carry us through the upcoming storms and difficulties of establishing a church that is for all people. What we have discovered is that once the novelty of a multiracial congregation wears off, it is easy to gravitate back toward homogeneous groupings.

In addition, as we grow numerically within each racial group, there is more selection from each culture or racial group to befriend. Some of our members reached out to individuals of different cultures because they had no one else from their own race. However, as each separate racial group grows in number, the temptation increases to return to their own racial group to have their needs met. If true repentance occurs, then there is a continual zeal that will fight off the temptations to go back to homogeneous units and drive each member to reach across multiple racial lines.

Restitution

The final mark of repentance is *restitution*, literally "avenging the wrong" or "making right the wrong."[18] This concept comes from the Old Testament priestly system, the guilt offering and its accompanying restitution for the damage done. Zaccheus demonstrated this mark by making restitution with the people he defrauded by giving them four times in return for the amount he stole from them. Furthermore, Zaccheus also pledged to give half of his possessions to the poor to cover anything else that he might have overlooked (Luke 19:1–10). We are still exploring what this facet of repentance looks like on the individual and the corporate levels. When God began to move in Wilcrest in this area of prejudice and racism, numerous individuals confessed to James Darby and to the church of their racism. Their confession took the form of private conversations with James and before the church during a confessional time. The contents of

---

[17] *Exegetical Dictionary of the New Testament*, ed. Horst Balz and Gerhard Schneider (Grand Rapids: Eerdmans, 1982), 3:172.
[18] *Exegetical Dictionary of the New Testament*, 1:408.

these confessions were personal feelings that the white person had against James individually, but some of these confessions were hateful feelings that the white person had against all blacks. Without a doubt, making personal and corporate confession is a monumental and initial step in the restitution process, but it does not stop there.

We have encouraged those who confess to engage actively in pursuing deep and personal friendships with people from different races. We have incorporated a "Dinner Eight" fellowship that encourages eight individuals from different races to eat in one another's homes on a monthly rotation in order to develop more meaningful relationships with people outside of the framework of Sunday services. There has also been the teaming up of members from different races during mission trips that has been an effective bridge and an expression of restitution. Formerly, Wilcrest established black and Chinese mission churches, separate from the primary white congregation. As an expression of making right our wrong, the church called a Korean children's minister and a black college minister. It is vital for the repentant church to portray and project diversified leadership to the rest of the world so that the God of all the nations would be glorified.

SUMMARY

Believers are often taught that if they can tack on the phrase at the conclusion of their prayers, "Father, forgive me of all my sins," then their relationship with God will immediately be restored. The apostle Paul instructed that prior to true biblical repentance, there must be an expression of "godly sorrow," which focuses on the damage done to God. Racism not only affects individual hearts, families, communities, and races, but ultimately, it is a sin against God (Ps 51:4). This "godly sorrow" will then lead to true repentance, a complete reversal from sin and a turning to God with one's entire heart. The evidence of true repentance is seven-fold, according to 2 Cor 7:11: (1) earnestness, (2) vindication, (3) indignation, (4) fear, (5) longing, (6) zeal, (7) and restitution. Although each of these marks of biblical repentance is distinct, they are not inseparable. True repentance envelops all seven, each one representing a different angle into the whole heart turning to God. For example, it is impossible to display a deep concern for every detail of one's prejudice as seen in one's earnestness without being willing to make right whatever wrong has been done with full restitution. Furthermore, if the repentant heart longs for the presence of Christ that racism had once separated, then one will not welcome segregation but meet racial division with a strong sense of indignation and disgust. When an individual, church, or denomination repents from prejudice and racism, it must do so according to biblical standards. The contemporary church in the United States remains segregated, which strongly suggests that true biblical repentance of racism has not occurred. The first words of John the Baptist and Jesus during their ministries still beckon us: "Repent, because the kingdom of heaven has come near!" (Matt 3:2; 4:17).

DISCUSSION QUESTIONS

1. Define repentance. Why is repentance so important in the biblical story, especially in the ministries of John the Baptist and Jesus?

2. Read 2 Cor 7:9–10. What is the difference between worldly sorrow and godly sorrow? What is the difference between repentance with regret and repentance without regret?

3. Write a brief description of the seven marks of repentance according to 2 Cor 7:11. In dealing with racial reconciliation, which of these marks are the most difficult to exhibit personally? What mark of repentance would be the most challenging to incorporate at your church?

4. If true biblical reconciliation were to happen among races, what do you believe it would look like from each race's perspective? What would the similarities and differences be among the Asians, Hispanics, African-Americans, and Anglos?

5. Do you see yourself playing a role in the racial reconciliation in your church or in your neighborhood? If so, what would that role entail?

CURRENT
REALITY

THE GREAT DIVIDE

---

*"I am obligated both to Greeks and barbarians,
both to the wise and the foolish"(Rom 1:14).*

CURRENT REALITY OF RACIAL DIVISION

There are so many different races, cultures, ethnic groups, and languages. Was that God's original plan? If racial division is by God's design, why are the lines so deep and violent, and where is God in this conflict? If it is not God's intended purpose, what went wrong? These questions are not confined to the United States, which over the last three hundred years has experienced the painful divide between whites and blacks. In the Middle East, wars continue to rage between the Jews and the Arabs. On the continent of Africa, there is a violent history between tribes and neighboring countries. In Europe, their lands have been stained with bloodshed of division for centuries. Divisions have a variety of causes, such as religion, territory, power, politics, money and resources, revenge, and injustice. Throughout history, many of these divisions resulted in war and bloodshed, but there are other rifts that are just as real and painful that are accepted and integrated into our daily existence. In the United States, some of these other lines of demarcation include the North and the South, the west coast and east coast, Republicans and Democrats, citizens and illegal aliens, the rich and the poor, the educated and the uneducated, English-speakers and non-English speakers, the religious and the nonreligious.[1] The great racial divide

---

[1] *Houston Chronicle,* January 27, 2007. The article describes the City Council of Pasadena's proposal of "English only" signs as an official city ordinance. Pasadena is a suburb in southeast Houston, Texas.

74

has tragically seeped into our churches as well. The congregations representing Jesus Christ do not look that different from our segregated society. According to Emerson, approximately 93 percent of our 300,000 religious congregations have at least 80 percent of the majority race.[2] Even after our Civil War and the Civil Rights Movement, the racial division in the United States is a reality. The question that we must ask as believers is whether or not these divisions within our churches, especially along racial lines, are affirmed or denounced by God. Is God silent concerning segregation? Does God convey with clarity that we are to cross racial barriers? We will begin by looking at the initial divide based on language.

THE INITIAL DIVIDE—THE TOWER OF BABEL

Racial tension and division did not begin recently; it has a long and destructive history. However, humanity began with one language. In fact, the writer of Genesis reported this truth that at the beginning of humanity, "the whole earth had the same language and vocabulary" (Gen 11:1). The Hebrew word used for "language" means "speech," and is also used in Isa 19:18, which states, "On that day five cities in the land of Egypt will speak the language of Canaan." Based on these two verses, it is evident that the reference in both of these passages is to spoken languages. The implication in Gen 11:1 is that there was basically one unifying language for all the inhabitants of earth.[3] In fact, the biblical writer emphasized the fact that humanity had one specific language before beginning the narrative in Gen 11:2. The writer apparently wanted the readers to know that the entire earth united using one language before the tower of Babel event. Unfortunately, this linguistic unity was used to further man's desire versus God's. God's purpose for His creation was to fill the earth with His glory (see Num 14:21; Isa 43:7). One way humanity was designed to mirror forth God's triune image was to exist as a multitude of diverse

---

[2] *United by Faith,* 2.

[3] Gordon J. Wenham, *Genesis 1–15,* Word Biblical Commentary (Nashville: Thomas Nelson, 1987), 238. According to Stephen A. Rhodes, the earth's inhabitants were multilingual before the tower of Babel based on Gen 10:5, "From these coastlands of the nations, were separated into their lands, every one according to his language, according to their families, into their nations." Rhodes adds that one of the blessings of creation was "linguistic, familial, and national diversity." *Where the Nations Meet: The Church in a Multicultural World* (Downers Grove, IL: InterVarsity, 1998), 24.

individuals living in complete unity throughout the earth. Ironically, the key verse in this text reveals that they did just the opposite: "Let us make a name for ourselves; otherwise, we will be scattered" (Gen 11:4). Thus the tower of Babel event reveals the depth of humanity's sin as they refused to employ their linguistic unity to exalt God's name and "fill the earth" (Gen 1:28).

Consequently God acted decisively by confusing and mingling their one language so they were unable to understand each other (Gen 11:7). God's purposes were not thwarted by humanity's sin. Instead, His judgment upon them caused them to scatter. The city was then "called Babel, because there the LORD confused the language of the whole earth; and from there the LORD scattered them abroad over the face of the whole earth" (Gen 11:9 NASB). The name "Babel" is possibly derived from a Hebrew word which means "to confuse or to mix."[4] The city of Babylon signified the place where God divided and scattered humanity into different language groups. This was the first recorded separation of humanity based on different languages and the subsequent disbursement of people groups due to sin. Scripture teaches that sin separates and divides us from God (Isa 59:1–2), but it also separates us from each other (Eph 2:13–14). Instead of humanity thriving as a multitude of diverse individuals in unity, Babel gave an outward expression to the inward reality that humanity had become divided by diversity.

As we reflect on our twenty-first-century American context, we may be able to deduce that the division between different languages initially began and continues to exist because of sin and a strong desire for people to make a name for themselves. However, this sin has not thwarted God's purposes. Instead, He has worked all things together to bring about His plan for the fullness of time, namely, to unite all things in Christ for the praise of His glory (Eph 1:9–10,13). God is now at work reconciling a new humanity to Himself and one another. Though we await the full expression of this reconciliation, we are to begin mirroring forth our new image in Christ among all nations. There is no more powerful expression of reconciliation than different races worshiping the same God at the same time in the same place.

---

[4] Wenham, 241. Interestingly "Nimrod," which means "rebel," is credited with the founding of Babylon (Gen 10:8–10).

THE INITIAL RACIAL REUNION—PENTECOST

The divine interruption at Babel pointed forward to humanity's need for a divine reconciliation. That is exactly what happened at Pentecost during the first century, at least 2,000 years after the tower of Babel. Pentecost is one of the three primary pilgrimage feasts in which Jews would travel to Jerusalem from all over the Roman Empire in order to celebrate the harvest and the ingathering of the first fruits. Pentecost was a joyous time that reminded the Jews of God's provision and blessing. Luke recorded the unusual movement and intervention of God that contained both auditory and visual special manifestations during the celebration of Pentecost. There was noise like a rushing and violent wind and tongues that appeared as fire which rested on the 120 believers in the upper room in Jerusalem (Acts 2:2–3). As a result of this divine visit, the believers spoke in many different languages, targeting the Jewish pilgrims who were "Parthians, Medes, Elamites; those who live in Mesopotamia, in Judea and Cappadocia, Pontus and Asia, Phrygia and Pamphylia, Egypt and the parts of Libya near Cyrene; visitors from Rome, both Jews and proselytes, Cretans and Arabs" (Acts 2:9–11). These Jewish visitors from all over the world were astounded because they heard these believers speak to them in their native tongues. The miracle of Pentecost was not only the miracle of the tongue, but it was also the miracle of the ear.[5] After hearing this message from God, this Pentecost audience could have exclaimed, "God speaks my language!"[6] The linguistic connection between the Galilean disciples of Christ and the Jewish pilgrims from all over the Roman Empire served as an impetus for an overwhelming response to the gospel.[7]

Although these pilgrims shared a common Jewish religious background, there were striking cultural and linguistic differences. In one sense Pentecost brought the tower of Babel full circle as the God who scattered people into linguistic fragments was now gathering them into a unified people. However, Pentecost revealed God's plan for humanity was not merely to fix what was broken at Babel. Instead,

---

[5] Eric H. F. Law, *The Wolf Shall Dwell with the Lamb: A Spirituality for Leadership in a Multicultural Community* (St. Louis: Chalice Press, 1993), 46.

[6] William J. Larkin Jr., *Acts* (Downers Grove, IL: InterVarsity, 1995), 51.

[7] Acts 2:41 records that there were approximately 3,000 converted after listening to the apostle Peter's message.

He would use their sin to bring about a more diverse humanity who would be bound in complete harmony through Christ alone. This was His plan for the fullness of time and will be completed at the culmination of all things (Eph 1:9–10; Rev 7). As a result, His excellence is seen more clearly and His name is exalted through the heartfelt praise of all the races. As diversity deepens, more grace and power are needed to sustain humanity in unity. Through this we are invited to marvel at His wisdom that transcends the foolishness of the wise, His grace as He has pardoned the miserable failures of men, and His power to replace racial divides with bonds of love, which flow from His triune being.

As believers in the twenty-first century, we must be moved by a deep desire to see God's name exalted through our lives individually and corporately. This desire will be fueled and shaped by perceiving God's plan for the ages as revealed in Scripture. God began the ages by creating humanity to reflect His triune image. As individuals were unified in diversity, they were to fill the earth and reflect their Creator (Gen 1:26–27). Though they were divided in heart by sin at the fall, they were divided by language at Babel. This was a consequence of the desire to use their linguistic unity to make a name for themselves instead of exalting God's. Consequently, God divided them by their diversity, while simultaneously moving toward His plan for the ages (Gen 11:1–9). In the fullness of time, God reconciled the different cultures and tongues through the blood of Christ and union in the Spirit. This spiritual reality is being worked out among His people as they are being unified in diversity through Christ alone. The converts at Pentecost were the first fruits of the multitude of nations who will be gathered at the great assembly in heaven to exalt the name of God through their heartfelt worship of His excellence. Though God's purposes will not be thwarted, we will miss the joy of glorifying Him in our day if we choose to wait until heaven to rejoice in the rich diversity of God's people and His magnificent plan for the church. When the 44 different nations gather at Wilcrest in worship connected only by their shared faith in Christ, this is the beginning of the fulfillment of the foreordained plan of God.

Since God's desire for humanity to be unified in diversity is clearly revealed from the beginning to the end of biblical revelation, we cannot simultaneously walk according to God's plan and maintain and propagate the racial divide among our churches. It is impossible for believers to eagerly anticipate the racial reunion around the throne of the Lamb in heaven, while advocating racial rifts in our churches here. We cannot attempt to gather around a name that is depicted by the color of our skin while simultaneously detaching ourselves from the name of Christ, the Savior of all people. Pentecost reminds us of God's plan to unite diverse races in Christ long before we arrive at His throne, so that His excellence may be marveled at in our lives and displayed among the nations.

LET THE WALLS FALL DOWN

There is no question that walls between races are real in society, but are there walls between races in our churches? During my initial interview with Wilcrest's Pastor Search Committee in March 1992, we met in the church library. As my wife and I followed the committee through the foyer, my heart exploded with excitement when I saw several Chinese people walking right by us. I initially thought I had finally found the multiethnic church of my dreams, both whites and Chinese in the same community of believers. I did not care how small or how large this church was, I was confident that this kind of church was what God had specifically designed for me!

What appeared on the surface, however, was in no way congruent with stark reality. As we walked through the church foyer, I noticed a deafening silence between the Pastor Search Committee and the Chinese individuals passing by us. As soon as we sat down in the library, I asked the committee members what kind of relationship the primary Anglo congregation had with the Chinese mission congregation meeting in the same facilities. Hesitantly, they informed me that there was not an intimate or interactive relationship between the Chinese mission and the sponsoring white church. In fact, only the former pastor communicated with the Chinese mission, and eventually the church wanted the Chinese to find their own facilities. Although Wilcrest was located in a racially diverse neighborhood, the walls between races, even in the foyer of the church, were pronounced. The silence in the church foyer that evening was from both racial groups. Whatever message was sent to keep the walls up, both racial groups understood it and accepted the racial parameters. Later, I discovered that the Chinese and African-American missions were established by Wilcrest in order to give each ethnic group their own place to worship and to keep these groups separate from the primary white congregation. On the surface, this format of sponsoring multiple mission churches gave the impression that Wilcrest had a heart for missions, yet it was disturbing that the different races would not worship in the same service together.

How long has this racial divide existed in churches in the United States? Historically, every evangelical church in the United States during the mid-1800s experienced some divide over the slavery issue. In 1845, the Baptists in the South seceded from the Baptists in the North and formed the Southern Baptist Convention. Earlier, in 1816, the African Methodist Episcopal Church (AME) was formed by Richard Allen. The Methodist Episcopal Church split in 1844 specifically over the slavery issue. In 1837 and again in 1857, the Presbyterian Church divided as well. In 1865, when the Civil War ended, there was an overwhelming black flight from white and biracial churches.[8] The Congregationalists attempted to stand against the flow of segregation, but finally succumbed to the overwhelming flood of pressure in the early 1880s. Even the small number of blacks in the Roman Catholic Church sought a racial refuge in the newly formed black Protestant churches.[9] If we as evangelical believers are to bridge the great racial divide that not only existed during biblical times, but also throughout the entire history of the United States, we must carefully consider how Christ and the early church took intentional and deliberate steps to bring down the dividing walls between different racial groups.

JESUS REACHES ACROSS THE SAMARITAN WALL

One of the first racial walls that Jesus reached across in His earthly ministry was with the Samaritans. This group of people initially emerged from the intermarriage between the conquering Assyrians and the Northern Kingdom Jews in the eighth century BC. Based on the influx of a foreign people group and their subsequent intermar-

---

[8] David Reimers, *White Protestantism and the Negro* (New York: Oxford University Press, 1965), 31–35. Reimers describes the black flight from the Southern Baptists, Methodists, Presbyterians, and Episcopalians, and the establishment of segregated churches and denominations.

[9] For an overview of how the churches split after the Civil War, see Emerson, *United by Faith*, 52–53.

riage with the Israelites of the North, the Southern Kingdom's orthodox Jews refused to allow the Samaritans to worship in the temple
in Jerusalem. Consequently, the Samaritans built a rival temple on
Mount Gerazim. This racial divide reached a peak in 380 BC with the
"Samaritan Schism,"[10] but maintained its momentum during the ministry of Jesus to such an extent that John recorded, "For Jews do not
associate with Samaritans" (John 4:9). It is insightful that the phrase
"do not associate" is equivalent to our phrase "are not synchronized."
There were no interaction, no connection, and no meshing between
the Jews and the Samaritans.

DIVINE MANDATE

The Samaritans lived in the province of Samaria, which was
located between Judea in the south and Galilee in the north. The
direct route through Samaria from Jerusalem to Galilee was a three-
day journey, but it was not the usual route for most Jews on their way
home from worshiping at the temple. They opted to cross the Jordan
just on the northern tip of Judea, bypass Samaria to the west, and
then cross back over the Jordan in the province of Galilee, a six-day
journey.[11] Interestingly, John records that Jesus "had to travel through
Samaria," which conveyed that Jesus was under compulsion or under
divine constraint; for it was under the guidance of the Father's will that
Jesus went to offer living water to the Samaritans. The divine mandate meant there was no other option for Jesus except to go through
Samaria. In addition, Jesus was weary, exhausted, tired, and hungry
because He walked north from Judea, approximately 42 miles. In
spite of this exhausting journey, Jesus reached this Samaritan woman
with the gospel across racial, religious, and gender barriers.

SIX APPEALS TO THE SAMARITAN WOMAN

In crossing this seemingly impossible racial barrier which had
existed for more than 700 years, Jesus utilizes six different appeals
with the Samaritan woman. The first appeal comes from Jesus' compassion and willingness to place Himself in a position of need. He

---

[10] D. A. Carson, *The Gospel according to John* (Grand Rapids: Eerdmans, 1991), 216.
[11] Gary M. Burge, *John,* The NIV Application Commentary (Grand Rapids: Zondervan, 2000), 140.

politely asks her, "Give me a drink." The Jewish Jesus gained admission to her Samaritan soul by asking her to do Him a favor to meet a basic need in His life. In reaching across racial lines, it is vital not to approach a person of another race with a sense of superiority. Jesus, with His rich Jewish heritage, humbles Himself by asking this ostracized woman for something that He does not have, a drink of water. This simple request seeks to disarm the common prejudices between Jewish men and Samaritan women.[12] Her initial response to Jesus' unexpected request reveals her attempt to distance herself from this Jewish man by quickly identifying herself as a Samaritan woman. It is as if she asks, "What are you doing? Do you not know who I am? Are you that blind? Don't you know the rules that Jews and Samaritans do not synchronize?" However, her racial paradigm does not derail Jesus' search for a connection with her heart.

Jesus then makes His second appeal to her curiosity by asking her if she knows or realizes that His offer is for living water. She sarcastically responds to Jesus' inference that He has nothing to draw to get the water, clearly focusing on the physical aspects of the water and missing His spiritual offer of eternal life.[13] In spite of her deflections, Jesus persists by appealing to her spiritual thirst. He draws a contrast between the well of Jacob and the well of Jesus. The former is unsatisfying and would run dry, while the latter would quench her spiritual thirst and never run dry. Every human being, regardless of race or culture, understands physical thirst. Jesus draws a parallel between her daily physical thirst that can be satisfied temporarily with water, and her spiritual thirst that can only be satisfied with the living water supplied by Jesus Himself. Yet her physical eyes refuse to see the spiritual source of living water standing right in front of her. In reaching this Samaritan woman, Jesus' model encourages us to locate the strongest spiritual thirst that would transcend all racial barriers, the need for Christ.

Now in the midst of a growing dialogue, Jesus then appeals to her family connection by commanding her, "Go, call your husband, and

---

[12] There was a popular Jewish sentiment that the daughters of Samaritans were "menstruants from their cradle" and therefore perpetually in a state of ceremonial uncleanness. See D. A. Carson, *The Gospel according to John* (Grand Rapids: Eerdmans, 1991), 217–18.

[13] Gerald L. Borchert, *John 1–11* (The New American Commentary; Nashville: Broadman and Holman, 1996), 203–4.

come here." Jesus hopes to startle her into an awareness of her need for a spiritual connection with the heavenly Father and with spiritual family. Jesus' principle of finding a point of contact in the area of family attempts to disarm another rigid racial barrier in His pursuit of her heart. However, the Samaritan woman concisely responds, "I have no husband." She does not volunteer any further details, but the desperate condition of her life is about to be in the open.

Although the Samaritan woman seeks to curtail her conversation with Jesus, family remains a viable conduit in reaching across racial lines. As immigrant believers incorporate into the Wilcrest family, they contend that their sense of detachment or loss of their blood family is replenished by their new spiritual brothers and sisters. In fact, showing interest and a willingness to connect as a spiritual family member has often permitted our church to enter arenas that were not on our radar. For example, a Nigerian woman whom we adopted into our Wilcrest family eventually led a mission trip with her spiritual family to minister to her physical family in her home village in a predominantly Muslim territory, just as the Samaritan woman went to her home village.

In his fifth appeal, Jesus targets her conscience. Jesus does not approach her with the moral question until He engages her in dialogue over a period of time by first gaining her attention and interest. It seems that Jesus strikes a vital nerve and she immediately deflects attention off of herself and onto a controversial religious issue of the day: where Jews and Samaritans should worship. Interestingly, Jesus does not ignore her question, but uses her worship question as a bridge to continue His progress to her heart. Finally, Jesus appeals to her to make a decision to place her belief and trust in Christ, for the object of worship was far more important than the location of worship. The Samaritan woman responds with somewhat of a delayed commitment, not realizing the full impact of having the Messiah staring her in the face and inviting her to place her trust in Him. Ultimately, Jesus boldly declares who He is to this Samaritan woman, ignoring racial, religious, and gender barriers. The need for salvation stretches across all of humanity. Jesus' interaction with this Samaritan woman gives us some clear guidelines in reaching across seemingly insurmountable barriers.

THE EARLY CHURCH REACHES
ACROSS THE GENTILE WALL

Right before Jesus ascended to heaven, He gave the disciples clear instructions concerning the mandate of crossing racial barriers: "But you will receive power when the Holy Spirit has come upon you, and you will be My witnesses in Jerusalem, in all Judea and Samaria, and to the ends of the earth" (Acts 1:8). The disciples heard the words of Jesus, but they did not yet grasp the difficulty and the resistance that they would face in the implementation of this formidable task. In fact, in spite of Jesus' overt command, all the apostles determined to remain in Jerusalem. Luke recorded an insightful observation concerning the apostles' unwillingness to cross racial lines: "On that day a severe persecution broke out against the church in Jerusalem, and all *except the apostles* were scattered throughout the land of Judea and Samaria" (Acts 8:1).[14] According to God's design, if His followers were not willingly going to reach other people groups, He would motivate them through divine measures.

TWO DIVINE VISIONS

Luke introduced a Gentile centurion stationed in Caesarea by the name of Cornelius who was connected to the Jewish faith as a God-fearer. As a God-fearer, he advocated most of the key tenets of Judaism but had not been circumcised.[15] Luke recorded that he was "a devout man and feared God along with his whole household. He did many charitable deeds for the Jewish people and always prayed to God" (Acts 10:2). Although a Gentile, an outsider, he sought to be connected to God regardless of the racial barrier between Jew and Gentile. In his daily prayer, a divine visitor gave Cornelius specific instructions to help him move closer to the Christian faith. While Cornelius received divine directions to where he needed to go, the apostle Peter simultaneously witnessed a divine vision that prepared his heart for his Gentile guest. In his vision, Peter saw both unclean and clean animals descending from the sky with the terse command, "Get up, Peter; kill and eat!" (Acts 10:13). Immediately, Peter objected to breaking his Jewish dietary habits by eating unclean animals. Yet this

---

[14] Author's emphasis.
[15] F. F. Bruce, *The Book of Acts,* NICNT (Grand Rapids: Eerdmans, 1988), 203–4.

vision occurred three consecutive times, reinforcing that God's Word and the mission to include all people took priority over all Jewish traditions.[16] Interestingly, although Peter saw the vision and heard the heavenly voice, he was still greatly perplexed (Acts 10:17). With the arrival of Cornelius's messengers at the front door of the house where Peter was staying in the city of Joppa, God supplied a personal contact and interaction with a Gentile to help Peter understand the necessity of crossing racial barriers with the gospel.

DIVINE INTERSECTION

God prepared the Jewish Peter and the Gentile Cornelius in order for both of them to understand that this salvation is for all people. After hearing Cornelius's servants relate what had happened to him, Peter traveled with them to talk with Cornelius in his home in Caesarea. Peter's entry into a Gentile home was an enormous breach for an orthodox Jew, who focused a great deal on maintaining ceremonial purity by avoiding any contact with Gentiles. Upon Peter's arrival, Cornelius recounted his divine encounter and eagerly awaited Peter's response. Peter then understood that God welcomes all people who come to Him on His terms, showing no partiality to any individual who comes with an open heart (Acts 10:34–35). The phrase translated "show favoritism" literally means "receiving face," which depicted a common practice; when a person greeted a superior, he could not look directly into the face of the superior, but would bow until the superior raised or received the face of the inferior.[17] God accepts and receives all people regardless of social status, color of skin, level of education, or nationality. God does not discriminate between persons, Jew or Gentile. The conversion of Cornelius represented an enormous breakthrough as Christianity began to spread to predominantly Gentile soil. In fact, Cornelius was the first Gentile to receive Christ in his own territory because of an apostle's testimony

---

[16] There were several instances in which Jesus utilized a series of three in order to communicate to Peter's unreceptive or unwilling heart. For example, Jesus woke Peter up three times in the garden of Gethsemane the night before the crucifixion (Matt 26:40–44). In the early morning hours during Jewish trial with the Jewish leaders, Peter denied any knowledge or association with Jesus three times (Matt 26:69–75). In addition, in Jesus' third appearance to His disciples after His resurrection, Jesus commanded Peter three times to feed His sheep (John 21:15–17).

[17] John B. Polhill, *Acts,* The New American Commentary (Nashville: Broadman Press, 1992), 260.

and witness. In the account of the Jewish apostle and the Gentile centurion, God demonstrates that He will go to whatever lengths necessary in order that the gospel may reach receptive hearts. In spite of Peter's initial resistance, God's activity to move Peter's heart proves God's patience with the majority racial group and His passion for the incoming minority group. What may not be visible on one side of the racial divide is that the God of all nations will prepare the hearts of both Jews and Gentiles. At Wilcrest, while God humbled the hearts of the white majority as different races began to infiltrate the church, He also encouraged the hearts of the nonwhites in their understanding that they are full members of the body of Christ.

NEITHER JEW NOR GREEK

In addition to speaking to the apostle Peter, God planted the same vision in the apostle Paul. Paul addressed the three primary walls of division or separation in human existence: racial, social, and gender. In his letter to the Galatians, he confronted and corrected the "Jewish missionaries" who contended that the Gentiles must keep the Jewish law and have faith in Christ in order to experience salvation. Paul asserted that all races were justified by faith in Christ alone, regardless of whether a believer was Jew or Greek, slave or free, male or female (Gal 3:28). When Christ abolished these distinctions, they did not cease to exist. Instead, they would no longer create barriers to fellowship with one another. Thus Christianity realigned the entire worldview of the lines of demarcation that separate people and races from one another.

The key issue in Gal 3:28 is unity in the body of Christ and equality of access to salvation through faith in Christ. Based on the foundational truth, R. B. Hays writes:

> Paul holds forth the vision of community of faith in which all are one in Christ (Gal 2:11–21; 3:26–29). . . . Jews and Gentiles are no longer divided because Christ's death brought us together. Therefore, all manifestations of racial and ethnic divisiveness are betrayals of the "truth of the gospel."[18]

---

[18] R. B. Hays, "The Letter to the Galatians," in L. E. Keck, ed., *The New Interpreter's Bible* (Nashville: Abingdon, 2000), 11:195–96. When Paul alludes to Jesus as the cornerstone in Eph 2:20, this stone joins two separate and distinct walls "without which the walls would never be united and therefore could not stand, so too Jesus unites the separate and

Paul broadened this theological truth that salvation is for all races, by adding the social-cultural term *Scythian*, which was applied to the Barbarian tribes that lived in the Black Sea area (Col 3:11). The Jewish historian Josephus depicts Scythians as "a little better than wild beasts."[19] God's salvation transcends all lines of demarcation, including social, cultural, ethnic, educational, and economic barriers.

THE GREAT DIVIDE IN THE UNITED STATES: BLACK AND WHITE

The great divide between the Jews and the Gentiles in the first century closely parallels the present racial divide between blacks and whites in the United States. According to Andrew Hacker, America is often seen as two separate nations, black and white, surpassing all other lines of demarcation in its intensity and subordination. This affirms the initial assessment of Alexis de Tocqueville concerning America's two principle races: they "are fastened to each other without intermingling."[20] In the same way, the Jews and the Gentiles coexisted but did not interact or cultivate friendships with one another. This is the reason Jesus' interaction with the Samaritan woman and Peter's dialogue with the Gentile Cornelius were so revolutionary. The Jews and Gentiles did not share the same worship places, schools, diet, or values, and strongly discouraged intermarriage.[21] The wall between the Jew and the Gentile pervaded every area of their existence. In the United States, the black-white racial divide also permeates every area of life. In 2000, the average American white family earned $56,442 while the average black family earned $34,192.[22] Hacker also argues that in addition to the inequality in income, there is a disparity in employment opportunities, education, and the perception of crime. In the face of this great divide, Jesus gave His disciples and the early

---

diverse factions of the church." Rhodes, *Where the Nations Meet*, 53. Only in Christ will the different racial groups connect and stand, and without Christ, each race trying to stand on its own will crumble.

[19] Josephus, *Against Apion* 2.269.

[20] Quoted in Andrew Hacker, *Two Nations: Black and White, Separate, Hostile, Unequal* (New York: Scribner, 2003), 18–20.

[21] The number of interracial marriages in the United States has increased tenfold from 1960 to 1998—from 149,000 to 1.4 million. This figure only represents three percent of all marriages, but the numbers seem to be growing. See *Against All Odds*, 166.

[22] Ibid., 111. Emerson adds that the black family has earned approximately 60–65% of what the white family has earned consistently over the last 40 years.

church a divine mandate to bridge the gap that had divided races, ethnic groups, social and economic classes. Dr. Martin Luther King Jr. echoes the New Testament command to cross the barriers and to "love one another" with these words:

> This call for world-wide fellowship that lifts neighborly concern beyond one's tribe, race, class and nation is in reality a call for an all-embracing and unconditional love for all men. This often misunderstood and misinterpreted concept has now become an absolute necessity for the survival of man.... Love is the key that unlocks the door which leads to ultimate reality.[23]

CROSSING THE GREAT DIVIDE

Intermittently some denominations attempted to reach across the racial barriers. In 1995, at the Southern Baptist Convention's annual meeting, there was the first denominational apology from the predominantly white evangelical convention: "We lament and repudiate historic acts of evil such as slavery.... We apologize to all African Americans."[24] This resolution led to the implementation of an annual Racial Reconciliation Sunday in which congregations are urged to offer sermons and Bible studies dealing with racial issues. In fact, there has been dramatic growth in the number of African-American churches who willingly aligned with the Southern Baptist Convention, adding more than 2,700 since 1990. Some of the reasons for this influx include the emphasis on conservative Christian traditions, strong family values, and global missions. The former leader of the North American Mission Board for Southern Baptists, Bob Reccord, contends, "Here's the bottom line, if we're going to spend eternity together, we better learn how to cooperate and learn how to enjoy each other right here."[25]

Undoubtedly, this is a monumental step for Southern Baptists who originally divided over the slavery and race issues in 1845. In this season of reconciliation, there is also a movement for Southern Bap-

---

[23] Martin Luther King Jr. *Where Do We Go from Here: Chaos or Community?* (New York: Harper and Row, 1967), 190.

[24] Amy Green, "Southern Baptist Surprise," *Christianity Today* 48:9 (September 2004): 55.

[25] Ibid., 56.

tists to establish black churches. The aligning of established black churches with the denomination and the planting of black churches does not adequately heal the racial divide. The inclusion of black, Hispanic, and Asian churches in a predominantly white denomination may project a multiracial denomination, but without the integration of different races within the local church, true racial reconciliation has not occurred. Before the Civil War, blacks and whites worshiped in the same churches on different pews; now blacks and whites worship in separate churches in the same denomination. This is not God's pattern established at Pentecost or portrayed around the throne of the Lamb of God in Revelation 7. If all the races are truly going to spend eternity together, it would be a taste of heaven here if believers began to worship together right now on earth.

CROSSING RACIAL BARRIERS LEADS TO CROSSING OTHER BARRIERS

Once Wilcrest began to develop the mind-set to overcome the racial barrier, we began to encounter other barriers that we needed to cross. It would have been inconsistent to contend that we were a multiracial congregation and at the same time establish other divisive parameters on what kind of people came into the church. One of the most difficult barriers that we experienced other than race or culture was that of lifestyle.

While I was playing golf in Houston, I paired up with a young man who worked in one of the prominent strip bars in Houston. Initially he was not aware that I was a pastor. After using excessive foul language throughout the first 16 holes and leading me by two strokes, I decided to implement a strategic move. As he was about to swing on the next to last hole, I enlightened him on the fact that he was playing with a pastor. As a result, he profusely apologized for his language and proceeded to lose total concentration on his golf game and eventually lost the match. After our initial time together, we quickly developed a strong and open relationship, and he opened his life to Christ and began to grow in his faith. One of the first things that he wanted to do was to bring his friends to our church. He told me that they probably could not attend the morning worship services because of their work schedule but could come to our Sunday night services. When he told me he wanted his friends to come, I did not actually think he was referring to his coworkers at the strip club. Subsequently, they came to our worship services without the knowledge of the full range of our unwritten dress code. They were dressed in extremely tight biker shorts and skimpy tank tops, but they came with their whole hearts. One by one they gave their lives to Christ. If we claim that our God and His people will accept and embrace all cultures and races, it would be hypocritical to restrict eager and willing followers of Christ who carry excess baggage. Once our people began to open their eyes to reach people who were different than they were, God begin to send all kinds of people to us.

As a result of the breaking down of the barriers of race, other barriers began to topple as well. One of our deacons suggested that we needed to alter our vision statement to include that we are more than a multiracial bridge, but that we are also a "multieconomic, multisocial, multieducational, multidenominational, and multigenerational bridge . . . and multimental." I simply had to tell him that we did not have enough space on our letterhead or placard in the foyer to put all those variations. Yet what he said was full of insight and truth because once the racial barriers began to crumble, there was a transformation in the hearts of our people that would not stop at the barrier of race. It is amazing that the crossing of such a visible barrier of race would open the floodgates for bridging other chasms.

STRATEGIES TO BRIDGE THE DIVIDE

There are pivotal encounters recorded in Scripture that give us insight into the heart of God and His love for all people. Not only does the Great Commission command all believers to make disciples of all nations (Matt 28:19–20), but the example of Jesus and His apostles lay the groundwork for us to do the same. Sadly many American Christians are content to interpret "make disciples of all nations," as something that missionaries do in other countries or making sure that we provide church buildings here in the United States where they can worship with their own race. Recent studies have shown that our population will no longer be a white majority by AD 2056.[26] We have people from many nations moving in from all over the world, and

---

[26] Leonard Sweet, *FaithQuakes* (Nashville: Abingdon, 1999), 176.

many of these countries are represented in the small southwest section of Houston called Alief. The world is moving in next door.

The New Testament church was somewhat reluctant to reach across racial and geographical lines in order to fulfill the Great Commission of making disciples of all the nations. As a result, God's strategy of moving the church out of its comfort zone entailed a great persecution against the church at Jerusalem. Yet the ones who heard the command of Jesus to cross racial lines were the very ones who refused to move out of their racial comfort zone (Acts 8:1). In addition to permitting persecution, God sent an Ethiopian eunuch to Jerusalem to hear the good news of Jesus Christ. It is insightful that Philip encountered this seeker on the road to Gaza from Jerusalem and not in Ethiopia. At that time, Ethiopians were considered to be living in the ends of the earth.[27] Amazingly, the Great Commission does not reach fulfillment by the apostles going to the ends of the earth, but the ends of the earth, Ethiopia, coming to them. In a similar global movement, the world has moved next door to the church in the United States. The global influx arrived early for the area surrounding Wilcrest, but the entire nation will feel its impact over the next several decades. The response from Wilcrest was to integrate 44 different nations into the body of Christ, thus beginning the fulfillment of the Great Commission. Yet the question remains: what will the church do about the painful divide that presently separates the church in the United States?

SENSE OF URGENCY

The primary racial divide in the United States is between blacks and whites, yet the division among races extends to all racial groups. In the immediate five-mile radius surrounding Wilcrest, there are approximately 70 languages spoken in the home other than English. Racial lines seem to intersect at every street corner near Wilcrest. The street signs near the church are in both English and Chinese. The divisions among races are growing sharper as each minority group becomes larger and more self-sufficient. In our immediate area, an immigrant could bank, shop for groceries, work, go to the movies, and

---

[27] Ajith Fernando, *Acts,* NIV Application Commentary (Grand Rapids: Zondervan, 1998), 283.

go to religious services and never have to speak English or interact with anyone outside his or her culture. Consequently, there is a growing sense of urgency that God gives us a brief opening to call all the races together under the color of Christ, but this moment may quickly pass. Bridging this racial divide takes on a new sense of urgency.

BRIDGING THE RACIAL LEADERSHIP DIVIDE

After my first year at Wilcrest, I was convinced that we needed to make some visible and sizable changes in regard to leadership if we were ever to begin bridging this widening gulf between races.[28] In March 1993, Wilcrest took a decisive faith step in the calling of an African-American minister to students, James Darby. This step not only affirmed our vision statement but it also provided the most visible evidence that we were moving in the multiracial direction. We could repeatedly say, "Wilcrest is a multiethnic bridge." However, until James joined the staff, the first-time visitor would only hear the claim. The words began to become a visual reality. Having a black minister to students in no way categorized our church as multiracial, but it moved us one step further away from being an exclusively homogeneous church.

BRIDGING THE RACIAL DIVIDE WITHIN

From my perspective, I thought this dramatic and bold change in leadership would not only make an enormous impact on our church but also bridge the gap between a white church and the blacks in the surrounding community. This change, however, did not initially alter our inroads to the immediate neighborhood, but calling James did produce a transformation within our community of believers. James explicitly contended that African-Americans would not come to the church based solely on calling an African-American on staff. I did not want to admit this assessment, but it was completely accurate. In my mind, I wanted the simple move of calling a black minister to students to transform Wilcrest suddenly into a racially diverse con-

---

[28] Culmore United Methodist Church in Falls Church, Virginia, attested that the key factor in the first year of institutional change was the church's willingness to incorporate its non-Anglo members into key leadership positions. This church was an all-white church that now has 32 nationalities gathering weekly for worship and ministry. See Rhodes, *Where the Nations Meet,* 93–94.

gregation. I realize now that in order to be a multiracial congregation, the process does not come from an "Affirmative Action" type of
maneuver; rather, it must emerge from the heart of the believer that
is touched by God. In fact, what surprised me most was the change
in the heart of the dominant white group in their interaction with
nonwhites. It was almost as if the relationship the church experienced
with James instructed the church body over a long and painful period
of time to understand believers and leaders of different races. Without
James teaching Wilcrest how to dialogue and follow a leader who
is not the same race as the dominant group in the congregation, we
would still be attempting in vain to add different races on the exterior
without deep and meaningful transformation from within the church.
The multiracial process does not begin on the exterior, but from the
heart of the believer aligning with the God who has a heart for all
people.

Before God instilled a clear multiracial vision in our church, He
needed to remove blinders of prejudice and racism. One of the spiritual barriers that inhibited much of Alief and Wilcrest from personally
experiencing a global community of faith was racism. This mind-set
gave birth to an exclusive isolation from different cultures or groups
other than middle and upper class whites. This racism filtered into the
church, and it was necessary to deal with it openly and with a heart
of repentance. The arrival of James as our minister to students challenged this exclusive mind-set every Sunday with his presence.

The racial divide had been evident in our area for decades. So
many people moved into Alief in the late 1960s and 1970s for the
excellent school district and the homogeneous makeup of the community. However, after the oil bust in Houston in the early 1980s, the
demographics around Wilcrest began to change dramatically. Many
whites began to move further west and southwest of Houston in order
to settle in more homogeneous schools, neighborhoods, and even
churches. Many who moved cited safety and education as the primary
reasons for their flight from Alief. As the white flight occurred, there
was an infusion of all kinds of people groups into Alief. A combination of the construction of several affordable apartment complexes
and the arrival of the Metro Bus routes to Alief encouraged many of
those living in the inner city to move out to Alief. In addition to those
who moved from the inner city, many immigrants began to settle in

Alief. In our area, we have the highest concentration of Chinese and Vietnamese in all of Houston. As fast as the immigrants and other people groups were moving in, the whites were moving out. In 1993, the statistics for Alief Independent School District demonstrated that approximately 50 percent of all the students were white and the other 50 percent were equally divided among the three major groups: Hispanics, African-Americans, and Asians. However, in 2002 there was a dramatic reduction in the number of white students in Alief schools, from 50 to 15 percent. In 2009, the process of white flight steadily continues in Alief, with the white students representing less than 6 percent of all Alief students.

COUNTRY CLUB VERSUS EMERGENCY ROOM

In bridging the enormous racial divide, we also needed a seismic shift in the way we perceived people as they came to our church. From the very outset of the implementation of this vision, I always wanted to instill a mind-set that our church is not a country club but an emergency room or an ICU ward. We assume that each person whom God sends to Wilcrest is in spiritual need regardless of the exterior cover or color. In an emergency room, the physical need takes precedence over any other characteristic that an individual possesses. In the same way, our church must consider the spiritual need of the individual over and above any other trait. In order to develop this mind-set, it is vital that we continually develop a keen spiritual vision that enables us to see and meet the need of the person who comes to Wilcrest. In addition, in the emergency room there is always a sense of urgency that a life may be hanging in the balance. In the same way, there are so many who come to our church in order to have their needs met immediately and then we never see them again. Wilcrest often attends to their pressing needs in order to get them back on their feet spiritually and send them on their way.

Wilcrest is in the midst of an extremely transient community. People pass through Alief for a short period of time. It is not surprising for our church to have 10 or 20 first-time visitors each week, so we often have only one valuable opportunity to make an inroad into their hearts. As a spiritual emergency room, each missionary member is on call and ready to help in any way they can. This abrupt shift in perspective caused some conflict in the fact that we were no longer a social gathering or a place to be seen or a place where your personal needs are the primary focus. The focus is no longer on what the members will receive for themselves, but on how the members can minister to those whom God brings to us in deep spiritual pain. It is impossible to be a missionary in this spiritual emergency room and demand that your needs take top priority over everything else. We have had many people leave the church because "their needs were not met." They came to Wilcrest expecting their needs to be perpetually satisfied but to their dismay saw a radically different paradigm. This shift in focus now attracts those truly in need and those who truly see themselves as missionaries in this unusual "mission field."

APPLICATION

One of the most frequently asked questions is "Do all the members of Wilcrest see themselves as missionaries?" Since the transformation of unbelievers into missionaries is a part of our spiritual DNA, we convey early and often what this looks like in and outside of the church. If their children are on a baseball, basketball, football, soccer, or swim team, we affirm them as missionaries to the players and to the parents on that team. If they are involved in the Parent Teacher Organization or the Citizens on Patrol, then they are the ambassadors to the members of those groups. Our children also see themselves as missionaries to their friends and teammates. Our teachers are also sent out as missionaries to their students, the parents of their students, and to other teachers and administrators. The work place has now become the mission field for Wilcrest missionaries. When God first called Wilcrest to become a multiracial congregation, most of our people were so excited because now they could invite all of their friends, coworkers, and neighbors regardless of the color of their skin. God's missionaries are now bridging the great racial divide. In the same way that God called the Israelites to cross the Red Sea for their freedom from slavery, He called them to cross the Jordan River to enter the promised land. Now He calls us to bridge the racial divide that separates us from one another and from God and enter the promised land of racial reconciliation.

DISCUSSION

1. From the biblical perspective, why are there so many different races and ethnic groups? What did God do to bridge the gap between races in Acts 2? Is it possible that God can do something similar in your church or area like Pentecost?

2. What were some of the racial barriers that Jesus or the disciples encountered in the New Testament? What are some of the racial barriers that you encounter at church, work, school, or in your neighborhood?

3. What are Jesus' six appeals to the Samaritan woman? Of these six, which one of these do you find easiest to implement? Which one of these six appeals is the most difficult for you when you are stepping out of your comfort zone in order to reach a person from a different race?

4. What are some of the things Jesus and the disciples did to bridge the gap between the races? What are some key steps that you or your church can imitate from Jesus and the early church to bridge the racial divide in your area?

5. In addition to the racial barrier, name three other barriers or walls that may be prevalent in your church, area, or city. Are these barriers more difficult than race? What are some possible strategies that you and your church could implement to bridge these barriers?

CHAPTER 6

TO CROSS OR
NOT TO CROSS

"Now you and all the people prepare to cross over the Jordan to the land I am giving the Israelites"(Josh 1:2).

I n Acts 2, God gave believers a taste of what it means to be a part of a racial reunion in the Pentecost event. Although in the spiritual realm, the wall between Jew and Gentile has been broken down in the work of Christ, the spiritual reality of seeing the nations come together needs to become a physical reality. We now are faced with a decision as believers. Do we wait until the second coming of Jesus and allow God to take care of the healing of the nations or do we immediately obey the command of Jesus to reach all nations and to follow His and the early church's example of crossing racial barriers? The question is: do we cross or not cross? To help us determine whether we need to cross this racial barrier, we will look at Israel's two most notable crossings and derive some devotional parallels. The first was the crossing of the Red Sea during the exodus, which liberated them from Egypt, while the second was the crossing of the Jordan, which was their first step into the promised land.

THE CROSSING OF THE RED SEA

After 400 years in slavery to the Egyptians, God called Moses to lead the people of Israel out of Egypt into the promised land. The nation of Israel initially entered Egypt with approximately 70 people under Joseph (Gen 46:27), and by the time of the exodus, they numbered more than two million. The bonds of slavery prevented the Israelites from functioning as a nation; thus their first act as a nation was the exodus. God trained Moses for this daunting task by placing him for 40 years in the royal court of Egypt and 40 years on the back side of the wilderness. God not only prepared Moses, but He also prepared the people of Israel in Egypt through the ten plagues. The final plague, the death of all the firstborn, propelled the people out of the land of Egypt to the edge of the Red Sea. The Lord's plan was not to lead His people directly to safety but to place them in a position in which they were forced to depend upon God and His intervention. When Moses and the people stopped at the water's edge, to the north were several massive Egyptian fortresses, to the south was the barren desert, to the east was the Red Sea, and to the west was the fast-approaching Egyptian army. Militarily speaking, they were in a most vulnerable position. Wedged between the army and the Red Sea, the people of Israel became frightened and cried out to the Lord. They quickly shifted the blame to their leader and accused him of taking them out of their "safe" Egypt. Moses responded with courageous tenacity, "Don't be afraid. Stand firm and see the LORD's salvation He will provide for you today. . . . The LORD will fight for you; you must be quiet" (Exod 14:13–14). The word translated "be quiet" is also translated "be speechless" or "hold your peace."[1] As the Lord miraculously created a path through the Red Sea, the people of Israel were faced with a crisis of decision: to cross or not to cross. The people of the Lord chose to cross what earlier had seemed to be an insurmountable barrier; yet with God's power, not only did they arrive on the other side, but also God destroyed their enemies who were chasing after them in the process.

The crossing of the Red Sea was the gateway to liberate Israel from more than 400 years of bondage. The exodus stands as the single greatest event in the history of Israel. It simultaneously released them from an oppressor and put them on the path to becoming a reputable and powerful nation. Their decision to cross the Red Sea reaped both immediate and long-term benefits. In the same way, when a church decides to leave the bondage of racism and injustice, they will also reap both immediate and eternal dividends. There are times when God places churches in the same position where Israel found herself, surrounded by trouble and enemies; yet there remains one way that

---

[1] F. B. Huey Jr., *Bible Study Commentary: Exodus* (Grand Rapids: Zondervan, 1977), 64.

God will provide a path that will simultaneously deliver them and give Him the glory that is rightfully due Him.

Wilcrest found herself facing its own Red Sea. Not only had the church suffered a steady decline for the previous ten years, but also the neighborhood no longer mirrored the church and the racial divide was quickly widening. Wilcrest's bondage represented the mind-set of "separate but equal," with each race worshiping the same God in different places. God wanted to set us free from the segregated paradigm by crossing our Red Sea. He allowed the circumstances of the changing neighborhood, the decline of the church, and the clear command from the Word of God to make disciples of all the nations to push us to the brink of our Red Sea. The church now needed to make a difficult decision: do we cross or do we not cross? Do we stay in our Egypt and subject ourselves to the increasing pattern of white flight to the suburbs? Do we stay a predominantly white congregation in a multiracial neighborhood or do we embrace a multiracial vision and enjoy a taste of heaven here on earth? Wilcrest chose to cross its Red Sea.

THE CROSSING OF THE JORDAN

The crossing of the Red Sea was an awesome display of God's power and love for the people of Israel. However, it did not provide that particular generation of Israelites with enough spiritual momentum to carry them into the promised land. The nation stalled because visible obstacles blurred their vision of Canaan and the opportunities that God promised them. Their lack of vision resulted in the forty-year wandering in the wilderness, which became an example of the truth of Solomon's words written centuries later, "Without revelation people run wild . . ." (Prov 29:18). God gave the new generation of His people a chance to dream again, but their barrier was different than the previous generation's. No longer was it the Red Sea that inhibited their movement and growth; now it was the Jordan River that stood between them and the promised land. The people of Israel needed both crossings to accomplish what God originally intended for them, but both required total dependence upon the power of God. One crossing signified freedom while the second crossing signified God's promise of blessing for the people of God.

God prepared the leader Joshua while he served as an understudy to Moses. He personally experienced the first crossing of the Red Sea, so he knew what God could do. In addition, God also prepared the people as a whole with the report of Rahab from the Canaanite city of Jericho. According to Rahab, the people of Jericho heard the reports of the Exodus and claimed, "When we heard this, we lost heart, and everyone's courage failed because of you, for the LORD your God is God in heaven above and on earth below" (Josh 2:11). Furthermore, God guaranteed His personal presence in the visible form of the ark of the covenant (Josh 3:1–13; see also 2 Sam 6:6–7). After the people spiritually prepared themselves with a time of purification, they approached the Jordan with the priests and the ark going before them. As the priests' feet entered the waters of the Jordan, God cut off the flow of the river until there was a dry path for the people to cross. The writer reminded the readers that the Jordan was at flood stage (Josh 3:15), which meant that the river was over its banks due to the melting of snow and the spring rains.[2] Scripture recorded that the waters were stopped as far as the town of Adam, 15 miles north of the crossing point (Josh 3:16). The priests stood in the middle, as if God Himself were holding the water back, while the nation made its way into the promised land. The crossing marked the completion of what began 40 years earlier. The Jordan represented the last barrier to the fulfillment of the promise made to Abraham centuries before that God would bless this nation with land, a country to call their own.

In many similar ways, Wilcrest needed to face both our Red Sea and our Jordan River. With the adoption of the vision statement, we crossed our Red Sea. We were liberated from the old mind-set of having a homogeneous congregation in a multiracial neighborhood. We were also set free from the need of comfort and the desire to have our needs met. Wilcrest was now free to look out into the neighborhood and the surrounding area with God's eyes. As we made our way from our Red Sea, we quickly approached our Jordan. Our Jordan included the promise of God that He would give us the land. Right now there are more than 30 different non-Christian worship centers in the Alief area, all representing strongholds that exert more control and influence than the spiritual base of Wilcrest and other evangeli-

---

[2] David M. Howard Jr., *Joshua,* The New American Commentary (Nashville: Broadman, 1998), 131.

cal churches combined. Our promised land has yet to be conquered, just as the land of Canaan had yet to be conquered when the Israelites crossed the Jordan. In fact, it took Israel more than 20 years to secure the promised land after they initially crossed the Jordan River. Although we adopted our multiracial vision statement and sent missionaries into the Alief mission field, we have yet to take the land completely for the kingdom of God.

EARLY IMPLEMENTATION OF THE VISION

After the adoption of the vision statement by the church body in 1993, I knew immediate and visible changes were necessary in order to send a clear signal that this decision, to cross "our Red Sea," was more than words. I was at a loss where to begin the implementation process on a churchwide level. I could see exactly what we would look like five or ten years down the road, but was not sure what precise steps to take the following week. As a result of my own personal experience and through the study of Scripture, God instilled the heart for multiracial ministry, but I had yet to lead a church in this path. A missionary colleague began to dialogue with me about the key elements that have to be present to see an all-white congregation make the transition to a multiracial congregation. The first two elements that emerged were *worship* and *leadership*. If we began to invite individuals of different cultures to come and join us, these two visible elements would speak volumes concerning our commitment to reach all people.

RESTRUCTURING OF THE STAFF

The week before my first official Sunday, May 19, 1992, the church hired a young white man to be the minister to students. I sat down and talked with him and his wife concerning the future vision of the church prior to my arrival, but I sensed that our visions for Wilcrest were not identical, thus limiting the effectiveness of the leadership team. In addition, I believed the church took an aggressive step of hiring the minister to students without thinking through all of the racial and spiritual implications. Their desire was to have as much as possible in place before I came so that I would not be entangled with the calling of a staff member. Their best intentions, however, took a sudden turn for the worse, as we released this staff member four months later. The entire process of the calling and firing of this minister to students was a very difficult process for me. I quickly realized that my leadership was about to be tested because, although they hired him, I fired him. Yet God was in the process of strategically restructuring our staff to align with the vision for a multiracial congregation.

THE CALLING OF THE FIRST AFRICAN-AMERICAN TO LEADERSHIP

Although I knew we desperately needed transformation in both areas of worship and leadership, I felt that it would be wise to deal with only one of these areas at a time. Due to the release of our minister to students, an immediate opportunity afforded itself in the area of leadership. Right at the time of the loss of staff, James Darby, an African-American, began to attend Wilcrest with his family. As we shared our vision to see all races come together to serve the same God in one church, we perceived that God was calling us to work together in order to see this dream become a reality. James and I began to pray that God would show us what exactly our working relationship would look like. God led both of us to believe that we should be open to James serving on our staff as our minister to students.

James Darby served as a part-time minister to students from March to December 1993. Toward the end of the year, we both sensed God calling him and the church to a full-time ministry capacity. During the fall of 1993, approximately 100 of our believers went through Henry Blackaby's *Experiencing God*. While we were in that study, God clearly brought to light the truth that He has a right to interrupt our lives any time He wishes. In addition, the leadership team felt that if God was in this move from a part-time to a full-time position, the entire church body must support it fully. We voted again in December of 1993, but this time we required a unanimous vote. In fact, we strongly encouraged the people if they felt God was prompting them that our church was not ready for a full-time African-American minister to students, then vote "no" or "later." To ensure that we would receive an accurate reading of the true pulse of the church body, we decided to utilize secret ballots that were not to be signed. If there was even one dissenting vote, we felt that we needed to wait to bring the issue before the church at a later time. The final vote was unanimous in favor of bringing James on in a full-time capacity.

In the process of calling James as our minister to students, the majority of the members on the Personnel Committee were convinced that we were going in the right direction, but they were concerned that this step was perhaps taken too rapidly. I still remember one member on the Personnel Committee gently correcting me by saying, "Pastor, I know your heart and where you are taking us, but I just want to remind you that we did not grow up where you grew up. So please be patient with us as we follow your leadership." He indicated that he believed in what we were doing and where we were going, but as a leader there would be times when I needed to wait for the rest of the body. There is no such thing as a leader without followers. In this case, God made it very clear that the entire body had to wait until everyone was on the same page going in the same direction at the same time.

I need to make a confession at this point. Waiting on God and the church body has always been extremely difficult for me to do. At times, my calling to lead out in this vision expresses itself with a strong will that moves ahead with or without any support. God taught me that this process does not involve one person or one leader but the entire body of Christ (Rom 12:4–5). It was imperative that this step in the process could only be taken as a cohesive and unified family. I admitted to the church body as a whole that I needed them and there would be no way my calling and vision would ever reach fruition without the coming together of the individual members under the head of Christ. All of us stood in desperate need of Christ and each other.

THE 20/20 MARCH THROUGH ALIEF

During the early stages of implementing the multiracial vision, God used a pivotal event to draw Wilcrest outside of its comfort zone and into the surrounding community. In the fall of 1993, while one hundred of our members were going through the *Experiencing God* study and were prayerfully contemplating bringing James on as a full-time minister, a drive-by shooting occurred within the Alief community, resulting in the death of a black teenager. This murder was connected with the heavy gang activity in the area. God moved James to lead the entire church on a march, beginning at the church and concluding at the very spot where the young man was shot. The verse that moved James to lead the church out on this march was Acts 20:20, which says, "I did not shrink back from proclaiming to you anything that was profitable, or from teaching it to you in public and from house to house." This last phrase convinced James that our church body needed to pray for our community house by house. This 20/20 March took place at night with approximately 125 of our members ready but not sure what God was going to do. As we began our march, two patrol cars from the Houston Police Department converged on our group and then escorted us through the entire neighborhood. As we arrived at the intersection in which the young man was shot, with his bloodstains still visible on the street, we knelt down and prayed and wept for our entire area. This was the most visible our church body had been in the community since I had arrived. Despite residing a half-mile from our facility, many of the people we encountered during the march did not even know that there was a church in the immediate area. In addition, some of our most timid members were out on the streets interacting with the onlookers. This march empowered them to speak on behalf of Christ with greater boldness. The 20/20 March has served as one of the most powerful spiritual markers in the history of Wilcrest as we entered the surrounding community at a critical time, representing Christ to a neighborhood full of fear. We crossed "our Jordan."

The 20/20 March also enabled our church body to see James in a completely different light. Here was an African-American minister to students leading an almost all-white group of believers through a racially diverse area to pray over a neighborhood which had just lost an African-American young man to a gang shooting. There are images in that march that will be etched in my mind forever. For a few moments, God gave us a chance to see that there were no color lines or barriers when it comes to the activity of the kingdom of God. It would be easy to see this march as a one-time event. However, God was beginning to write a rich spiritual heritage in the area of walking by faith across racial and cultural lines in our immediate area. The very lines that the world used for demarcation, God used as a rallying point to get His people on their knees over the bloodstains of a slain young man.

PENETRATION INTO THE SURROUNDING COMMUNITY

The 20/20 March laid the initial groundwork for the more thorough penetration into our community in the future. Subsequent walks through our immediate neighborhood became consistent as we passed out flyers concerning upcoming events, such as Vacation Bible School, the Jesus Video Project, children's events, sports clinics, karate camps, musical and drama productions, and prayer walks. The more our members walked the streets, the more burdened they became for the spiritual condition of our immediate area. Right after the Mexico Mission Trip during the summer of 2001, several of our missionaries returned with a desire to show the Jesus Video in Spanish to our neighborhood. The entire planning team of lay persons took responsibility for the setting up of chairs in the church parking lot, making popcorn, translators, greeters, and publicity. This project attracted approximately 50 of our Spanish-speaking neighbors. As we canvassed our neighborhood, walking up and down the streets, we realized how many people exclusively spoke Spanish in close proximity to the church. As a result, a Spanish worship service was introduced in September 2002 on Sunday nights. We also implemented simultaneous Spanish translation during the morning worship service.

YOUTH CHOIR MISSION TOURS

As Wilcrest began to reach its immediate area, our Jerusalem, God called us to reach out to the next area, our Samaria (Acts 1:8). God used James as the primary prompter in organizing mission trips for our young people to different parts of the South. He had a two-fold purpose: (1) to initiate our young missionaries to a mission field that was radically different from their comfort zone at home; and (2) to expose other areas of the Deep South to what God can do through a multiracial congregation. These mission trips targeted the states of Louisiana, Oklahoma, Mississippi, Tennessee, Alabama, and parts of Texas, and involved either all-black or all-white congregations. As in any great spiritual movement in the United States over the past 200 years, God initially worked through the younger generation in order to set the pace and the direction for the rest of the congregation.[3] These mission choir tours transformed our youth and our youth workers in such a way that when they returned home their zeal and excitement became infectious. The initial trips within the United States laid the essential foundation for the worldwide mission trips that eventually emerged.

RISKS AND REWARDS OF CROSSING

In the New Testament, Jesus clearly establishes the necessity and value of calculating the costs, the risks, and the rewards, for whatever spiritual endeavor His disciples will pursue. Jesus illustrates this truth with two common first-century analogies: going to war and building a tower (Luke 14:25–35). In each of these examples, Jesus concludes that it would be foolish to begin a task without first knowing both the resources that are required and the difficulty of the task. In the same way, when God called the Israelites to cross the Red Sea and the Jordan, they had to calculate what resources they had available and the difficulty of the task. In each case, the difficulty of both crossings proved to be beyond their own human resources, yet with God, nothing would be impossible. Furthermore, the people of God received clear instructions from God to cross the water barriers (Exod 14:15; Josh 1:2). If Israel refused to cross the Red Sea, the cost of disobeying the command of God would result in oppressive slavery under the Egyptians. If the Israelites did not follow Joshua across the Jordan, they would have to wander in the wilderness without any direction or a place of their own. In both cases, the rewards of crossing the Red Sea and the Jordan, which included freedom from the bondage of slavery and the occupying of the promised land, outweighed the risks of not crossing. God also calls us to calculate the risks and rewards of crossing racial barriers.

---

[3] For an extended survey of how God used young people in revivals, see Alvin L. Reid, "The Zeal of Youth: The Role of Students in the History of Spiritual Awakening," in *Evangelism for a Changing World,* ed. Timothy Beougher and Alvin L. Reid (Wheaton, IL: Harold Shaw, 1995), 233–48.

SURVEY SAYS

Over the course of 2006 and 2007, a survey was given to the members of Wilcrest asking them to convey both the risks involved and the rewards received by incorporating into a multiracial congregation. The survey form also asked the members their age group, predominant race, and length of time at Wilcrest.[4] We encouraged the members to be anonymous if they desired in order to give them a format of expressing their true feelings and insights.

Rewards of Being a Part of a Multiracial Congregation

According to the responses of our Wilcrest members, the most predominant reward of crossing racial, cultural, gender, and age barriers has been the value and *celebration of diversity*. One white member (age 31–35) who was a part of the racial transformation for several years offered the following insight:

> Seeing the great diversity of people in the kingdom is a constant reminder of just how big our God's kingdom is. Since Jesus is the only common factor among our congregants, it serves as constant encouragement to keep our focus on Jesus. Learning that unfamiliar cultures are not threats to be avoided, but are opportunities to learn.

Another white member (age 41–45) affirms the same sentiment: "The multiracial church reinforces the messages of the New Testament that Jesus died for everyone and is Lord of all." Another white respondent (over age 55) views the racial mixture in this way: "The world has come to me as I remained planted at Wilcrest. I have been blessed." One white woman (age 46–50) admits this celebration of diversity did not come easily: "Trying to get over my prejudice of other colors was difficult at first. Today, it is not even an issue. The more people of different color the better." A highlight for one of our white women (age 20–25) was being invited into the homes of members of different races. She explains the impact of this connection by saying, "This has helped me become a more complete and mature person as my eyes have been opened to the cultures around me, which has allowed me to develop a better sense of who God is and how to interact with other

---

[4] See appendix 1 for the full survey.

people." This perspective is not limited to the whites who have witnessed these changes over a period of time, but also comes from all the other races. An Indonesian member (age 36–40) relates, "I felt at home and so welcome, as there are so many nations in one body and it seems like a picture with a lot of color in it. I do not feel different and awkward." An African-American woman (age 51–55) confirms this multicolor portrait: "I feel this is a peek at what heaven is going to be like, every race, creed, and color together." A Hispanic woman (age 31–35) added that when she looks out into the congregation from the choir, she loves "seeing the splashes of color all throughout the sanctuary. It is a glorious sight." A Korean believer who is not a member of Wilcrest confirms this truth by stating, "The convergence of such different cultures, represented by unique music styles, clothes, and appearance, reminds me that God is sovereign over all peoples."

The second most prevalent reward is the *strong sense of acceptance*. A white member (age 41–45) asserts, "I am loved for who I am and not what I look like, the language I speak, not what I wear." One Cuban member (age 41–45) conveyed:

> It is okay to worship God and not have to change or hide my ethnicity. There is such freedom of being able to be from a different culture and not be afraid of being looked down on or made fun of. I love to hear their "story" and to learn songs from their country about our Lord Jesus.

An African-American woman who had visited Wilcrest in the early years of the transition did not see but one other African-American man during her initial visit, but "he didn't count as diversity since he was married to a white woman." Since this African-American lived near the church but felt out of place, she sent the children to activities without going herself. Two years later she joined the church and the reason is: "We noticed a change. Now there are so many blacks here, I don't even know them all. I don't know all the Hispanics. My husband said, 'Now we are welcomed. This is the place for us.'"[5]

Not only is there a new feeling of acceptance by others, but the multiracial congregation challenges each person to be accepting of

---

[5] Brad Christerson, Korie L. Edwards, and Michael O. Emerson, *Against All Odds: The Struggle for Racial Integration in Religious Organizations* (New York: New York University Press, 2005), 56.

others. A white member (age 31–35) expresses this feeling: "I have been challenged to grow out of my prejudicial attitudes I was raised with about race, economics, and mixed marriages. It has taught me to look at a person or couple and see a child of God, not color or status." The openness and acceptance of different races and cultures overflow in the acceptance of other areas, such as divorce. One white member (age 46–50) observes that after her divorce, "without the support of Wilcrest family, who knows what the turn out would have been." It would be hypocritical to announce that the church accepts all races and ethnicities but then dismiss others who come to Wilcrest with their lives fragmented and in need of God's acceptance. A black member (age 31–35) recalled his first visit:

> When I first visited I looked hard at the cover of the bulletin. It drew me in, saying this was a church for everyone. I looked up at the people in the sanctuary. They seemed to be from everywhere. It was beautiful. I felt like they said, "Welcome to the family. This is your new home." And I thanked God.[6]

Another reward is the further *development of a global Christian perspective*. For one white member (age 26–30), one of the best benefits of being a part of Wilcrest has been "the shift in focus from 'community' to 'global'." Within a uniracial congregation, it is difficult to see a Christian worldview, especially when insulated by only those who share the same color of skin, educational background, social and economic privileges, and church traditions. A Korean believer who is a member of an all-Korean church expressed his lack of understanding when a Korean friend joined Wilcrest. He acknowledged, "I appreciated that she at least gave the issue some thought, whereas most Korean people in my church give it no thought at all." In racially homogeneous congregations, other racial perspectives on church, family, relationships, and spiritual issues are not on their spiritual radar. The global Christian perspective pushes each member out of their racial, ethnic, cultural zone and challenges them to see those around them through a different set of lenses. For example, the way Africans perceive in-laws is extremely different from the way that most of our whites perceive in-laws. One of the white members

---

[6] Quoted in *Against All Odds*, 41.

(age 31–35) describes his change of understanding of family in this way after interacting with one of West Africa's members: "I learned that in the West African culture, there is no concept of the in-law. A person is either a part of the family or they are not." The new sense of family now permeates throughout the entire church family.

Another fresh global perspective that many of our third-world members embody is the value of suffering. Many of our Christians who have grown up in the United States define suffering as going without air conditioning during a worship service, only having one car for the entire family, not being able to eat at a restaurant whenever one wants, or having to wait an extended period of time to see the doctor. Yet when our members who originally fled Liberia or Sierra Leone because of a revolution or upheaval in the government and were forced to live in refugee camps for a number of years hear the complaints of American Christians, they simply shake their heads in disbelief. As our immigrants from war-torn countries tell their story, there is little complaining about the temperature of the worship center or the number of cars others have.

Another reward, especially from the nonwhite perspective, is the *knowledge in navigating the American social, economic, and educational system*. As immigrants search for a safe place to adjust to a new nation, they also develop social networks and gain access to resources outside of their racial circle. Many of the international members "develop relationships with believers from different cultures that eventually help them search for jobs, negotiate the immigration system, get medical treatment, or pursue education."[7] This advancement is not only in the economic, social, and educational realm, but also in the spiritual realm. With one of the church's primary goals of reaching every nation from which the members have come, the church places the international members as key spiritual leaders in the mission trips. For example,

> We rely on them to make contacts, arrangements, and serve as liaisons during the entire trip. They are needed by the congregation. They become the mouths and the voices for the rest of the church body as ministry takes place in their country and in their language. Their spiritual status exponentially

[7] Quoted in *People of the Dream*, 110.

increases not only in their own eyes, but also in the eyes of the rest of the members as well.[8]

The final reward that many of our people relish is the *value of passing on the multiracial vision to the next generation*. One white woman (age 26–30) asserted, "My child is able to make friends with children of different cultures and can better understand the meaning of the song, 'Jesus loves the little children, all the children of the world'." One African-American man (age 40–45) added that if his children are in a multiracial neighborhood, a multiracial school, why should he and his family be in an all-black church? He expressed a strong desire that his children would receive a multiracial perspective in every area of their lives, especially in the spiritual arena. One of my goals for this prototypical multiracial congregation is that the impact would not just be experienced by the first generation of believers who have adopted this vision, but that it would exponentially expand to the next generation. As the psalmist urges the people of Israel, "That they should teach them to their children, that the generation to come might know, even the children yet to be born, that they may arise and tell them to their children, that they should put their confidence in God and not forget the works of God, but keep His commandments" (Ps 78:5–7 NASB).

The primary rewards of being a part of a multiracial congregation according to the members of Wilcrest include: the value and celebration of diversity, a strong sense of acceptance, the development of a global perspective, especially in the areas of family and suffering, the knowledge of navigating the American economic, social, educational system, and the possibility of introducing and incorporating children into a multiracial mind-set from a biblical perspective. All of these benefits are encouraging and even inspirational, but are they worth the risks or sacrifices to move in this multiracial direction?

Risks of Being a Part of a Multiracial Congregation

A variety of responses seemed to be in regard to the sacrifices or risks that individuals take as they incorporate into a multiracial congregation, especially along racial lines. A prominent fear among the whites at Wilcrest is feeling that they must *relinquish control of*

---

[8] Ibid.

leadership and the ability to make decisions. In what was formerly an all-white church, now there is representative leadership from all races. One white member (age 46–50) admitted, "I believe I had more of a voice in the past than I do now in regards to matters in the church, especially where the money in the church is used." This is one of the most difficult struggles for some of our whites who have been at Wilcrest for a long time. In fact, many of our white members left as the church became more racially diverse. One of our older white members (over age 55), who eventually left, contended that if the music changes any more then he would be afraid to invite any of his friends to the service.[9] Another white member (age 31–35) initially thought there was a bias against whites at Wilcrest in the pursuit of having multiracial leadership, but he confessed, "The kingdom of God is bigger than my personal ambitions. We have to be ready to forfeit our rights and desires for the sake of the body of Christ. Besides, we do not serve for a position or recognition; we serve because we love the Lord."

However, according to Emerson, "Numerical minority group members bear the highest relational costs of being involved in interracial organizations. The costs are reduced as representation increases."[10] Emerson adds that some of the areas of representation include "raw numbers, worship styles, leadership, or organizational practices."[11] During initial changes at Wilcrest, all of these areas were either nonexistent or at the embryonic stage of development. Consequently, the nonwhites at Wilcrest had to sacrifice the most relationally as they incorporated into the church. According to Eric H. F. Law, "Whenever two or three culturally diverse groups come together, the white English-speaking group most likely sets the agenda, and does most of the talking and decision making."[12] Yet Emerson concludes,

---

[9] According to Emerson, white adults are often unwilling to sacrifice the potential experiences, privileges, and opportunities for their children despite their desire to be a part of a multiracial congregation and their belief that this vision has intrinsic benefits for them. Some of this is due to the perception that nonwhites are inferior to whites and may be detrimental to their children's life chances. See *Against All Odds*, 170.

[10] *Against All Odds*, 156.

[11] Ibid.

[12] Eric H. F. Law, *The Wolf Shall Dwell with the Lamb: A Spirituality for Leadership in a Multicultural Community* (St. Louis: Chalice, 1993), 2–3. Law identifies the coming together of whites and nonwhites as the "wolf and lamb" scenario. When a lamb is with other lambs or a wolf is with other wolves, everything is peaceful. However, when a lamb and a wolf are placed together, "something bad is going to happen."

"The acceptance felt by minorities is related to the structural inclusion they witness, such as the vision statement of the organization, the worship styles, leadership representation, and other structural arrangements."[13] Once Wilcrest reached a point when there was no racial majority and had over forty-four different nations represented, there was less expectation that each group have representation and that each group would have to sacrifice.

Another key area of sacrifice or risk for all racial groups is the area of *worship*. A woman from Trinidad (age 51–55), a Hispanic woman (age 31–35), and a white woman (51–55) all expressed that they miss the old traditional songs of their culture and religious heritage. One black woman (age 51–55) adds that "I miss the clapping and dancing during the praise and worship and offering time." One of our African-American women (age 31–35) conveys that on the way to church she often has to listen to her black gospel music in order to "get her fill before coming to Wilcrest." It was also a challenge to adjust to different cultural or racial aspects of worship. A white member (over age 55) had to make some adjustments with "women serving as ushers." Some of our whites have also experienced frustration with the differences in how each culture views and values time. One white member (age 31–35) contended that at his previous all-white churches, "when Bible Study started at 9:30 a.m., the people were there at 9:30 a.m. There was no 'island time' like there is at Wilcrest." Interestingly from another perspective, one of our leaders (age 51–55) argues that in the Hispanic culture, to show up "on time" is an expression of arrogance, implying the event could not start without their presence.

Another risk that our people take when they leave their homogeneous church or religious roots and move into a multiracial congregation is with *family*. One of our Hispanic women (age 41–45) said that she heard from her own blood family, "You stick to your own kind and they stick with their kind. It is okay for you to speak with them, but it is not good for them to be your friends or have them come for dinner." She adds that her grandparents were absolutely "horrified that we embraced and went to church with people of a different color of skin, even those from another Latin American country." Another Hispanic woman (age 31–35), who grew up in the Catholic faith,

---

[13] *Against All Odds*, 159.

contends that the most difficult sacrifice in following Christ and joining a multiracial congregation is with her family. She explains, "That
still hurts, and that one thing has been my family. My family refuses
to see Jesus Christ in my life." Many of our church members are
deeply grieved that their families of origin do not understand why
they would embark on something so difficult and dangerous. The sacrifices and risks are not limited to relationships with family members
but also with friends. A white woman (over age 55) who has been a
member for almost five years adds, "I have lost friends from my former all-white church because I go to a multiracial church." Abraham
truly understood the call to leave family when God commanded him,
"Go out from your land, your relatives, and your father's house to
the land that I will show you" (Gen 12:1). Leaving nation, relatives,
and immediate family is a high price of following the call of God
in order to be the conduit of blessings for "all the peoples on earth"
(Gen 12:3). Though about the offense of the gospel, Jesus' promise
to His disciples who left everything remains applicable to those who
join a multiracial congregation: "There is no one who has left house,
brothers or sisters, mother or father, children, or fields because of
Me and the gospel, who will not receive 100 times more, now at this
time . . . and eternal life in the age to come" (Mark 10:29–30).

Another predominant risk that is expressed by the vast majority of
our responders is in the area of *leaving their comfort zone.* An African-American member (age 26–30) conveyed, "I was in an all-black
church, so this took me some getting used to." A white woman confirmed, "I definitely forfeited being comfortable as I was in previous
churches. It was a time to reach out, stretch, and get involved." One
white member (age 46–50) conceded that it was difficult to transition
from being a "majority to a minority, but it is not necessarily a bad
thing, but it has required some adjustments in thinking and attitudes."
A black member (age 31–35) expresses her discomfort with the following words: "I am more used to being in a church with clean-cut
Christians than being with members from different backgrounds who
have tattoos and gold teeth; that has been a challenge for me." One
Korean member (age 26–30) relates her experience about first coming to Wilcrest:

> I initially experienced a kind of cultural loneliness since I
> was used to being in a church heavily infused with one cul-

ture. I felt constantly reminded of my "Korean-ness." I also felt as if I lived in two different worlds: Korean Christian and Wilcrest Christian. I really wanted these two worlds to collide, but my feeble attempts in bridging these two worlds usually consisted of conversation that felt polite and unnatural. Even now, I feel like there's an invisible wall that makes it a stretch to build an interpersonal bridge.

A Korean believer who is not a member of Wilcrest provides insight into the difficulty of moving out of one's comfort zone: "Naturally I am drawn to and can connect with people who share the common things other Korean Americans experienced growing up, such as growing up with parents who do not speak English, eating kimchee, getting certain types of haircuts, following parents to an ethnic church on Sunday, and being pushed to get educated." He then adds, "If there was a solid biblical church with a bunch of people with all the following characteristics, but were of a plethora of different ethnicities, I would probably go there because I can connect with them." Yet his interaction with other races is somewhat guarded as he admits, "When this African-American brother let loose and is himself in front of me, I find his energy a little overwhelming at times." Another Korean believer from an all-Korean congregation confirms this awkwardness: "I think it is obvious that different ethnic groups are just different in enough ways that most people find it socially awkward to interact across racial lines. I often feel this social awkwardness, which I find unfortunate since I should love people regardless of ethnicity." A black pastor adds, "I realize that external comfort and familiarity is of great value to all Americans, but for different reasons. Whites want comfort simply because they do not do well with change. It is a white world. Minorities want comfort because they cannot find it elsewhere in this country." Moving out of the comfort zone of a racially homogeneous congregation into a multiracial one requires a willingness to place oneself intentionally in the arena of ongoing discomfort.[14]

If a person remains in a racial comfort zone, the perspective toward race and culture becomes narrow in its focus. For example,

---

[14] In the study of a multiracial church plant in Los Angeles, in which the predominant racial group is Filipino, the findings indicate that the numerical minority groups bear the greatest relational costs of being in a diverse congregation. See *Against All Odds*, 22.

one Hispanic member was previously incorporated in an all-white church so much that she admitted, "I actually started looking down on Hispanics. I look white; I do not have an accent, even though I am fully bilingual. I actually had to reconcile who I was when I got to Wilcrest." By removing themselves from their comfort zones, many of our people are challenged to deal with prejudices, identity, and ministry from totally different perspectives. One Hispanic woman (age 41–45) adds that she has to watch "how I say things and my body language. I have to be more sensitive to others who are not used to the American way of saying or doing things." However, if a person is out of their racial comfort zone for an extended period of time, as one white member (age 20–25) contends, "It can be tiring!"[15]

The final area in which all races expressed a major change is in their *prejudices toward other races*. One Hispanic woman (age 41–45) emphatically stated, "The most difficult experience for me was letting go of the racial prejudice that I was raised with. I realized that if I was going to be a part of a multiracial church, I had to let the prejudices go." A young white woman (age 21–25) was forced to deal with her own prejudices each Sunday as she interacted with people from different races in a church setting. Yet through her experience at Wilcrest, she contends, "overcoming the prejudices was not as hard as recognizing and accepting that they existed."

In summary, the primary risks or sacrifices for those who incorporate into a multiracial congregation include the following: loss of control as a majority to the shared representation among leaders with other races, the shift from a uniracial to a multiracial worship service, resistance from one's immediate family, the necessity of leaving one's comfort zone, and the biblical necessity to release prejudices against other races. It is interesting that many of the risks in becoming a multiracial congregation involve sin, such as demanding control, refusing to sacrifice, leaving the comfort zone, and releasing prejudices. Yet these risks transform into rewards because God uses

---

[15] For an extended discussion of "racial fatigue" see George Yancey, *One Body, One Spirit: Principles of Successful Multiracial Churches* (Downers Grove, IL: InterVarsity, 2003), 98–101. Yancey adds that "most Americans are either tired of dealing with racism or are frustrated at the lack of results we have experienced in removing racism from society. Overt efforts to eradicate problems connected to racism and racial prejudice generally meets resistance from both whites and racial minorities. What may be called 'racial fatigue' has plagued contemporary efforts to deal with racism."

the process as His instrument of purifying the church. Thus, "We know that all things work together for the good of those who love God: those who are called according to His purpose" (Rom 8:28). Indeed God is working not only to unite His people, but also to purify His people. All of these risks serve as sober reminders that moving in a multiracial direction as an individual and as a church will come at a great cost and sacrifice. The questions emerge again: Do we cross or not cross? Do the rewards and blessing outweigh the risks and sacrifices required to leave our Egypt and to cross our Red Sea and Jordan River? Are the immediate and eternal dividends worth the spiritual investment in the face of resistance and rejection from our own family, friends, church, denomination, and race? However, the risk and reward analysis pales in comparison to the mandate of God. Can we risk living in disobedience to the will of God?

SUMMARY OF SURVEY

According to the survey conducted at Wilcrest, the primary risk of being a part of a multiracial congregation, ironically, is the same as the primary reward: the racial diversity within the church. Moving out of one's racial comfort zone in a congregational setting comes as a costly sacrifice for many of our people, which will possibly entail resistance from their own family members and racial group, discomfort in worship, and releasing or sharing control in the decision-making process. However, the rewards for doing what God calls us to do reach beyond what many of our people have ever imagined. When believers learned the part in the Lord's Prayer (Matt 6:9–13) that says, "Your kingdom come. Your will be done on earth as it is in heaven," those who choose to cross into a multiracial church will see and experience heaven right here on earth. The racial diversity that is so aptly depicted around the throne in Rev 7 is one of the last Jordans for the people of God to cross before the second coming of our Lord Jesus Christ. The question remains: Will you cross the Jordan with all the nations to the promised land of Rev 7?

DISCUSSION QUESTIONS

1. Read the accounts of Israel's crossing of the Red Sea (Exod 14) and the crossing of the Jordan (Josh 3). What were some of the

primary obstacles that the nation of Israel faced? What did the
Red Sea represent to Israel and to Egypt? What did the Jordan
River represent to Israel as they came out of the forty-year wilderness wandering? What role did God play in each of these
crossings? What role did the people of God play in each of the
crossings? What was the immediate response of the people after
they arrived on the other side?

2. What is your personal Red Sea or Jordan River in regard to
   reaching across racial barriers? What is your congregation's
   Red Sea and Jordan River in reaching all nations in your Jerusalem and to the ends of the earth?

3. What steps can you take to get ready to cross the racial barriers in your life or in the life of your church? Are there any
   events, changes, or circumstances around you that may provide
   an opening to begin to cross your Red Sea or Jordan?

4. List every possible risk that you or your church would take
   when you decide to cross the racial or cultural barriers. List
   every possible reward that you see in Scripture, experience, or
   in the testimony of others. Compare the risks and rewards. Are
   the spiritual rewards worth the potential risks that would be necessary to cross your Red Sea or Jordan?

C H A P T E R   7

GIANTS IN THE LAND

"To ourselves we seemed like grasshoppers, and we must have seemed the same to them" (Num 13:33).

The apostle Paul reminds us of an important truth concerning new opportunities and beginnings as he writes to the church at Corinth, "a wide door for effective ministry has opened for me—yet many oppose me" (1 Cor 16:9). In his address to the church at Ephesus, Paul warned them of the dangers of doing effective ministry: "I know that after my departure savage wolves will come in among you, not sparing the flock" (Acts 20:29). In fact, Jesus warned His disciples that upon His departure troubled times would lie ahead of them: "They will ban you from the synagogues. In fact, a time is coming when anyone who kills you will think he is offering service to God" (John 16:2). Any time God opens a new door of service or opportunity, obstacles and enemies will come against His people. In the same way, as the people of Israel journeyed from Egypt through the wilderness to the edge of the promised land, they encountered "giants in the land."

In his preparation for the conquest of Canaan, Moses selected one representative from each of the 12 tribes of Israel to spy out the land and return with a status report. He gave them specific instructions concerning the parameters of the search: to determine the strengths and weaknesses of the enemy, and bring back a sample of the produce of the land (Num 13:17–20). The 12 spies spent 40 days surveying the land and reported that the produce was everything that God promised, but the people of the land were strong and the cities were well-fortified. The scouting report was somewhat divided; ten of the spies were overwhelmed with fear in the face of giants, while two spies courageously challenged Israel to invade. The longer the ten spies spoke, the more they regressed from what God called them to do, thus forfeiting the promises of God. The ten spies said that the inhabitants of Canaan were "strong" (Num 13:28), and they were "stronger than we are" (Num 13:31). Instead of focusing on "the land flowing with milk and honey," they redirected their attention to the obstacles that stood in the way of their victory. The ten spies looked "on the presence of these other nations as an insurmountable obstacle to entry, not as a confirmation of God's purpose."[1] The spiritual eyes of the Israelites were set on an overwhelming enemy that would conquer them instead of on an overwhelming God who would conquer their enemy, thus giving the Israelites possession of the promised land. Finally, they contended, "'We even saw the Nephilim there.' (The offspring of Anak were descended from the Nephilim.) 'To ourselves we seemed like grasshoppers, and we must have seemed the same to them'" (Num 13:33). After this cowering majority report, it appeared that since Israel was small and insignificant in their own eyes, they were already defeated. Much of their report was accurate, but they failed to take into account God's powerful presence on their behalf. Caleb, one who stood in opposition to the majority report, boldly claimed, "We must go up and take possession of the land because we can certainly conquer it" (Num 13:30). There was no hesitation on his part because his vision was God's vision.

When God calls us to enter a new territory or embark upon a new season, there will always be conflicting reports and "giants in the land." The enemy will not shrink back and allow the people of God to follow His vision without seeking to steal the joy and destroy and kill what God has in store for His obedient children (John 10:10a). How much more opposition will we encounter if we embrace the vision of reconciliation among the races, of building a bridge between estranged sinners and a loving Savior, and preparing the bride of Christ for the marriage supper of the Lamb with every nation enjoying the presence of God? There will always be the "ten-spy report" that relates an accurate picture of reality but is devoid of God's presence, power, and vision. At Wilcrest, we heard many from both inside and outside the church who joined the "ten-spy report." They claimed that there was no way that a multiracial congregation would survive

---

[1]   Gordon J. Wenham, *Numbers* (Downers Grove, IL: InterVarsity, 1981), 120.

in Alief, in Houston, in the Deep South, in the Bible Belt, as a Baptist congregation, with a Chinese pastor, in a transitioning community, with our facilities, and with little or no resources. Here are some of those reports and how God raised our many "Calebs" to announce to the world the greatness of our God.

OBSTACLES FROM WITHOUT

During my first year in Houston, I communicated this multiracial vision with several local Houston pastors from a variety of cultures. There was a great diversity in response to the proposal to lead Wilcrest from a homogeneous congregation to a multiracial congregation. On one hand, most of the white pastors with whom I shared this vision seemed to respond with either a sense of curiosity or doubt. On the other hand, one prominent African-American said, "Woo, it will never work, especially from the black perspective." I challenged his response, but he would not budge. The pastor did not say that statement to me in animosity or hostility, but I believe it originated from the mind-set embedded in the racial reality of the Deep South. Over the last 15 years, I have primarily followed God's vision inside my heart while secondarily trying to prove this African-American pastor wrong. Even after all this time, energy, and prayer, there is a sense that he spoke truth to me on that day. We have been able to reach almost every racial group to some extent except the African-Americans, until recently. Our church has many African-Americans who are married to a person of a different race, a few African-American teenagers and children, many Africans, and many from the Caribbean Islands. The only African-American family that Wilcrest had for the first several years was our minister to students and his family. However, these past three years we have witnessed a steady flow of African-American families joining and participating in the ministry of Wilcrest. There may be a variety of reasons for this recent influx, but the primary one seems to be that in the overall composition of Wilcrest, there is no one racial majority in the church. One of our black women visited our church years ago when it was all white and then returned years later and joined due to the changes that occurred in implementing the multiracial vision.

Another prominent African-American pastor in Texas encouraged me in our vision of reaching all racial groups. In a phone conversation, I described to him the difficulties we were having in incorporating African-American believers into the fabric of the church body at Wilcrest. In fact, we had several who visited us regularly and were loosely connected with our church family, but demonstrated no sustained commitment. This pastor suggested that radical changes would have to be made in the worship and the style of preaching. Yet he quickly added that if those changes were implemented then we might lose a major part of our present makeup of our congregation. He concluded by saying that it may not be worth gaining "the one" at the cost of losing "the many." In my zeal to reach all people groups, this reality grieved me. Yet through this struggle, God gave me hope in the form of a different perspective that focuses on what is gained and not solely on what is lost.

After the initial conversation with the African-American pastor my first year in Houston and this last conversation with the other pastor ten years later, I concluded that we can reach and incorporate African-Americans into our congregation. It was never a question of *if* we would reach African-Americans—it was *how*. The initial wave of blacks that came was believers who were involved in other ministries or who had a falling out with their former churches. When these believers came they were accustomed to the uniquely African-American style of worship and leadership, but Wilcrest offered a combination of multiple styles. If Wilcrest would grow in the number of African-Americans in our congregation, it must be through conversion, and that is exactly what has happened.[2] It is an extremely slow and tedious process because so many of the African-American unbelievers are so heavily influenced by the African-American church that they still have remnants or memories of their church tradition. They may not have attended church in the last several years, but someone in their family who was rooted in church kept tabs on them and still influenced the way they think church should be. The way African-Americans experience church or the way whites or Hispanics experience church is not an issue of right and wrong, but there are measurable differences, especially in the area of worship. Dur-

---

[2] See appendix 2 for the number of African-Americans who join by baptism compared to those who join by transfer.

ing this stage of our transformation, there was an ongoing struggle between individual people groups vying for their own unique style of worship and at the same time celebrating with other cultures in their expression of worship. I discovered that this tension is healthy, for it reminds believers from various cultures that God cannot be confined within cultural or racial parameters. Each culture and race bring a unique worship expression that will give us insight into the character of God that would otherwise be impossible to see and understand without the multiracial context.

AN ENCOURAGING WORD

At the end of 1995, Monty Jones, our worship leader, and I felt that we should have a special emphasis on worship, especially with all the changes we were trying to implement. Consequently, we invited a professor of music to come and lead our church in a "Worship Revival." This professor addressed multiple issues in the area of biblical worship that transcended all races. What stood out to me during this time was a spontaneous conversation with the professor concerning our vision of seeing all the races worshiping together as depicted in Rev 7. He asked a pointed question that both encouraged and instructed me: "How long do you think this change will take?" I responded that I believed it would take only a few years to see this transformational process implemented. He clarified, "It is going to take several years, maybe as many as ten years, for the entire process to complete the turn." As I heard his words, my heart sank because I had gauged the change process to be much quicker. Yet at the same time, I knew God was speaking to me and instilling inside of me a vivid and accurate picture of a long and deliberate pilgrimage that would require a decade of my life. I left that conversation with a renewed sense that this seismic change would only occur with the power of God over an extended period of time.

DIVINE DELAY

The conversation with this seminary professor reminded me that every time God placed a call on an individual in Scripture, it was several years or generations later when the vision finally reached fruition. For example, when God called Abraham to be a great nation, he did not see the birth of the promised Isaac until 25 years later. When Joseph had the two dreams of seeing his brothers bow down to him, he did not see the dream come true until 15 years later. When God revealed to Hosea and Amos that He would destroy the northern kingdom of Israel during the middle of the eighth century BC, it was not until 722 BC when the Assyrians eventually conquered the Israelites. When God gave Jeremiah the prophecy of the new covenant that would be written on the hearts of believers, the prophecy did not come to fruition until the time of Christ (Jer 31:31–34). The reason God let people know what He would do before He carried out His promise is seen in the words of Jesus the night before His crucifixion: "I have told you now before it happens, so that when it does happen *you may believe*" (John 14:29).[3] God led the corporate body of Wilcrest to become a multiracial congregation in 1992, yet we did not reach critical mass until 2002, when there was no longer one racial majority within the church body. Only from our perspective is there a delay, for God's timing is perfect.

OBSTACLES FROM WITHIN

Decrease in Attendance

Our church continued to battle numerous tangible "giants in the land" throughout this painstakingly slow process. In fact, several things became worse before getting better. The first of these was a dramatic decrease in attendance. White flight affected Wilcrest in the number of people leaving and in the finances decreasing. Wilcrest averaged approximately four or five hundred white people each Sunday in the early eighties. With attendance dropping below two hundred people each Sunday, the congregation went into a tailspin throughout the decade of the eighties and into the early nineties. This decline had a tremendous impact on the morale and spirit of the church. As one member told me in his description of the church in the seventies and early eighties, "All we had to do was open the doors and they would come." Wilcrest was one of the few Baptist churches in this new and developing suburb of southwest Houston. Wilcrest had a tremendous youth ministry, choir ministry, and a strong Mother's Day Out pro-

---

[3] Italics mine.

gram. The Mother's Day Out program had almost 200 children at its peak; in 2002, there were just under 20 children enrolled, and in 2005, the program shut down completely. When I came in 1992, we had approximately 30 deacons, all white. We presently have 17 deacons, 9 of whom were deacons when I originally arrived. The departure of our deacons is indicative of the white flight that has happened on a wider scale throughout the church and the neighborhood.

Decrease in Giving

The second "giant in the land" was an accompanying decrease in our giving. When I first arrived at Wilcrest our annual operating budget was right under $400,000. Over the next eight years our budget would fluctuate around the $400,000 mark, while our receipts would often be below that mark. The decrease in giving was due to the number of stable tithers (people who give ten percent of their income to the church) who were leaving the Alief area and the number of people who were moving into the church who were not giving consistently or substantially. The number of people attending gradually increased but our giving did not. Our financial base now required many more people to maintain the same budget. I have come to believe this is one of the initial costs of leading an Anglo church to become a multiracial church. During this entire eight-year period, we kept approximately $100,000 in savings for emergencies. While maintaining the bare essentials in ministry, the chairman of the deacons (this office is held for only one or two years and then another deacon is required to serve in this capacity) noted that perhaps the whites who set this money back for emergencies were preparing for the lean years of transition from a homogeneous to a multiracial congregation. Ironically, many of the whites who wanted to keep the blacks and Chinese separate in their own mission churches in the seventies and the eighties were, at the same time, ensuring that these people groups would be incorporated into Wilcrest years later.

A Caleb Moment in Giving

Not until October 2000 did our church experience a sudden and spiritual turn in the area of giving. At the beginning of October 2000, we were about $40,000 below budget for the year, which was not unusual for us. In September, God placed on my heart the burden to challenge our people throughout the month of November to practice tithing (giving ten percent of your income to church) as a spiritual experiment. We called the month of November, "Prove the Tithe" month. At the end of that year, we had received a total of $470,000, about $1,000 below our God-sized annual budget. We had never received this much money in the general operating budget since my arrival in 1992. As the new budget year arrived, I thought our people would revert to their old pattern, but giving continued to increase. This exponential increase ultimately permitted the church to hire a full-time associate pastor in charge of students for the first time since James Darby left. In addition, we were also able to retain the part-time staff members. In 2002, we increased our total operating budget by 18 percent over the 2001 operating budget and since then have been staying on track with the challenge budget.

As Wilcrest made the transition from an all-white congregation to a multiracial congregation, I knew finances were going to be a major challenge. Based on what studies have shown, white Americans make and give more to churches and to ministry than any other people group. Consequently, if Wilcrest was a financially stable white church that had grown steadily in its first 15 years of existence, then what would happen to the church if a great number of the white givers left and were replaced with nonwhites? What we have learned, especially from the "Prove the Tithe" project, is when a challenge is given to people based on vision, the level of consistent giving increases dramatically. Our church does not have and probably will never attract the affluent, but those who are connected have demonstrated a passion to give and support the vision that God planted in their hearts.

For example, our first mission trip to Honduras involved 25 people at the approximate cost of $800 for each person. In addition, there would be an additional cost of $6,000 for supplies. Needless to say, this was a cost that was out of reach for the majority of our people who wanted to go. When I announced to the church in December 2001 that we were going and God would take care of the finances, we had 20 people immediately sign up. The majority of them had little money, but they wanted to go and they would trust God to make a way. Following that announcement, one of our members who had moved out of Houston heard about the mission trip to Honduras and gave $12,000 for the trip. In addition, a man in our church family wanted to go but was unable, so he contributed $4,000 towards supplementing the cost of the trip. Furthermore, there was another individual who ultimately gave $3,000 towards the trip because of his passion for missions. As a result, we were able to provide each missionary with a $400 scholarship. The flood of funds arrived only after our people committed to go on mission. Our church continues to offer as much financial assistance as possible for any individual who is low in funds and high in missionary zeal. In this context, we are able to see how God provides as long as we choose to walk by faith in total obedience.

Initial Passive Resistance Within

During the first several years, the church staff encountered so many pockets of opposition to the change process that I felt like we were constantly in the midst of a spiritual battlefield. Although more than 90 percent of the members initially voted for me to come as the new pastor, continuous conflict over what it meant to be open to other races made me question whether Wilcrest called the right pastor. I felt the church needed aggressively to pursue other races to come and join us, yet many of our white members were content with just making sure that if and when other races came, they would feel welcome.[4] Furthermore, if other races would come, then they could learn to assimilate into the present structure of Wilcrest. Yet it became evident that until there was a systemic change, there would be no long-lasting transformation. Initially, I interpreted this passive approach as an unwillingness to pursue the vision, but I now realize that the church took a monumental step in this new direction by releasing the control of the former direction of the church to an entirely different vision. It was not a question of direction but the pace and the method of implementation of the vision. During one of my many frustrating moments in dealing with the slowness of change, a deacon from rural East Texas calmly and correctly chided me, "Pastor, you must remember that we did not grow up where you grew up." This statement immediately put the pace of change in proper perspective. My roots in the ghetto were tremendously different from the perspective of rural east Texas. I have to remember that an all-

---

[4] This is an apt description of the "hospitality mind-set" in all-Korean churches.

white congregation took a chance on a twenty-nine-year-old Chinese pastor with a Hispanic wife to lead them to a place they could never imagine. This spiritual gamble was a release of control as Wilcrest willingly sacrificed a homogeneous congregation to move toward a multiracial vision. This initial step of faith cannot be underestimated in the impact that it would have in years to come.

The First Test of Trust

The week before my arrival at Wilcrest, the church decided to hire a white minister to students. From their perspective, the church felt they were helping me by saving me the trouble of locating and securing an individual for this staff position. However, the person did not exhibit the work ethic or the passion to help Wilcrest make this dream become a reality. After being at Wilcrest for only four months, we released him. The abrupt departure of a new staff member could have easily created dissension or immediate distrust in their new pastor. I feared that the members would ask, "What does this new pastor think he is doing by firing the person we hired?" or "Do we trust the decision we made to hire this minister to students or do we trust the new pastor?" What was very surprising to me is that the release of this staff member produced the opposite effect. After this difficult decision, the church began to gain confidence in my leadership skills. As a result of passing this initial test, they also trusted me to wait an entire year before inviting Monty Jones to become our worship leader.

SPIRITUAL MOMENTUM THROUGH UNIFIED LEADERSHIP

The first several years of watching the homogeneous Wilcrest congregation move through the transformation process to become a multiracial congregation was extremely exhilarating. Everyone told us that the task was impossible, the church was dying, the neighborhood was changing, all the church people were moving out, and the immediate area was dangerous. However, we knew we were witnessing the unexplainable with our own eyes, something that was beyond us. In the midst of this arduous journey, I knew having gifted and unified leadership would be paramount to ensuring the fruition of this vision. In the Wilcrest story, the three ministerial staff members rode the wave of spiritual momentum through a vast array of difficulties and obstacles for the first five years. It was such a difficult process that resistance became the primary confirmation. The apostle Paul assured the church at Corinth that the open door invites adversaries. In the work of the ministry, there are no open doors without opposition. When one of the ministerial staff members was challenged, questioned, or opposed, the other two would immediately rally around him. The primary target seemed to be James, our African-American minister to students. The actual points of contention were seldom vocalized as being racial, but it was what James was doing or not doing that seemed to draw the majority of criticism from the members. The strength of the adversaries was somewhat weakened by the strength that we drew from one another. We would often disagree privately and engage in some lively debates with each other, yet we projected a united front before the congregation. This strategy carried us through the majority of the initial battles and proved effective as long as we leaned on and learned from each other.

FLUCTUATING STAFF

The first five years of the transition process felt like one enormous tidal wave with constant change. It was very satisfying to see a potential "white flight" church not only survive in the transitional neighborhood but also steadily grow. The pastoral staff was together more than five years. This offered a great deal of stability within the leadership when everything else around us was in a state of flux. Yet in 1997, the winds of change targeted the staff. James felt he needed to leave Wilcrest in order to begin his ministry of speaking to young people across the country. Although we experienced many spiritual victories during the first five years, the Wilcrest ministerial team lost one of the key leaders with his departure. While the church was making adjustments, I felt I had lost not only a partner in the vision but also a brother.

Another major shift in our staff occurred in December 1999 when our associate pastor of worship informed me that he had begun to grow detached from the church and the multiracial ministry. During this initial season of shadows, we began to encounter multiple obstacles. One of these struggles involved Monty trying to discern exactly how he fit into the increasingly diverse congregation. Consequently, he left for a worship position in the southeast part of the United States. In my mind, I understood that whomever the church would call as full-time vocational minister, none of them would have a shared history with me or with Wilcrest like James and Monty. With their departures, I felt my right hand and left hand had abandoned me. James and Monty were such vital parts of the formation and the implementation of the multiracial vision, and now I felt completely alone. Amazingly, during this period the church grew in a way we had never experienced with the highest average attendance since my arrival in 1992.

In these three difficult years, we experienced the exodus of two full-time vocational staff members, numerous deacons, and other leaders due to job relocation or retirement. The decrease in visible leadership and resources caused a great deal of anxiety for me and the rest of the church. There were moments when we really did not know if or how we were going to make it through this turbulent period. Throughout all of this tremendous shifting, there was the truth that was being instilled that the vision was bigger than an individual or a budget. This exodus of key leaders and missionaries initially created a spiritual vacuum, but eventually drove the entire church body to a new level of ownership of the vision that was implanted and cultivated in them. In the early years, I adamantly believed we needed a certain number of people and money to implement this vision adequately, but all we needed was passion and commitment to the vision. Now I look back and I see that everything was provided exactly when we needed it. This painful and extracting lesson reminded me of the people of Israel wandering in the wilderness, awaiting their daily provision of manna, which eventually instilled in them a daily trust in following what they saw through their spiritual eyes. Throughout this particular season of shadows, I often questioned if we were on the right path and if we heard the right voice. The dilemma was if this vision was so right, why were so many of our key people moving away?

The Recall of Monty Jones

During the intense search process for new staff, there was an unusual interruption. In June 2000, I received a call from our former associate pastor of worship, who wanted to return to his home base of

Wilcrest. Monty had gone to an all-white church in December 1999. What caught me off guard was the fact that the Personnel Committee and I were moving in an entirely different direction of searching for an associate pastor from a nonwhite racial group. Yet the committee continued to run into multiple obstacles in their search process. After an extensive interview process with Monty and his wife, Wilcrest then issued a "recall" to Monty and his family to return to Houston. In the midst of facing a fearful future, a part of our past returned to play a vital role in our future. Monty came back with a renewed passion for leading our church into a new dimension in the area of multiracial worship.

THE SHORTAGE OF LAY LEADERSHIP

For some reason I assumed that if the ministerial staff members were brought up to speed in the area of vision and direction, the lay leaders would naturally follow the staff's example. However, this assumed automatic osmosis did not occur within our lay leaders. From what we have discovered, leadership development within a multiracial congregation offers a wide range of difficulties.[5] As a reminder of the history of growth of Wilcrest, we rarely received any non-Anglos into our community of believers from other congregations. The majority of our non-Anglos became Christians when they initially connected with Christ through our church. As a rule, mature believers, regardless of race, have their spiritual roots in homogeneous congregations. Our believing visitors may express some initial interest, but very few move from the fascination stage to a firm commitment to the vision because Wilcrest is so different from their familiar spiritual heritage. Consequently, we needed to develop our new leaders from adults who had recently become believers or from those who had been out of the church for an extended period of time. From our experience, we discovered that it requires years of intense discipleship, mentoring, and affirmation to see these new or renewed believers become spiritual leaders within the church. Along this spiritual journey, there were many casualties. In addition, the process has taken much longer than I expected. One of our constant themes is that

---

[5] For an extensive discussion on the role of leadership in a multiracial congregation, see chapter 11.

we are a spiritual ICU: targeting those who are outcasts and discon-
nected from God and church. Consequently, Wilcrest continues to see
a steady influx of hurting people whose lives are shattered. Our future
leaders then come from this group, making the process of leadership
development painfully slow and tedious.

Some of our key leaders have experienced setbacks in their spiritual pilgrimage. Each setback possesses its own reasons, yet there
seems to be a common thread through most of them. With the permanent departure of James and the temporary departure of Monty, I felt
that there were vast holes in the spiritual leadership of Wilcrest. Consequently, we began to place several growing believers in leadership
positions. Initially, I felt they were ready to step up to the challenge
of teaching and leading particular ministries or committees. Looking
back, there were several unhealthy reasons why we placed people in
leadership positions prematurely. The first reason was the great need
for leadership. The willingness of the growing new believers coupled
with their development convinced me that they could handle the rapid
transition. Another reason was that many of these leaders were non-
Anglos and I felt a sense of urgency that we needed our leadership
to reflect the church as a whole. During one of my interviews with a
pastor from another multiracial church on the West Coast, I repeatedly
heard how vital it is to have the church's leadership be an accurate
reflection of the vision and the community of believers. Unknowingly,
I made several decisions that forced many of our new believers from
all races into positions of leadership before they were ready. Consequently, having undeveloped leaders impaired the spiritual growth and
blurred the spiritual vision of the church as a whole.

THE GIANT OF THE TEMPORARY

Another shadow area of a multiracial congregation is the transitory nature of our church. My wife, Sasha, has always called Wilcrest
the "Stop-n-Go" church because of the number of people who stop
for a short period and then quickly leave. In the area immediately surrounding our church facility are a large number of low-income apart-
ments and rental houses. In this socioeconomic context, very few
people stay in our area for a lengthy time, much less retire in Alief.
Consequently, when our Anglos reach retirement age, the majority of

them move out of our area of Houston. We lost several key leaders
and supporters as a result of the rapidly changing neighborhood. Just
when we gained spiritual momentum with a flood of new believers,
their quick exodus completely disheartened the church.[6]

Another factor that accelerated the transition of our people was
that many of them returned to their home countries because they
completed school or wished to be reunited with their families. Many
of our international members were on student or work visas, which
are temporary by law. This transitory nature also served as a primary
strength because the church was able to send missionaries all over
the world after their exposure to a multiracial congregation. However, during the first several years, I felt we were losing some of our
strongest advocates while the home base was continually weakened.
There were times when I have wanted to alter our vision statement
for a year or two and require members to stay longer before they were
sent to a different mission field. As a matter of fact, on February 4,
2004, I asked how many of the people were at Wilcrest 12 years ago
when I came. Out of the 450 people in attendance that day, only 50 of
the people were there 12 years ago.

Some of the people who left were the members who had seen
Wilcrest transform from 99 percent Anglo to less than 40 percent
Anglo, and had grown weary of the racial transition. It was almost
as if too many changes occurred in too short a time period, and their
systems overloaded. During this shadow period, I felt that some of
them lost their passion and vision, but eventually I came to have a
different perspective. I was reminded that this pilgrimage of transforming a homogeneous congregation to a multiracial congregation
was not a hundred-meter sprint, but a grueling marathon. It was as if
the first group faithfully carried the baton the first several laps and
now have handed the baton to the next spiritual generation in the congregation. No one person or group can carry the spiritual load alone.
I believe that is why I found myself originally slipping deeper into
this spiritual shadow. I felt that I was all alone because I often saw
only the people who were leaving and not the ones who were arriving
to help carry the church to the next dimension. The lack of continuity among members and staff often conveyed to me that the people

---

[6] See appendix 2 for the number of additions by baptisms and transfers from other
churches from 1992 until 2007.

did not embrace the vision, or they tasted it and opted for something more palatable to their spiritual systems. At times I questioned if this vision was from an eternal and unchanging God, then why were so many people coming in and out of this vision process? While in the shadows, I could not see clearly past my own sense of isolation, but over a period of time, I began to understand that Wilcrest is actually fulfilling the vision by sending so many people out to other ministries and mission fields.

During the past five years, we experienced a greater sense of stability within the congregation. More people are coming with a strong sense of mission to a multiracial ministry. Many of our members have moved geographically out of our immediate area but continue to commute because of their commitment to the vision. This aspect has greatly encouraged me because I know that transformation requires a long period of time, and having some of the same people in leadership accelerates the process.

THE GIANT OF SPIRITUAL FATIGUE

Another "giant in the land" is spiritual fatigue. As a pastor, there is a call and demand on one's life that is 24 hours a day and seven days a week that never desists. Before I came to Wilcrest, I served as a pastor of a growing rural church in central Texas. Although this ministry was difficult at times, there would always be a pastor or leader who had experienced what I had experienced, which would provide an encouraging model. What I have discovered in the multiracial process is that few paradigms provide guidance and even fewer leaders know how to lead a church through this process. Spiritual fatigue not only comes as the result of being a pastor, but also is compounded by having very few who have gone before and paved the way.

At times I am overwhelmed by the sheer number of cultures and races in one local body of Christ. When God began to send different races into our church family, I would often cringe when our Anglos spoke to our non-Anglos. The whites often displayed a lack of sensitivity to racial and cultural differences. For example, one of the primary points of contention has been in the area of schedules and being on time. Many of our white members are accustomed to starting at the announced time, yet many of our believers from different races view time in a completely different manner. Our Sunday morning worship services often begin with only half of the people there, but by the time the service comes to a conclusion, the other half has arrived. The late arrivers then want to spend a large amount of time visiting with each other after the worship service is over. However, the ongoing exposure and interaction with believers of different races eventually began to instruct all of our people how to interact, support, and learn from each other, regardless of the race and culture.

The year 2001 was the first year since my arrival in 1992 when I felt we turned a major corner in the area of finances and vision. After Wilcrest began to emerge from the "dark night of the soul" toward the end of 2000, I began to think God wanted us to move into the next dimension. This new sense of expectation was precipitated by the personnel committee offering me a sabbatical from the intense pilgrimage. This would give me an opportunity to study and to reflect on the past and future of Wilcrest. When the offer was made to me on December 10, 1999 at 9 p.m., a spiritual marker was planted in my own spiritual journey. I had never been offered an opportunity to rest and to study by a church body. However, the church was sending me a signal that I needed some outside help to go to the next level. It was as if God led the church through me to a certain point, but could not go any further until I rested and refocused. I had invested heavily in the vision and in the church, and this sabbatical was a powerful signal that the church was investing in its leader. This multiracial ministry is a painstaking journey that extracts even more from the leader than does a homogeneous ministry. At times, I received antagonism or opposition from all the different people groups, and it was difficult to mediate between the various perspectives. I desperately needed the time away from the twenty-four-hours-a-day pressure from serving as pastor in the multiracial context. God met this need by calling me to withdraw to Him in a place of solitude for a time of rest (see Ps 46:10; Isa 40:31; Mark 6:31).

FACING THE GIANTS: A BIBLICAL
MODEL—DAVID AND GOLIATH

The most famous giant that Israel ever encountered was Goliath, the Philistine. He stood nine feet six inches tall, protected by 125 pounds of scale-like armor and a bronze helmet, and wielded a spear with a tip weighing more than 15 pounds.[7] This giant invoked fear in the most courageous of all the Israelites. The biblical writer conveyed that because of this fear "they lost their courage and were terrified" (1 Sam 17:11), which means to be faint-hearted to the point of being crushed under pressure.[8] Yet in the face of this physical giant, God sent a spiritual giant, the shepherd David. In contrast to his fellow countrymen, David responded by asking, "Who is this uncircumcised Philistine, that he should taunt[9] the armies of the living God?" (1 Sam 17:26 NASB). In David's conversation with King Saul, David related his previous combat experience in protecting his father's flock and his immeasurable faith in God: "The LORD who rescued me from the paw of the lion and the paw of the bear will rescue me from the hand of this Philistine" (1 Sam 17:37). In Saul's vain attempt to assist this giant of God, he placed military armor on the young man as he made himself ready for battle. As Ralph W. Klein affirmed, "Humanly speaking, they were grossly inadequate for attacking Goliath who was dressed in armor from head to toe and armed with a scimitar and an enormous spear."[10] David refused to use what King Saul had offered and opted for five smooth stones and his sling.

The battle that ensued pitted the giant of the Philistines against the giant of God. In his provocative dialogue with Goliath, David challenged him with this divine claim: "You come against me with a dagger, spear, and sword, but I come against you in the name of the LORD of Hosts, the God of Israel's armies—you have defied Him" (1 Sam 17:45). Although the battle was confined to David and Goliath, the spiritual victory would declare to the entire earth the greatness and glory of God (1 Sam 17:46). At the climax of the confrontation, David fearlessly ran toward the battle line in order to meet this giant, face to face, with absolute confidence in God. David removed a smooth stone from his pouch and calmly hit Goliath squarely in his forehead, his only vulnerable opening. This great Philistine giant who had boasted

---

[7] Howard F. Vos, *Bible Study Commentary: 1 and 2 Samuel* (Grand Rapids: Zondervan, 1983), 63.

[8] See Wilson, 127.

[9] The term *taunt* conveys the sense of blaspheming the God of the Israelites. See Wilson, 41.

[10] Ralph W. Klein, *1 Samuel,* Word Biblical Commentary (Waco: Word, 1983), 179.

that he would serve David as food to the birds, immediately collapsed with his face on the ground.

In David's battle with his giant, we are able to glean several principles when we are facing giants in our spiritual battle in becoming a multiracial congregation. *The first principle is that God often calls the most unlikely and uniquely gifted individual to lead the charge.* David, a shepherd and the youngest in his family, was not his older brothers' or King Saul's first choice. After David volunteered to fight Goliath, King Saul attempted to impose his traditional military armor on this spiritual giant. However, God had already trained David in his own battleground with lions and bears. Each person who will engage in the spiritual battle of establishing a multiracial ministry or congregation will need the gifts and experiences that God has provided uniquely to them.[11]

The second principle is that the battle requires that we release all human resources as we place our absolute faith in the God who will crush Satan under His feet (see Rom 16:19–20). When Wilcrest faced the giants of decreasing attendance and finances, lack of leadership, the transitory nature of the church, and spiritual fatigue, we had few options remaining if we wanted to survive in this spiritual battlefield. In confronting each of these giants in our promised land, God provided exactly what we needed in His perfect time.

The final principle is that each battle that is fought and won on the racial battlefront will announce to the world the greatness and glory of God. As David announced to Goliath and to the rest of the Philistine army, "Today, the LORD will hand you over to me. Today, I'll strike you down, cut your head off, and give the corpses of the Philistine camp to the birds of the sky and the creatures of the earth. *Then all the world will know that Israel has a God*" (1 Sam 17:46).[12] As the multiracial church gathers together, the body of Christ will announce to the entire world that God is the God of all peoples and "in every nation the person who fears Him and does righteousness is acceptable to Him" (Acts 10:35).

---

[11] The characteristics of a multiracial leader are discussed in chapter 11.

[12] Emphasis mine.

SUMMARY

When God called the people of Israel to cross the Jordan River into the promised land, the first set of eyes envisioned the opposition and obstacles and not the opportunity. Every new land has giants to face and conquer. Some of the giants that Wilcrest encountered in their journey toward becoming a multiracial congregation included: discouraging words from outside of our congregation, fluctuation of staff leadership, shortage of lay leadership, decrease in attendance, decrease in giving, the temporary nature of the people we attracted, and spiritual fatigue. Each one of these by itself could easily cause a detour from the pursuit of the vision, but cumulatively, it would be impossible to stay focused on the God-given vision. However, the giants become peripheral when we lock our gaze upon God. The biblical example of David's encounter with the Philistine giant provides evidence that God empowers His people to face insurmountable barriers. In David's battle with Goliath, God used an unlikely instrument who placed his absolute faith in his great God, thus bringing glory to God alone. As with David, God orchestrated our journey to testify to His surpassing greatness. He did this by giving us a vision in advance that we may believe and stripping us of all resources, allowing us to see. The greatest joy that comes from pursuing a God-sized vision is seeing the God who alone can accomplish it.

DISCUSSION

1. In your spiritual journey, what are some giants that you have encountered that caused you to lose focus or take a spiritual detour? Have your primary points of resistance been outside the church among unbelievers or from within the body of Christ? What is the difference between opposition from without and opposition from within?

2. In the crossing of your Jordan, what are some of the giants that you have faced in reaching across the racial barriers on a personal and church level? Would some of the giants include racism, prejudice, tradition, your comfort zone, lack of personal exposure and experience, and fear? Which one of these giants has invoked the most fear in you?

3. What was the difference between the "ten-spy report" and Caleb's report after their return from the promised land? Read Num 13:17–33. What did both groups see? What did Caleb see that the "ten-spy report" did not see? If there is a "ten-spy report" in your ministry regarding the racial landscape, what would it say? In contrast, what would Caleb see and report if he saw your promised land?

4. What steps can you take biblically in not only facing your giants but also defeating them from the example of David's military engagement with Goliath? What are the three principles gleaned from the battle between the giant of the Philistines and the giant of God? Of these three principles, which one encourages you the most and why? Which one challenges you the most and why?

CHAPTER 8

COUNT THE COST

"For which of you, wanting to build a tower, doesn't first sit down and calculate the cost to see if he has enough to complete it?" (Luke 14:28)

It is not an easy task for a homogeneous church to know when it is ready to make the transition to a multiracial congregation. It is even more difficult for a church planter to determine if the core group or the surrounding geographical area is ready for the establishment of a multiracial church. If the pastor is ready, there are no guarantees that the church body or the core group is ready. Since every church is unique in its composition, history, location, and purpose, the starting point may vary for each individual congregation. When the leader and the congregation are ready to begin this difficult but rewarding journey of reaching across racial and cultural barriers in order to bring salvation to all the nations, there are costs in navigating this unknown path. As the apostle Paul conveyed to the church at Corinth, there are times when God opens doors, yet these opportunities are often accompanied by potential danger (1 Cor 16:9). Since so few multiracial congregational models exist, the question of readiness is not a simple question. Perhaps to give a little taste of the complexity of this issue, let me deal with the simple and yet diverse practice of greeting each other in church.

FORMS OF GREETING

Greeting is a vital part of every culture because it indicates an individual's willingness to reach out to another person. In a homogeneous context, each person understands the acceptable forms of greeting, such as hugging, kissing, shaking of hands, and bowing.

Other elements that determine the form and expression of greetings are culture, age, and gender of the individuals involved. However, when there is a convergence of multiple cultures and racial groups in one local church family, greeting one another can become somewhat confusing and awkward. What is deemed appropriate by one culture may be perceived as offensive in a different culture. The call of God to reach across racial and cultural lines mandates that we discover the most effective bridge to an individual's heart regardless of their background. In the same way, the apostle Paul adapted to different cultures, "To the Jews I became like a Jew . . . to those under the law, like one under the law. . . . I have become all things to all people, so that I may by all means save some" (1 Cor 9:20–23). The initial greeting with all people groups can often determine if the doors to their hearts will be open to the gospel or closed to Christ.

GREETINGS FROM THE APOSTLE PAUL

In the early church, there was evidently some flexibility when it came to greeting one another. When Paul wrote his epistles, he utilized a general form of greeting that was acceptable to the first-century context. For example, he introduced himself as the author and often added the names of those who were helping him in the ministry. He then identified the recipients, either by function or by their location (cp. 1 Cor 1:1; 2 Cor 1:1; Phil 1:1; Col 1:1; 1 Thess 1:1; 2 Thess 1:1). Finally he conveyed the Christian triad of blessing: grace, peace, and mercy to the recipients of the letter (cp. 1 Cor 1:3; 2 Cor 1:2; Gal 1:3; Eph 1:2; Phil 1:2; Col 1:2; 1 Thess 1:1; 2 Thess 1:2; 1 Tim 1:2; 2 Tim 1:2). "Grace" and "peace" communicated effectively to his audiences. In most cases, he expressed both forms of greetings because Gentiles and Jews were integrated in the churches that he addressed. He usually utilized the acceptable form of greeting, but then, based on his purpose and the need of the recipients, he adjusted to different expressions of greeting. In all of his greetings, Paul's purpose was to communicate the revelation of God to his recipients. In the same way, the multiracial church needs to be sensitive to each culture to ensure that the lines of communication remain open to convey the heart of God for all the nations.

GREETINGS IN WILCREST

Greetings come in a vast array of forms at Wilcrest due to the global composition of the community of believers. For example, there is a man who is in his early seventies from Ethiopia. Every time I greet him and attempt to embrace him, he shuns any bold physical contact, but rather bows and addresses me as "Father" or "Abba." Since most of our new believers come either from no religious background or a Catholic tradition, this form of greeting has set off numerous alarms in my spiritual system. Yet this brother patiently explained that since I am his spiritual leader, he renders respect for the position of pastor. On any given Sunday, while he bows to his pastor in respect, there are several young children of all races running up to me and knocking me over with hugs. I would offend my brother from Ethiopia if I embraced him, and I would offend the children if I did not hug them. These are examples of two extreme expressions of greeting, but both indicate the need to be aware and sensitive to different cultures within the same local body of believers, while still conveying the love of God.[1]

Another example of the cultural tension in this area of greeting comes in the form of how to address the pastor. This issue does not seem like it should be that volatile, yet in our multiracial setting, what to call the pastor can cause confusion and conflict. When I came to Wilcrest, I was 29 and the majority of members were white and between the ages of 40 and 60. The atmosphere of the church was somewhat formal, with the majority of our members being middle to upper middle class Anglos. In order to convey the desired intimacy, I encouraged the members to call me by my first name. I did not want a formal title to be a hindrance in reaching a person with the good news of Christ. For some the title erected a barrier that was difficult to cross. Although some of the members continued to address me as "Dr. Woo" or "Brother Rodney" or "Pastor Woo," most eventually

---

[1] In the Filipino culture, shaking hands between males is the most appropriate, preserving an appropriate distance between each other. Men usually do not hug unless it is a time of crisis. Men and women may embrace, but only if they are close friends. In the Latin America cultures, it is acceptable to kiss each other on the cheek and hugs are very important, for they are signs of warmth and affection. In the Korean culture, bowing is a noble way to greet one another, especially if there is a difference in age. In addition, there is a tendency to avert the eyes when addressing each other in the Asian culture. Consequently, when a multiracial church gathers, navigating with understanding through these potential landmines is an absolute necessity. See Rhoads, *Where the Nations Meet,* 165–67.

identified me simply as "Rodney." Yet with the influx of different cultures, the informal manner in which many of the white members addressed me proved to be inappropriate to some of our nonwhite members, who insisted on addressing the pastor in a more official manner. The use of the variety of titles caused some confusion when the newer members heard different people address me in different ways. In fact, our Korean minister to children finally asked me in a staff meeting, "What do I need to call you?" I responded by telling her to call me "Rodney" in personal meetings, but perhaps addressing me in a more formal manner in public. She nodded, but still remained reluctant to address me by my first name under any circumstances the next two years. Now after five years, she feels somewhat comfortable addressing me by my first name in private.

The multiracial community of believers experiences a multitude of risks of including or excluding different people groups in something as simple as the form of greeting. Many people find the challenge of greeting and other cultural contrasts insurmountable within the framework and fabric of the church structure. Consequently, they choose either to avoid a multiracial ministry or they actively oppose the mixture of races and cultures in one church. Many of our members, however, see this clash of cultures in the area of greeting as an opportunity to learn from and minister to different cultures.

COUNT THE COST

The different ways people greet each other is a microcosm of the larger picture of the barriers that the body of Christ must cross in order to be a racially integrated congregation. Other barriers include: worship style, leadership, length of services, communication, trust, how to handle conflict, and dealing with prejudices. Jesus counseled those who counted the cost of following His gospel call with these words: "For which of you, wanting to build a tower, doesn't first sit down and calculate the cost to see if he has enough to complete it? Otherwise, after he has laid the foundation and cannot finish it, all the onlookers will begin to make fun of him" (Luke 14:28–29). In the same way a builder must know the resources and requirements to complete the project, the commander of an army must also count the cost of engaging an enemy in battle. Similar to counting the costs of the gospel, in the spiritual struggle of developing multiracial congregations in the battlefield of prejudice and racism, leaders must count the cost of what it requires to integrate believers into the local church. How does a church know if they are ready to become a multiracial congregation? Before a church can move in this multiracial direction, it is vital to assess exactly where they are. I have developed a hand model to help individual believers and churches understand where they are in the process of becoming a multiracial congregation. In addition, once they know where they are, then it becomes clearer to see what steps they need to take to move toward this goal.

THE HAND MODEL

According to our biblical survey, crossing racial and cultural barriers presented a difficult challenge for every generation since the fall of Adam. In spite of overwhelming resistance, there continue to be pockets of grace that encourage movement toward racial reconciliation, which are often located in individuals rather than corporate entities such as churches, schools, and governments. If building bridges to different people groups is to occur at a corporate level, it will require a unified group of people committed to a God-sized task over a long period of time.

The hand model will serve as a spiritual gauge or a biblical barometer of discovering where people are when they come to a multiracial congregation for the first time. It will also provide a method of measurement as churches progress toward becoming multiracial congregations. This model is an adaptation of a model that Alvin Reid shared with me in regard to worship. Alvin Reid is presently serving in the Bailey Smith Chair of Evangelism at Southeastern Baptist Theological Seminary. In his model, there are five fingers on the hand and each finger represents a strong desire for a certain style of worship. His primary point is that wherever an individual falls in his leaning toward a particular style or form of worship, a church generally can move that individual no more than one finger over from where he or she originally began. In addition, it often proves futile to attempt to move an entire congregation or an individual more than one finger or one space over from where they started. My multiracial hand model also has five fingers, each representing a particular perception of the integration of races within the congregational framework. Each of these groups has both modern and biblical characters that fit into the distinct categories. Although these are somewhat arbitrary in nature, this model communicates in a tangible form the necessity of seeing where people are and then determining if the congregation is ready to move to the next level.[2]

Advocates of Prejudice

On the far right are the *advocates of prejudice* who want to maintain the purity of the separate divisions between races and cultures within the religious or church context and will utilize whatever means necessary to keep these divisions intact. The individuals in this category during the first century included the Jewish zealots, who aggressively acted out their prejudice against the Roman government.[3] There was even a subgroup of zealots known as the "Sicarii," who used stealth in order to kill Roman soldiers during the crowded Jewish festivals. The Sicarii would immerse themselves in the crowds, approach the Roman soldier without his knowledge, and kill him with a hidden dagger.[4] Violent aggression was a visible expression of commitment to their cause and to their God. The zealots opposed any element that would infect Judaism and would go to great lengths to protect the purity of Judaism at all costs.

In modern times, these would include "racial purists" of the church, who aggressively combat any attempt to cross any racial or cultural lines. They are opposed to any interaction or dialogue between the different people groups because it would compromise or infect the purity of their belief. This racial attitude was clearly depicted in the 1920s, when there were "approximately forty thousand ministers of the Ku Klux Klan with Protestant ministers serving as Grand Dragons in Pennsylvania, Texas, North Dakota, and Colorado."[5] Individuals from this category perceive their own racial group as superior and all others as inferior. For example, the whites in this group would contend that the curse placed on Canaan would entail a curse against

---

[2] This concept was first introduced in *People of the Dream*, 169.

[3] Simon the zealot, one of Jesus' twelve disciples, would be an example.

[4] Clayton Harrop, "Jewish Parties," in *Holman Bible Dictionary,* ed. Trent C. Butler (Nashville: Holman Bible Publishers, 1991), 791–94. See also "Assassins," in *Holman Bible Dictionary.*

[5] *United by Faith,* 60.

the black race, thus arguing from a biblical base for the superiority of the white race and inferiority of the black race (see Gen 9:25–27).[6] This group would also strongly oppose any interracial marriages and would use the Ezra and Nehemiah passages to support their belief that God commanded the Jews not to intermarry with other races (cp. Ezra 9:1–2; Neh 13:23–29). The Bible often becomes their weapon to inflict their doctrine of separation of races on others, while at the same time they refuse to understand the biblical model and mandate to alleviate the division between the Jew and the Gentile in Jesus Christ. This was also clearly evident in the way the Nazis contended that their race was superior to everyone else, ultimately resulting in the Holocaust. This group is intentionally blind to any biblical teaching or practice that does not support their erroneous presuppositions. This category applies not only to individuals, but also to churches and denominations.

Homogeneous Advocates

The *homogeneous advocates* are entrenched in their distinct racial traditions and represent the second category or finger on the hand. This group sees nothing wrong with churches of different races and even encourages their separate existence, but they refuse to cross racial lines and interface with different people groups. One example of this group found in the New Testament was the Pharisees, who acknowledged other groups but wanted to ensure the purity of their own group by distancing themselves completely from others. In fact, the name "Pharisee" means "separated ones."[7] The Pharisees and other such groups were not militant toward the different groups, but they intentionally withdrew from any contact with people who were not exactly like them. They took great pride in the fact that they did not include others who were different from them and believed outsiders would contaminate their beliefs and lives. They acknowledged the validity of the existence of other groups, but strongly contended that groups needed to remain separate and distinct. The influence of the Pharisees may be one of the primary reasons why the early Christian

---

[6] During the time of the Civil War, many southern Christians argued that slavery was biblically valid because Canaan, Ham's son, was made a slave to his brothers. See *Divided by Faith*, 34.

[7] Merrill C. Tenney, *New Testament Survey,* rev ed. (Grand Rapids: Eerdmans, 1985), 105.

Jews had so much difficulty incorporating the Gentiles into the body of Christ.[8]

The homogeneous advocates would encourage the formation of distinct Jewish and Gentile congregations. However, if the two groups were to merge, the Jewish advocates contended that the Gentiles were to discard much of their background and incorporate Jewish practices. The prevalent thought was that if new Gentile believers wanted to participate in their Jewish form of Christianity, then they were to become like Jewish Christians in belief and practice. This was the primary debate at the Jerusalem Council in Acts 15, in which a group of Jews contended that unless Gentiles were also circumcised, then they shared no part of the family of God. This Jewish imposition created a potential spiritual inferiority within the Gentile Christians. In fact, Paul confronted this group of Judaizers, who insisted that in order for Gentiles to become full Christians, they must not only put their faith in Christ and but also keep the Mosaic Law (Gal 3:1–14).

In our contemporary context, the homogeneous advocates celebrate the existence of distinct racial congregations, but believe that real and meaningful growth will only come if the different people groups remain isolated and separate. During America's history in the 1950s, the term *separate but equal* depicted the black/white issue in the South. In the same way, the homogeneous advocates echo this battle cry. Many of these churches actually plant missions for "those people" in order for them to have a separate place of worship. The Southern Baptists historically fall into this category as they encourage ethnic mission churches. Some of the reasons given to justify separate churches have included: "They need their own place"; "They worship differently than we do"; "They need freedom to express themselves without any restraints"; and "They speak a different language." The Church Growth Movement, which originated at Fuller Theological Seminary, even claimed that maintaining separate identities actually propagates a more effective evangelism.[9] C. Peter Wagner contends,

---

[8] For further discussion, see Robert H. Gundry, *A Survey of the New Testament,* 4th ed. (Grand Rapids: Zondervan, 2003), 63–64. This group numbered only about 6,000 at the time of Herod the Great, but greatly influenced the religious landscape during the time of the New Testament.

[9] In his book *Our Kind of People: The Ethical Dimensions of Church Growth in America* (Atlanta: John Knox, 1979), C. Peter Wagner claims that the issues of race and culture are amoral, people prefer to worship in their own cultural group, growth is more vital when

"For optimum conditions of growth, the composition of the congregation should be compatible with the needs for social companionship felt by the unchurched people in the community."[10] One note of constructive criticism to this evangelistic approach encourages the members of the local congregations to look like one another. The multiracial congregation, however, is racially diverse by design but drawn together by a factor other than the common color of skin, the person of Christ.

In the early history of Wilcrest, the common belief that each racial group needed to experience their own place of worship permeated the white majority. In fact, Wilcrest played a key role in the establishment of an African-American and a Chinese mission congregation, which both eventually formed independent churches. Each of these congregations initially utilized our physical facilities but maintained their separate identity from the sponsoring white church. Often times, when African-American or Chinese individuals visited the white church, the white leaders gave their names to the pastors of the mission congregations. According to the evangelical standard prevalent during that period, Wilcrest viewed itself as a mission-minded congregation because the church had planted two ethnic congregations. As I look back on that chapter in our church's history, God gave Wilcrest an opportunity to integrate different races into one body of believers. However, the formation of separate and distinct congregations was the manner in which Wilcrest dealt with the upcoming wave of nations that would eventually envelop the surrounding area of the church.

Seekers

The third group or finger on the hand model is the *seekers*, which include people who are curious and fascinated by the multiracial congregation. During the first century, this group is represented by the Greek seekers in John's Gospel (John 12:20–26), Cornelius (Acts 10), and other God-fearers. These peripheral observers were originally attracted to Judaism for its monotheistic (worship of only one God) emphasis and a high moral code. The God-fearers were willing

---

done in a homogeneous environment, and growing homogeneous churches is an essential tool for Christian growth.
    [10] Wagner, 15–16.

to cross over the racial and cultural lines because of their desire to seek the one true God, yet many of them refused circumcision or to become proselytes (full Jewish converts).[11] Both monotheism and the moral code of Judaism helped prepare the God-fearers for the introduction of Christianity. Yet Christianity offered the God-fearers what Judaism could not, namely, a personal relationship with God through the blood sacrifice of Christ. In fact, the God-fearers were the first Gentiles targeted by the apostles.[12]

The New Testament seekers also served as a bridge between the homogeneous and rigid Jews and the Gentiles who had no religious background. When the God-fearers converted to Christianity, they already understood and embraced the key tenets of Judaism, so they could still make connections with the Jewish elements within the New Testament church. At the same time, their Gentile background provided them with a point of contact and understanding with the Gentiles who had no religious or monotheistic background. This new bridge builder of the New Testament church modeled to the Jewish Christians how to understand and embrace the Gentile Christians and vice versa.

In the contemporary context, this group of seekers includes people who come to our church looking for something different than their homogeneous congregations. They feel that something is missing in their Christian and church experience. They see or hear fragments of Christianity from other cultures and deduce that everything from these separate Christian groups cannot be totally wrong. They question why there are racial lines of demarcation at all, especially in light of what the Bible says about reaching all nations. These seekers discover and experience the crossing of racial lines at work, school, community, and are perplexed why the church refuses to cross these blatant barriers.

Many of our initial seekers who come to Wilcrest are those who are in interracial marriages and find no acceptance in churches of their respective racial groups. They are simply looking for a place of intimate connection in which both husband and wife can find acceptance and love without the race factor provoking a point of contention. The children of these interracial couples also are in desperate

---

[11] Larkin, 153–54.
[12] This is evident in Peter's connection with Cornelius in Acts 10.

need of a place to belong. The incorporation of the interracial families in the multiracial congregation is one of the first fruits of a greater multiracial harvest. I believe the interracial marriages will serve in the same role that the God-fearers served in the early New Testament church. As a family, they possess connection and understanding with two distinct races, but are committed to the integration of different races into one church family.

As a church, Wilcrest fell into this category when I first arrived. Some of the reasons the Wilcrest members were curious seekers included: the homogeneous method was not working, the surrounding neighborhood was extremely diverse, and the community was in transition from an all-white neighborhood to a multiracial community. Consequently, the church opened itself to multiracial ministry in order to save the life of the church. It was an issue of survival. If Wilcrest failed to reach across racial barriers, the church was going to die. Since Wilcrest experienced a ten-year decline with many of the church's primary targets quickly exiting the area, there were few viable alternatives. Some within the leadership proposed to join the white flight and relocate to more predominantly white suburbs, but the core of the church stood firm with a strong sense of calling to Alief. Once the church determined to stay in the original location, the desire to survive ignited the possibility of ministering to more than one racial group.

Seekers are motivated for a variety of reasons, but what connects all of them is their desire to see something different than what they are presently experiencing. For Wilcrest, the numerical and spiritual decline prompted the church to seek solutions measurably different than its former experience. Among Southern Baptists, seekers offer the most fertile ground to transform our denomination from homogeneous to multiracial. Many Southern Baptists contend that we are already a multiracial denomination because we now have black, Latin, Chinese, Vietnamese, Nigerian, Indonesian, Laotian, Filipino, and Korean Southern Baptist churches. Yet all of these churches remain subdivided into separate racial entities without meaningful integration. One of my students at Houston Baptist University observed:

> While Jim Crow Laws were outlawed and segregation was deemed illegal, there is still little to no integration within the confines of church buildings. This is seen in present-day

Houston when you drive down a street. There will be First
Baptist Houston, then there is *Primera Iglesia Bautista His-
pana*, and down the street from this church, there will be
First Baptist Chinese Fellowship and Crossing Point Church,
which is an African American Baptist church. So, how can
this be what God intended for his people and the worship of
him?[13]

I am confident that the apostle Paul did not contend that Christianity
in the first century was multiracial because there were separate Jewish and Gentile congregations (cp. Acts 13:1; Rom 9–11).

Fully Integrated Believers

The fourth group is the *fully integrated believers* in the multiracial
congregation. There are numerous examples of those who led out in
the early New Testament church in the incorporating of different people groups within their sphere of ministry. For example, the church
in Jerusalem sent out the Jewish Barnabas to encourage the church at
Antioch and their ministry to the Gentiles (Acts 10:19–27). Timothy
also served in a similar capacity. Timothy's background laid part of
his foundation for a multiracial ministry, for his father was Greek and
his mother was Jewish (Acts 16:1). In addition, he served with Paul
in both the synagogues to the Jews and to the Gentiles while on their
missionary journeys. The church at Jerusalem is another example of
an integrated congregation. The church elected spiritual men in order
to serve food to the Hellenistic widows because they saw the potential problem of racial division between the Jews and the Gentiles. All
seven men elected by the church possessed Greek names; thus they
were able to identify closely with the widows who had Greek backgrounds (Acts 6:1–7).

There is no doubt that these individuals and groups did not fully
integrate immediately, but it followed a long and slow process of
transcending former lines of demarcation and embracing Christ's
activity in other cultures. For example, the early Jewish church continued to worship on the Sabbath, while adding Sunday worship for
the celebration of the Messiah's resurrection. As Christianity spread

---

[13] This observation comes from an assignment given to students in the course titled
"The Multiracial Church" offered at Houston Baptist University in the fall of 2002.

to the exclusive Gentile regions, the primary day of worship was Sunday. This is one example of releasing the Jewish lines of distinction because the day of Christ's resurrection now took priority over all Jewish traditions.

In the contemporary setting, the fully integrated believers are the people in our church family who caught and embraced the multiracial vision. The majority of our integrated believers began their pilgrimage as seekers, but through intense spiritual growth and the process of time, they now adopt God's heart for all the nations as their own. During this process, they expose themselves to biblical texts, experiences, and models of what it means to be part of a multiracial congregation. In addition, they have numerous personal friends who are of different cultures and races other than their own. They participate zealously on our mission trips to extend themselves beyond their racial comfort zone. In their desire to develop and sharpen their multiracial skills, they place themselves intentionally in an arena in which they are the minority. As a result of this internal transformation, they now experience discomfort in a homogeneous setting. For example, when our integrated believers visit the place of their homogeneous upbringing (usually in the Deep South), they return to Wilcrest amazed at how different they are now, as opposed to their original roots.

Among the integrated believers, there are a variety of expressions and levels as they mature in this ongoing process. One example is a young man whom I baptized at the end of 2001. He accepted Christ and reconnected with his wife after a prolonged period of separation. After his baptism, he confided in me that he was half-Hispanic and attempted to conceal this fact all of his life. One of his reasons for doing this was that it never benefited him to announce to others that he was Hispanic. Most of the time people perceived him to be white and consequently treated him better. At times, there was also a sense of shame that others would look down on him because of his heritage. After becoming an integral part of Wilcrest, he felt safe enough to reveal and celebrate his Hispanic heritage, knowing that Wilcrest accepted and embraced him for who he is in Christ and for his culture. The reality of having a safe area for authenticity has an immeasurable impact on individuals who live in a culture that outwardly coerces recognition of distinct cultures. The multiracial congregation provides an arena that encourages diverse cultural expression out of an intimate connection with other believers and not external coercion from legislation.

Missionaries

The final group is the *missionaries* for the cause of multiracial congregations. The primary biblical examples are Jesus and Paul. Both of these shattered ancient racial barriers in order to incorporate all people groups into one body and one family. Even though they encountered stiff opposition from their own race, they both intentionally and persistently reached out to all people groups. A large number of these individuals does not need to be in each congregation, but each church needs a core group who are willing to lead, cast the vision, and set the pace.

In the life and ministry of Jesus, He set both the pattern and pace for reaching all people groups. Jesus knew His mission began with the Jews first (Matt 10:6; 15:24), and then He opened Himself to the Syrophoenecian woman (Matt 15:21–28), the Samaritan woman (John 4), and the Greeks (John 12:20–26). Going to the Jew first and Gentile second was the model and direction of both Jesus and Paul (Rom 1:16). Jesus laid the groundwork with His message and ministry for Paul and the early church to follow.

When the apostle Peter withdrew from table fellowship with the Gentiles because of the pressure from the zealous Jews, the apostle Paul passionately opposed this racial exclusion. This apostolic confrontation is an excellent example of why this process requires at least one missionary who is willing to do whatever it takes to ensure that the multiracial vision reaches fruition. Paul stepped in and called Peter out on his refusal to eat with those from another culture. Paul's passion for the nations allowed no room for arbitration; thus he stood firmly on the truth that a leader needed to lead in this very difficult direction even in the face of opposition (Gal 2:11–14).

During the transitional period at Wilcrest from a homogeneous all-white congregation, there were many junctures when the church felt content to stop short of fully integrating into a multiracial congregation. It is tempting to conclude that when we reach a certain percentage in each primary racial group or we have representative leadership, then our task is accomplished. Another danger is the perception that since the church reached the numerical quotas espoused by Affirmative Action, we are a biblical multiracial congregation. Yet within the contemporary American Christian context, we are not close to where God wants us to be. Numbers and percentages are only a small part of the overall gauge of multiracial ministry. The God-given vision in accordance with Scripture is what drives and directs the multiracial congregation, while the hearts of the participants constitute the soil in which this vision takes root and ultimately bears fruit. The representation from different races and cultures is merely the outward expression of what has already occurred within the mind of God and His people.

SUMMATION OF THE HAND MODEL

The hand model offers only an arbitrary description of the spiritual location of where many believers are in relation to multiracial congregations. Participants in all of the categories or fingers strongly believe in their expression of the Christian faith. The primary reason I want to present this model is to challenge individuals, churches, denominations, and institutions to examine carefully exactly where they fall in the area of crossing humanly constructed barriers. This model will not only aid in the discovery of where one is, but also help move a ready heart in a new direction. I would also have to agree with Alvin Reid, who contends that it is difficult to move an individual or group more than one finger or category at a time. If God placed the desire to plant or to transition a church toward becoming a multiracial congregation, it is advantageous to target seekers who could move into the integrated believer category. When Wilcrest began this arduous process, not one member fell into the integrated believer category. However, 15 years later, the vast majority of our people now are either in that category or moving rapidly toward it. God will raise missionaries for multiracial churches out of multiracial churches in order for them to plant churches or assist those who are open to making this transition, but lack leadership. One of our former members just recently left Wilcrest to continue the education process. She is now determined to go to an all-white church and help it transition to a multiracial congregation.

Early in this process, I thought that if other churches witnessed what God did at Wilcrest, they would eagerly join this unusual movement. After interacting with a large number of church leaders and members, what I discovered is that they readily acknowledge that the multiracial model is biblical and necessary, but they claimed that this model is not specifically designed for them. There are numerous reasons for their hesitation and reluctance, such as: "We are in a different neighborhood than yours"; "Our people are not ready for that"; "That model has worked well for you and your situation"; "The process will take too much time"; "We will lose the majority of our people"; "I do not believe that our staff will buy into this model." All of these responses call into question the obedience to the biblical mandate to reach and incorporate all people groups into the body of Christ.

Fifteen years into this process at Wilcrest, there is no doubt that modeling a multiracial congregation is a powerful part of leading other congregations down this path. When people see all the races in one place worshiping together, serving together, and loving each other, they are personally encouraged that this can happen and divinely convicted that this should be happening in more places. If the God of all the nations can draw all the different people groups together at Wilcrest, there is proof that what will be happening in heaven around the throne can happen here on earth.

DISCUSSION

1. Where do you fit personally on the hand model? What biblical character do you most closely identify with in relation to reaching across racial and cultural lines? Do you feel content to stay the same or have you been challenged to move to the next stage? If you are open to moving to the next stage, what appropriate steps could you take to start moving in that direction?

2. Where does your congregation fit in the hand model? What group in the New Testament or Old Testament most closely models your present church situation? Is your church locked in on their present condition or do they sense a need to move to the next stage? If your church is open to move to the next stage, what are some of the appropriate steps that your church could take in order to move in a new direction?

3. Read Luke 14:28–32. What are the builder and the king about to do? What is Jesus' primary point about the building of the tower and the king going out to battle? On a personal level, what is your tower that God is calling you to build or what battle is God calling you to fight? What will the cost be for you to build or to fight? As a congregation, what is God calling you to build or fight in the area of multiracial ministry? What will this building or battle cost your church?

IMPLEMENTATION

CHAPTER 9

RULES OF ENGAGEMENT

"Be strong and courageous, for you will distribute the land I swore to their fathers to give them as an inheritance" (Josh 1:6).

INTRODUCTION

The first section of this book establishes the biblical foundation for multiracial ministry, beginning with creation and concluding with the racial reunion around the throne of God. Since Scripture clearly indicates that God has a heart for the nations, the biblical vision for reaching the nations mandates that the church develop a strong working theology of what it means to live in unity in the midst of diversity. However, the primary obstacle that undermines the reconciliation among the nations, races, and cultures is racism. This first section calls the church to repentance and to produce deeds of reconciliation that are appropriate to repentance (Acts 26:20). The second section provides a clear picture of the current reality depicting relationships among the races in our society and churches. A church that captures the vision for multiracial ministry must decide their willingness to pursue this vision despite numerous obstacles from both within and outside the church. This section gives help to churches and individuals to assess their progress in the process and to give them insight concerning the cost of this multiracial vision. This final section offers practical guidance, with help to implement multiracial ministry. It also includes specific rules of engagement as the spiritual battle for reaching all the races ensues. The key battlefields of worship, leadership, and missions will be addressed through the lenses of multiracial ministry in chapters ten, eleven, and twelve respectively.

THE NECESSITY OF BATTLES

One common vehicle in God's fulfillment of plans for His people is through battles. From emotional to spiritual to literal, we see many biblical figures receive a vision from God that is made real through their personal battles. Initially, Abraham had to battle against unbelief through a twenty-five-year waiting period from the time he first received a vision of his seed's future blessing to all nations to the final fulfillment at the birth of his son, Isaac. Moses had to engage in a military battle with the Egyptian Pharaoh for his people's freedom, only then to battle emotional discouragement in the face of his people's numerous desert rebellions. As Israel emerged as a new nation, they too had to learn to fight according to God's Word in order to experience the fruition of God's vision to Abraham to reach all nations. Additionally, Joshua first engaged in a spiritual battle where he aligned himself with the "angel of the Lord" before the physical battle over the promised land. In fact, the initial stages of the conquest of the promised land did not become a reality until six centuries after God's promise to Abraham. The final conquest of the promised land was not completed until the time of David, a thousand years after Abraham. Although God promised Israel the land of Canaan as their inheritance, the people still had to engage in battle over an extended period of time.[1]

THE NECESSITY FOR RULES OF ENGAGEMENT

Battles are time consuming, difficult, and discouraging. However, in the case of Israel, battles were a necessary trial to bring to fruition God's vision for His people. As the young nation of Israel formed over a four hundred-year period while in bondage in Egypt, they did not have much time to develop and sharpen their military skills before their first battle with the Canaanites in the promised land. With so much difficulty in battles, regardless of the time era, it is necessary to formulate rules of engagement (ROE):

---

[1] God told Moses, "I will drive them out little by little ahead of you until you have become numerous and take possession of the land" (Exod 23:30). Later God reminded Moses, "The LORD your God will drive out these nations before you little by little. You will not be able to destroy them all at once; otherwise, the wild animals will become too numerous for you" (Deut 7:22). God's design was to grow Israel's faith as they conquered the land a little at a time.

In military or police operations, the rules of engagement (ROE) determine when, where, and how force shall be used. Such rules are both general and specific, and there have been large variations between cultures throughout history. The rules are . . . typically only fully known to the force that intends to use them. . . . In any engagement, the ROE need to balance two competing goals: The need to use force effectively to accomplish the mission objectives and the need to avoid unnecessary force.[2]

The emergence of multiracial churches in the United States comes in the context of the historical battlefield of racial prejudice and segregation. These prototypical multiracial churches have had little time or practice honing their skills in how to take possession of their promised land. Yet knowing that the war will be long and costly, God still calls us to engage in the spiritual warfare. In all congregations, many battles emerge, but it is vital to know when to fight and when to flee. However, once Wilcrest understood and embraced God's vision of all races and cultures worshiping together as the body of Christ, we chose to fight this spiritual battle. The ongoing struggle, marked by numerous setbacks and multiple battle scars, serves as a constant reminder of the cost of racially integrating a congregation.

In the multiracial church context, there are so many potential battlefronts. This chapter will introduce the five multiracial rules of engagement (ROE) that Wilcrest underwent in battling for the vision of becoming a multiracial congregation. Each of these five ROE will be introduced with a biblical example. The biblical example will then be elaborated and accompanied by one life lesson from Wilcrest.

MAKE SCRIPTURE THE SOLE AUTHORITY
IN DETERMINING COMMON GROUND

The first ROE is: *Make Scripture the sole authority in determining your common ground.* If a church proceeds in the incorporation of many nations into a unified congregation, there has to be one source of authority that is acceptable and immutable across all ethnic, racial,

---

[2] Wikipedia contributors, "Rules of Engagement," *Wikipedia, The Free Encyclopedia,* http://en.wikipedia.org/w/index.php?title+Rules of engaemtn&oldid+141837806 (accessed July 29, 2007).

age, political, social, and economic lines: the Word of God. This ROE was first applied in the first-century New Testament church's battle with a strong Jewish element that demanded faith and circumcision for all the new Gentile converts.

Jerusalem Council—Dealing with a Religious and Cultural Crisis (Acts 15:1–35)

In Acts 15, a racial and cultural issue emerged as Gentiles began to join the predominantly Jewish church. This influx of non-Jews prompted a Jewish subgroup, who espoused circumcision as a necessary addition to faith in Christ in order to become a Christian, to protest the departure from a ritualistic Judaism.[3] This claim obviously targeted the new Gentile believers who embraced Christianity by faith in Christ alone. This group sought to impose the Jewish custom of circumcision on the Gentile converts, arguing that circumcision was necessary in order to come into the family of God. Paul and Barnabas took the matter to the church at Jerusalem for invaluable feedback that would also help them on their upcoming Gentile mission. The Council convened in order to determine the terms under which Gentiles should be admitted to the church, and how to promote table fellowship between the Jewish and Gentile segments of the church.[4] James, the leader of the church at Jerusalem, utilized Old Testament prophecy in his quotation of the prophet Amos, "So that the rest of mankind may seek the Lord, and all the Gentiles who are called by My name" (Acts 15:17 NASB). The biblical foundation asserts that God calls the Gentiles to be a part of God's family. If the Gentiles have always been a part of God's original plan, then there should be no unnecessary hindrances placed on their path to Christianity. Yet when the Jewish segment of Christianity maintained strict adherence

---

[3] The practice of circumcision represented adherence to the entire law of Moses, which they perceived to be necessary for salvation. Consequently, if the Gentiles refused to be circumcised, this would mean that they rejected the entire law and could not experience salvation. See John B. Polhill, *Acts,* New American Commentary (Nashville: Broadman, 1992), 323. In fact, it was natural for Jews who were grounded in the Old Testament to believe that in the last days, Gentiles will flow to Jerusalem and be incorporated into Israel, the true people of God. See William J. Larkin, *Acts* (Downers Grove, IL: InterVarsity, 1995), 219. These Jews were not opposed to the Gentile mission, but they were determined that the incoming Gentile believers must fall "under the umbrella of the Jewish church," thus making the Gentiles into Jews. See John Stott, *The Spirit, the Church, and the Word: The Message of Acts* (Downers Grove, IL: InterVarsity, 1990), 242.

[4] F. F. Bruce, *The Book of Acts* (Grand Rapids: Eerdmans, 1988), 282.

to the Jewish dietary laws, they would inevitably defile themselves when they fellowshipped with the Gentiles.[5]

Furthermore, the Jerusalem Council ultimately decided that the Gentile converts only needed to do four things: (a) abstain from food sacrificed to idols; (b) abstain from fornication; (c) abstain from the meat of strangled animals; (d) and abstain from blood (Acts 15:29). All of these requirements focused on the fellowship between the Jewish and the Gentile segments of the early church. The Council knew that if the Jews and the Gentiles were to experience true community, the eating of certain foods would be a cause of division between them. Consequently, the final decision of the church in Jerusalem did not impose Jewish culture and tradition on the vast array of other cultures coming into the early church. The probability of a culture war was inevitable unless a common ground was found, while at the same time affirming the different cultural identities.

In the same way that the Jerusalem Council determined what was biblically essential for both the Jews and the new Gentile converts, Wilcrest also had to establish the absolute authority of Scripture that would transcend all racial and cultural differences. Once the common biblical foundation was established, the church would not place any unnecessary religious burdens or practices on new converts. The Jews in the early church made allowances with the Gentiles in the area of the ritual Judaism, yet both Jews and Gentiles agreed on faith in Christ and to avoid any offensive practice that would disturb the faith of the other racial group.[6] In the case of Wilcrest, the mature believers had to be the first to make allowances to ensure the acceptance and the growth of our new converts that were coming in from all over the world. Styles and methods can change but the gospel does not.

Change in Preaching Format

One of the first adjustments that I discovered that was necessary in Wilcrest, transitioning from a declining homogeneous white congregation to an increasingly younger racially diverse congregation,

---

[5] Polhill, 330.

[6] Michael Pocock summarizes the two primary points of the decision of the Jerusalem Council: (1) Do not make life unnecessarily difficult for believers from other cultures, and (2) the new generation or culture should not do things that would disgust the older generation or culture. See Michael Pocock, "The Compass for the Journey," *Cultural Change and Your Church*, 95.

was in the area of the format of my preaching. In 1995, I also discovered that the vast majority of our new people only came to the Sunday morning worship services. The growing majority of our new members were nonwhite adults who recently converted to Christianity. If I wanted effectively to instill a more thorough biblical theology of a multiracial ministry, I knew I needed to do this teaching during the Sunday morning worship services. Up until that year, I preached on a variety of biblical texts in light of the spiritual maturity of our people: many members had been involved in a stable ministry for a number of years. As new believers began to incorporate in the church, I needed to find a way to unify the entire body in one direction with one mindset. However, if we were to grow together into a new dimension of spiritual maturity, I had to challenge the Sunday morning worship participants. Consequently, I began to print an outline that accompanied the biblical message, thus encouraging them to take notes and study the biblical text throughout the following week. By using this format, I explained and applied the more intricate and difficult biblical texts. This minor adjustment produced a hunger and expectation for the explanation of the Word of God in detail each week.

During this period of teaching new converts on Sunday morning, I made a special effort to explain exactly where the particular Scripture text was in relation to the entire Bible. For example, when I preached a series on the "Ten Commandments," I asked the people to turn to the very front of the Bible, and the second book or section that they saw. The first is Genesis and the next book is Exodus. After doing this several times, a mature believer made an appointment with me in my office concerning this approach. This member felt insulted when I instructed the congregation in detail how to find the book of Exodus in the Bible. This person asked me if I really did not think the majority of the believers at Wilcrest knew where Exodus is in the Bible. I responded that I was confident that the vast majority of the Christians knew the exact location of the "Ten Commandments," but my concern was for the few who did not know. I described to this person the increasing need of many of our new believers in understanding the Bible, even the location of certain books in the Bible.

The ongoing preaching challenge extended not only across the different levels of spiritual maturity, but now the difficulty of preaching reaches across racial and cultural lines. What connects with one culture may not connect with another culture. As a result, I gather feedback from key people from different racial groups to ensure that I am making spiritual contact with the congregation as a whole. Our students from Taiwan listen and process differently than our refugees from Liberia and than our second-generation Hondurans. Many of our Nigerians know the Word of God in great depth, while our converted Muslims have never opened the Bible. Consequently, it is necessary to preach the Word of God with a global perspective when dealing with different races. The multiracial congregations force the church to depend upon the sole sufficiency and authority of Scripture, whereas homogeneous churches are more susceptible to begin leaning on cultural bias in preaching. The multiplicity of cultures creates a healthy and necessary tension that helps protect Scripture from cultural bias, thus promoting a more pure preaching of Scripture. Since the Word itself possesses a global perspective, then our preaching transcends all cultural differences. Jesus commands us to make disciples of all nations (Matt 28:19), while the apostle Paul testifies that he is obligated to both the Jew and the Greek (Rom 1:14). In addition, when Paul lists all the spiritual armor that the believer is to wear, the only offensive equipment is the Word of God (Eph 6:10–18). When a congregation determines to reach all races, the Word of God has to be the primary weapon against whatever forces that come against God's mandate.

As stated earlier, a ROE helps us know when "the need to use force effectively to accomplish the mission objectives and the need to avoid unnecessary force."[7] Therefore, one example of utilizing force effectively is the changing of the preaching styles.

MAKE THE NECESSARY ADJUSTMENTS WHEN
THE NEEDS OF THE CONGREGATION CHANGE

Another example of knowing when to utilize force effectively to accomplish the mission objectives leads us into the second ROE: *Make the necessary adjustments when the needs of the congregation change.* We first witness this strategy during the time of Israel's King David.

---

[7] Wikipedia contributors, "Rules of Engagement."

General Joab—Be Ready and Flexible War Strategy (2 Sam 10)

In the midst of battle, unforeseen difficulties demanded some drastic changes to ensure victory. Joab, the general in King David's army, implemented a skillful strategic adjustment due to the fact that Israel was being attacked on two different fronts.[8] In this particular battle, Joab divided his troops into two groups, with his brother Abashai leading half of the army against the Ammonites, while he led the other half against the Arameans. He gave his brother these specific instructions: "If the Arameans are too strong for me, . . . then you will be my help. However, if the Ammonites are too strong for you, I'll come to help you" (2 Sam 10:11). These were adjustments in the midst of the battle due to the changing needs.

The Addition of a Second Morning Worship Service

Due to the growth of our church in 2001, we made an organizational adjustment by adding another morning worship service. Up until this change, we averaged approximately 400 in our one morning worship service. Once we instituted this additional service, we increased our attendance immediately by ten percent to a total average attendance of 450. Our worship center can comfortably seat 400 people, so the limited space placed restrictions on our numerical growth. Since its inception, the early worship service fluctuated between 40 and 80 people in attendance. It was difficult to gain a grasp on the exact personality that would emerge in this service. After searching diligently for a clear purpose the first year, the staff felt the need to make this service different and distinct from the second worship service. The second and better-attended service was a time of celebration, but early service began to be a time of intimacy. Consequently, I physically moved closer to the people on the floor of the auditorium and began to encourage interaction with the people. This dialogical and intimate service began to attract some individuals from all people groups. Many of our young couples also indicated that their young children actually paid closer attention without the distraction of the larger crowds. As a result of the implementation of this additional

---

[8] Eugene H. Peterson, *First and Second Samuel* (Louisville: Westminster John Knox, 1999), 177.

service, we have experienced a growing spread of influence as more people are now able to participate in worship.

The staff originally introduced the idea of this new service about three years before we implemented the change. Initially, this idea met some resistance because of the fear that the second service would potentially divide the church into two fragments. Another concern was the possibility that one of the services would not have the choir, which is one of the primary drawing strengths of our church. This was such a concern that our choir members volunteered to sing in both services on a trial basis. The participation of the choir in both services lasted approximately six months, and the choir eventually gravitated back to the celebration service. The other challenge was the additional support needed for this service in the area of nursery and musicians. Both of these groups, however, made adjustments, and the entire church is now enjoying the benefit of two unique and diverse services. After almost six years of leading this intimate and dialogical service, I see more of our members from various people groups connecting with one another through the times of spontaneous testimony. The format of the first service also encouraged an openness and transparency that could not occur in the larger service.

One of the limitations of making adjustments in the heat of battle is that the leader makes a decision with only the knowledge that is available. Even with the best intentions, however, the decision does not always work out. In the growing context of a multiracial congregation, an abundance of knowledge or wisdom is not readily accessible, so we have to learn through trial and error. It is a slow and painful process, but it is necessary.

EMPOWER REPRESENTATIVES OF EACH RACIAL GROUP TO BE INTEGRAL VOICES IN THE DECISION-MAKING PROCESS

In the context of a growing multiracial congregation, each race flourishes when they are confident that their leaders will fairly represent their interests. One way to build this confidence leads us to the third ROE: *Empower representatives of each racial group to be integral voices in the decision-making process.* Studying the early church helps the contemporary church in understanding how important it is to make sure all cultural, ethnic, linguistic, racial, economic, social, and educational groups are adequately represented within the leadership of the church. Yet the early church moved one step beyond representation: they gave empowerment to those who were the most effective in ministering to the neglected and overlooked. This ROE was initially established in the first-century church.

The Faithful Seven—Delegating Racial Representation in Leadership (Acts 6:1–7)

At this time, the church in Jerusalem was growing at an exponential rate (see Acts 2:41; 4:4). In order to counter this growth, Satan utilized a variety of measures such as external opposition (Acts 4), deception (Acts 5), and internal division (Acts 6). If the enemy forced the multiplying church to turn their focus inward, then the expansion would suffer greatly.

What essentially divided the first-century church was a complaint concerning the ministry of feeding the widows. These women had no relatives to support them and were utterly dependent upon others to sustain their basic needs. Earlier, the Old Testament singled them out with orphans as primary objects of benevolence. In the early church, James writes, "Pure and undefiled religion before our God and Father is this: to look after orphans and widows in their distress . . ." (Jas 1:27). The ministry of feeding the widows was a legitimate concern that Satan used to divide the overall ministry of the church.[9]

Both sets of these widows were Jewish, yet they possessed different experiences and mind-sets. There was a cultural, ethnic, and perhaps linguistic barrier between these two groups. The Hellenistic Jewish widows were from outside the region of Palestine. They spoke Greek and were immersed in all aspects of the Greek culture.[10] In fact, the Hellenistic Jews had separate synagogues from the Hebraic or Palestinian Jews. The primary reason these widows were back in the Jerusalem area was because of the proximity of the temple. For

---

[9] Michael Pocock adds that the equitable distribution of food also secured a sense of justice. See Michael Pocock, "The Compass for the Journey," in *Cultural Changes and Your Church*, 94.

[10] William Neal, *The Acts of the Apostles*, New Century Bible Commentary (Grand Rapids: Eerdmans, 1973), 102. Dunn adds that there were two groups of widows: (1) the Greek speakers and (2) the Aramaic speakers. See James D. G. Dunn, *The Acts of the Apostles* (Valley Forge, PA: Trinity Press International, 1996), 81.

years they had been removed from the ability to worship and offer sacrifices in the temple, but since they were approaching death, they desired to be close to this important and sacred site. In contrast, the Hebraic or Palestinian Jewish widows were natives of the Palestine area and spoke Aramaic. They immersed themselves in the Jewish culture, which often drew distinct lines of demarcation between them and anything non-Jewish.

An important observation is that the people in charge of distributing the food were Hebraic Jews. The writer of Acts tells us that there were no problems prior to this because "there was not a needy person among them" (Acts 4:34). The expansion of the early church began to include all kinds of Jewish people, but somehow the feeding of Hellenistic Jewish widows was neglected.

The apostles then assembled the church together to participate in the solution because the entire church was affected by the problem. The approved solution was for the church to select Hellenistic Jewish men who would understand and empathize with those who were neglected. All seven of these men had Greek names, indicating their cultural connections. This selection speaks clearly of the grace of the Hebrew majority as they released authority to those who were in the minority.

The Calling of an African-American to Leadership

With the biblical model of racially representative leadership clearly established in Acts 6 with the "Faithful Seven," God provided a clear mandate to incorporate racially diverse leadership. In God's sovereignty and grace, an African-American minister, James Darby, began to visit Wilcrest in the fall of 1992. There was an immediate connection between his family and the body of Christ at Wilcrest. We began to take the necessary measures to bring him onto our staff. However, since the calling of a nonwhite was a monumental step for our church family, I knew we needed to do a churchwide interview and dialogue with James as one of the initial steps in this critical process. During the course of this interview, all types of questions were posed, ranging from "Do you like Michael Jackson?" to "Do you believe in interracial dating?" The members also expressed their fear that James would take the youth group to an all-black church, thus possibly exposing them to a style or form of worship that was not appropriate for their children. James patiently responded to all those questions but also demonstrated a strong sense of God's call on his life.

When the day of the vote came, I distinctly remember sitting on the front row of the auditorium all alone, wondering what would happen if the church did not vote in favor of James coming to Wilcrest. I was so immersed in the process of taking this enormous step in the direction of becoming a multiracial congregation; it had never occurred to me that the church might not follow my leadership in this direction. In my heart, I knew I would not be able to stay at Wilcrest if the church did not call James onto our staff. Since I was convinced that the Bible clearly called the church to have racially representative leadership, I did not know how Wilcrest would accomplish the mission of reaching all the nations without racially diverse leadership. The final vote was more than 75 five percent in favor of calling James to Wilcrest. If the church did not walk through this open door, then it would be a long time before it would be ready to repeat this step, and it might not ever see this opportunity again. Looking back on the vote of that day, I felt like we walked through the Red Sea and left our slavery in Egypt. There was a strong sense of liberation from the bondage of racism. It was going to be a long road ahead, but on that eventful day the body of Christ at Wilcrest took one decisive step toward the mission of seeing all the nations coming together. The words of Jesus came to my mind: "No one who puts his hand to the plow and looks back is fit for the kingdom of God" (Luke 9:62). In this task of the kingdom of God, we could not afford to take our hands off the plow and look back.

DO NOT BE AFRAID TO TAKE RISKS THAT CONTAIN LEARNING BENEFITS TO ACCOMPLISH THE MISSION

This process of including all races in the decision-making process was accompanied by numerous trials. However, the benefits greatly outweighed the hardships. This leads us to our fourth ROE: *Do not be afraid to take risks that contain immense learning benefits to accomplish the mission.*

The Apostle Paul—The Faithful Risk-taker (2 Cor 1:15–22)

The apostle Paul described his desire to come and see the Corinthians in 2 Cor 1:15–22. Apparently the timing was not right, but Paul contended, "Our message to you is not 'Yes and no.' For the Son of God, Jesus Christ . . . did not become 'Yes and no'; on the contrary, 'Yes' has come about in Him" (2 Cor 1:18–19). Paul's struggle was determining whether his coming to Corinth was in the best interest of the church there. No matter what obstacles and setbacks Paul faced, his response was always a willing "yes" if it meant the promotion of the Corinthian joy.[11] In the same way, Wilcrest is in the ready position of "yes" when it comes to attempting the unknown in view of seeing the vision of all people groups coming together as one body and bringing joy to our heavenly Father.

During a one-year period, Wilcrest attempted to step out of its comfort zone with two major visionary ministries in order to multiply the multiracial vision. Both failed; however, both the lessons we learned and a special gift within God's hidden plan far outweighed the hardships. This included: (1) a multiracial church plant and (2) the attempt to incorporate an Indonesian Baptist church into Wilcrest.

The Multiracial Church Plant

In the fall of 2002, a church planter from Seattle made contact with Wilcrest. This Chinese pastor and his Anglo wife successfully planted a multiracial congregation in Seattle, and now they expressed a desire to plant a multiracial church in Houston. Wilcrest, along with several other churches and the area association, connected and committed to help in this new work. Prior to our connection with this church planter, Wilcrest sought to explore ways to multiply this multiracial vision, yet we experienced little success. This new multiracial church plant provided Wilcrest with the perfect opportunity to extend the vision with a new strategic approach. The immediate area surrounding Wilcrest is fertile ground for a multiracial ministry based on the enormous and overwhelming diversity of people groups in a compressed region. Working together, the church plant and Wilcrest implemented several ministry tasks in order to gain attention for this new church plant, including a diverse Easter concert featuring black gospel, rap,

---

[11] Garland, 101.

contemporary, and traditional music. Yet after eight months of net-working and laboring, only five core members remained. Eventually, this church planting effort derailed, and what I thought was the most effective method of reproducing our vision came to a grinding halt.

The Indonesians Are Coming

During the same year that the multiracial church plant failed, the pastor from the Indonesian Baptist Church of Houston asked us to rent space because they needed to move from their facilities they had used for the previous thirteen years. From our history of renting space to nonwhite congregations (African-American and Chinese congregations), we had learned that the strategy of including other racial congregations through leasing property only widened the racial gap. During our conversation, I asked the pastor if he would consider the Indonesian congregation joining in a multiracial congregation. He responded, "God placed the ministry to all races on my heart for a long time." The following week the pastor called and invited me to preach at their monthly English-speaking service; this brought us one step closer to seeing the fruition of coming together. As a result of ongoing dialogue, we saw the need to connect the two congregations in two consecutive steps: (1) an informal meeting between the leaders of each congregation in order to discuss the vision and direction in which the churches were going; and (2) a coming together in a joint worship experience, with the Indonesians taking some leadership roles.

Our two leadership groups met on a Friday evening in order to discuss the possibility of joining our two congregations under one vision. Although both groups anticipated the potential connection, no one had any idea exactly what that would look like. As the night progressed, there was an amazing openness from both sides in regard to our hopes and our fears. The primary hesitation from the Indonesian perspective was the fear of loss of identity and mission clearly depicted in their name, "Indonesian Baptist Church." They were first and foremost Indonesian believers with the clear mission to reach the Indonesians in the Houston area. If they joined a multiracial church, then they assumed they would lose their name and perhaps even their identity and mission. One of Wilcrest's members responded that our church has a Hispanic ministry and yet it still remains a vital part of Wilcrest. The name of the ministry is *Iglesia Bautista de Wilcrest*

(Wilcrest Baptist Church), and when spoken in Spanish, it conveys that we have a ministry and mission for Hispanics. We left that night committed to praying for God's will. Before concluding the meeting, one of the Indonesian members challenged the leaders of his church with an illustration from the Spanish conquistador, Hernando Cortez. Upon arriving on foreign territory, the Spanish ruler admonished his soldiers to burn their boats for there was no turning back. The burning of the Indonesian boat was the day they had to move out of their facilities. The sense of urgency was clearly felt.

Nine days later, our churches came together for a worship service in which their members led in singing and the pastor shared his testimony. Wilcrest was so excited about the possibility of seeing such a large people group integrate with us. The reality of seeing an influx of 40 Indonesian believers at one time was beyond our comprehension. The visible presence of the Indonesians gave the Wilcrest family a concrete picture of the possibility of the two churches merging together in one direction under one vision. The next week, the Indonesian church met and voted to join in with a Vietnamese church, and by doing so they retained their Indonesian identity and name. I knew God was in control, but this decision crushed me and our church family at Wilcrest. I really thought God orchestrated this entire process of seeing the converging of more cultures into the Wilcrest family. I knew God had called us to reach the Asian section of our community in a comprehensive manner. If this connection occurred, our Asian representation would have increased from four percent to thirteen percent in one day. How could that not be from God?

God's Gracious Gift within His Hidden Plan

The following Sunday, an Asian woman expressed her desire for believer's baptism. We made an appointment to discuss her baptism for the following Wednesday. While she was in my office, she prayed and committed her life to Christ, and I baptized her the following week. I asked her, "What country are you from?" She responded, "I am from Indonesia." I could not believe my ears. I quickly asked if she was connected to the Indonesian Baptist Church and she said she was not, but she had lived in our neighborhood for 20 years and wanted to grow in her commitment to Christ. God taught me through this experience that the Indonesians are really coming, not as a church but one person at a time. In addition, Wilcrest took and passed the test of being willing to embrace and do whatever it takes to see God connect different cultures and races in one congregation. The baptism of our first Indonesian signified a major breakthrough in a new people group. I know it was God's timing in order to remind us that God has called us to reach the Indonesians one by one.

Two Strikes . . . Is This Really Worth It?

During this one-year period, Wilcrest attempted to step out of her comfort zone with two major visionary ministries in order to multiply the multiracial vision. These included: (1) the multiracial church plant; and (2) the incorporation of the Indonesian Baptist Church. Although both of these endeavors afforded great opportunities to stretch beyond our safe parameters, both failed.

Our first strike was the multiracial church plant. Based on the large number of difficulties that Wilcrest experienced in transitioning a homogeneous congregation to a multiracial one, we perceived planting a multiracial church was the most effective method to reproduce the vision of Wilcrest. Although some key elements of the spiritual foundation of the multiracial church plant needed more attention, some other obstacles emerged. For the nonwhites, several strong homogeneous churches were available. In addition, the combination of attending a church that is both small and multiracial proved an insurmountable challenge for newcomers. Each racial group continues to grow in number and in strength in the surrounding area, so there is not as great a need to connect outside of their own race and culture.

Although it offered a rare opening with a racial group we wanted to reach, our second strike was the failed attempt to merge the Indonesian church with Wilcrest. Yet the Indonesian church maintained a strong commitment to retain their Indonesian name and individual identity in order to reach the immigrants and first-generation Indonesians coming into Houston. Although the risk of simultaneously integrating one large people group was great, the reward of seeing an entirely new racial group incorporated into Wilcrest was worth the risk.

Interestingly, three years after the Indonesian Baptist Church decided not to merge with Wilcrest in order to maintain their unique cultural identity, the multiracial seed is beginning to sprout. Their new pastor has asked me to preach in their English-speaking services three or four times each year. Each time I return, the pastor and members report the growing diversity in their congregation due to the challenge that Wilcrest's vision and example provided for them. They first targeted Asians who were not Indonesian. Now that racial line has been crossed, they are reaching out to other racial groups.

At that time, both setbacks hit me simultaneously and caused a great deal of discouragement and disillusionment. After my experience over the previous 12 years, I knew that Wilcrest needed to take these risks, but it was with no apparent success. The issue that continues to emerge is whether we need to hold on to what we have since we made so many advancements in the area of multiracial ministry, or do we continue to forge ahead? Do we give our people a chance to catch up with where the vision has taken us, or do we continue to take risks? From the beginning, we possessed a passion to be risk takers and that often included multiple setbacks throughout this journey. We tried to adopt the apostle Paul's strategy in 2 Cor 1:15–22 in describing his desire to come and see the Corinthians. Although the timing of his visit to the Corinthians was not right, Paul contended, "Our message to you is not 'Yes and no.' . . . On the contrary, 'Yes' has come about in Him." No matter what obstacles and setbacks Paul faced, his response was always a willing "yes." In the same way, Wilcrest is in the ready position of "yes" when it comes to attempting the unknown in view of seeing the vision of all people groups coming together as one body. After we walked through the transformation process, it was easy to forget the failures and only remember the victories. These risks and their subsequent failures and setbacks were a reminder that this would always be a learning process.

DEAL WITH ANY RACIAL OR CULTURAL DIVISION THAT THREATENS CHURCH UNITY

We are fortunate that in our failures, the name of Christ was not profaned. Not all failures are so fortunate. In fact, many times when church leaders fail, their failures began with a failure of accountability. Therefore, what must be done brings us to the fifth ROE: *Take decisive measures to deal publicly and immediately with any racial or cultural division that threatens the unity of the church.* If leaders are not willing to do what it takes to protect the unity of the troops, then the mission has already failed. One of the devil's schemes is either to keep the nations from unifying or to raise divisions among them. Therefore, a lesson from Galatians can help us better prepare to protect against division.

Paul versus Peter—Showdown at the Table (Gal 2:11–14)

At times the battle involves invading the enemy's territory or taking necessary risks for the kingdom of God. However, some of the fiercest and most damaging battles are when leaders turn against one another. Jesus affirms this truth by stating, "If a house is divided against itself, that house cannot stand" (Mark 3:25). By the time God called me to Wilcrest and the church adopted the multiracial vision, the vast majority of those who desired to worship in a homogeneous congregation had left. Even though the remaining leadership possessed little or no experience in a multiracial congregation, they were willing to begin the journey. Thus, the church as a whole began to move in the same direction with one vision. If one leader believes in the multiracial vision and the other leader regresses to the homogeneous model and mind-set, conflict is inevitable. This is exactly what happened between the apostles Paul and Peter.

In Gal 1:18–20, Paul described his initial meeting with the apostle Peter in Jerusalem. During his fifteen-day stay in the holy city, Paul stayed as Peter's guest. As Gal 2 opens, Paul depicted Peter as a fellow apostle whom God assigned to the Jews and Paul to the Gentiles (Gal 2:7). Yet when Gal 2:11 described Peter's arrival in Antioch, Paul narrated an intense confrontation over Peter's withdrawal from table fellowship with the Gentiles.

The Jewish law did not prohibit eating meals with Gentiles but advocated a strict code of dietary restrictions that were not shared by Gentiles. In order to maintain cultural and religious purity, they practiced a policy of separation. Just as the Old Testament Jews had turned exclusively inward in their zeal to maintain their cultic purity and had lost their original mission of becoming priests for all the nations (Exod 19:5), Peter turned inward toward other Jews and lost sight of the Great Commission of reaching all nations with the gospel.

Consequently, Paul opposed Peter because he acted in contradiction to Peter's conscience and the revelation he received in Acts 10 concerning Cornelius. In addition, Peter behaved in a totally different manner than his previous custom.[12] Paul confronted Peter because he failed to perceive the implication of the gospel when applied to the Gentiles. The same table that served as a symbol of unity had now become a table of division. In Gal 2:12, Paul described Peter's withdrawal with a verb that implied a gradual retreat under external pressure instead of an abrupt departure from his former practice. Peter's withdrawal sent a clear signal to the Gentiles that they were not as good as the Jewish Christians. Acts 10 reminds us that God deemed it necessary to use a vision to persuade Peter that it was acceptable to eat with the Gentiles in the first place. Yet now the same Peter who denied the Lord in fear of a slave girl the night before the crucifixion, now denied the Lord for fear of a Jewish segment in the church.

According to Paul, Peter deceived through pretense and acted as a hypocrite. This word *hypocrite* literally means to cover your face with a mask or to play act.[13] This action was hypocritical because their previous practice indicated that there was nothing wrong with eating with the Gentiles. This contagious deception spread rapidly among other Jewish Christians, including Paul's first missionary journey partner, Barnabas. In fact, Barnabas traveled with Paul during that first journey in which both witnessed so many Gentiles coming to Christ in faith without any suggestion that it was necessary for them to be circumcised. The change in the clientele of Peter's table fellowship demoted the Gentiles to a second-class category within Christianity.

Many scholars have contended that Peter initiated withdrawal from table fellowship with the Gentiles because this practice caused additional persecution to the Jewish church in Jerusalem from Jewish zealots.[14] Yet it is one thing to become a Jew to the Jew in order to win the Jews for Christ (see 1 Cor 9:19–23), and it is completely different to force the Gentiles to become Jews. Whatever Peter's motives were, they paled in comparison to the overarching mission to the Gentiles. The damage was done publicly, and now Paul needed to address this sin publicly and decisively. The action on the part of Peter and the Jewish Christians obscured the truth that all believers are one in Christ. At the beginning of 2007, the adversary attacked Wilcrest's unity through the failure of a leader's openness and humility to seek accountability.

---

[12] R. A. Cole, *The Epistle of Paul to the Galatians* (Leicester, England: InterVarsity, 1984), 74.

[13] Frank J. Matera, *Galatians* (Collegeville, MN: The Liturgical Press, 1992), 86.

[14] F. F. Bruce, *Commentary on Galatians* (Grand Rapids: Eerdmans, 1982), 128–30.

Deacon Defection

Since my arrival at Wilcrest, we have consistently practiced church discipline. Several members have committed offenses that required the church to remove them from leadership and service positions in the church, including staff, deacons, Bible study teachers, choir members, and committee members. The more visible the leader has been, the more painful the process. The biblical guidelines are clear when a brother or sister steps into disobedience: (1) go to the individual in person, (2) then take two or three witnesses, and (3) then go before the entire church (Matt 18:15–18). The apostle Paul adds that the individual in rebellion needs to be specially marked out and fellowship is to be withdrawn. This removal of intimacy with the body of Christ will then produce a profound sense of shame. Yet Paul conveys that the person in sin should not be treated like an enemy but be admonished as a brother (2 Thess 3:11–15).

Satan's most ferocious attack came against one of our deacons the church entrusted with the mission work in Central America. His admission of inappropriate behavior led the church body to place him under church discipline. This was a very unusual case because his actions were done while on the mission field representing both Christ and the church. Due to his failure to meet the requirements of repentance and restoration, the body of deacons had to take multiple measures in the discipline process. This revelation of sin attacked the unity of the body of Christ at several levels: the unity within the church in Central America, the unity within Wilcrest, and the unity within marriages. The church commissioned a restoration team to return to Central America to humble ourselves and seek restoration of the relationship that had been severely damaged by these sins. Throughout this painful discipline process, the members of Wilcrest and the church in Central America have witnessed compassionate and firm church discipline based on biblical guidelines. The potential racial, congregational, and marital divisions mandated that decisive and public measures be taken to ensure the integrity of biblical theology for multiracial ministry. As the apostle Paul confronted the apostle Peter over a practice that created a rift between races, churches need to be willing to confront any sin that divides and contaminates the body of Christ.

Answering the Tough Questions

Once the church captures, embraces, and embarks on the multi-racial journey, the spiritual battle begins. When Wilcrest adopted the vision statement in the first stage of its racial transition, little did we know the obstacles that would come from every conceivable angle. Many times, the resistance from our whites expressed itself in subtle forms such as: "Pastor we did not grow up in an all-black neighbor-hood"; "Our experience is different than yours"; "I do not think that the blacks or Hispanics or Asians would enjoy our worship style"; and "The other races may want to be with their own kind." At other times the expressions were much more blatant, such as: "Having a black youth minister may encourage my white daughter to date a black guy"; "Having those people may run off some of our good people"; and "If we change that much, we will lose our identity." It is impossible to avoid confrontation and conflict when the new vision of the church challenges a paradigm that strongly encourages the separation of races within the family of God. If a church chooses to engage in this spiritual battle, then it is necessary to understand what the Scriptures say about how to wage this war. We must be ready and willing to take decisive measures to deal publicly and immediately with any type of division that threatens the unity of the troops.

SUMMARY

Based on our battles in the implementation of the multiracial vision, we discovered five primary rules of engagement (ROE). Many of these battles have parallels within the biblical framework. The biblical principles used in Wilcrest's struggles include:

1. Make Scripture the sole authority in determining your common ground (Matt 28:19; Rom 1:16; Eph 6:10–18; Acts 15:1–35).

2. Make the necessary adjustments as the needs of the congregation change (2 Sam 10:6–19).

3. Empower representatives of each racial group to be integral voices in the decision-making process (Prov 11:14; Acts 6:1–7).

4. Do not be afraid to take risks that contain immense learning benefits to accomplish the mission (2 Cor 1:15–22).

5. Take decisive measures to deal publicly and immediately with any racial or cultural division that threatens the unity of the church (Gal 2:11–14).

DISCUSSION QUESTIONS

1. What is the one racial issue that would cause the most difficulty in your congregation or to you personally? Some examples may include: style of worship, interracial dating or marriage, painful racial history, political perspectives, socioeconomic differences, educational gaps, family structure, following a leader not your race, and language barriers. Based on the first rule of engagement, what does Scripture say about the issue?

2. If your church wanted to become more integrated, what are some necessary changes that would help bridge the gap among the different races? What adjustments would be needed in structure, personnel, leadership, and style to make sure that each group would know that they are included?

3. If you could take any risk to reach across racial barriers, what would you do? What would be the costs and benefits of such a risk? Is there anyone who would be willing to join you in this endeavor?

4. Who is in charge in your congregation? This is the individual or group of individuals who make the important decisions. Do they decide the direction and vision of the church? Does your leadership look like your congregation as a whole? If you want to be a multiracial congregation, do you have multiracial leadership? What are some positive steps that you can take to move the church in this direction?

5. Read Matt 18:15–18; 2 Thess 3:11–15; 1 Cor 5:1–5. Based on these passages, is church discipline biblical? Does your church practice church discipline? If so, what forms of expression does it take? Read Gal 2:11–14. If there is a public sin of prejudice or racism in your congregation, what does Paul say to do? Ultimately, who is responsible for the discipline in your congregation?

CHAPTER 10

THE ROLE OF WORSHIP IN THE
MULTIRACIAL CHURCH

---

*"All the ends of the earth will remember and turn to the LORD. All
the families of the nations will bow down before You"(Ps 22:27).*

DEFINING WORSHIP

What is worship? Worship is our response to God's revelation of Himself. Worship occurs both privately and
publicly, but in this chapter, the focus will be on worship in the public gathering of believers. Some of the elements of
corporate worship that will be emphasized are music, preaching, testimony, length of services, greeters, bodily expression, and the use
of different languages. Furthermore, one of the key issues that will
be dealt with is whether worship looks or sounds different in a multiracial congregation than it does in a homogeneous congregation.
Yet before we can describe what multiracial worship looks like, it is
vital to lay the foundation of biblical worship. It is necessary first to
introduce the concept of "the audience of One," which points to the
primary focus of our worship. Then, two key biblical passages will
be provided that have helped shape our understanding of worship in
a multiracial congregation.

THE AUDIENCE OF ONE

In our contemporary landscape of the struggle between contemporary and traditional worship styles, it may seem like adding the
multiracial variable will further complicate the dialogue. However, it
may actually simplify the issue. A common misconception is that a
worship service should be created and designed for the audience of

the many who come. But in a true worship service, God is the "audience of One." Understanding the "audience of One" will remind the worshiper of the focus and purpose of our worship. However, many churches inversely start at the other end of the spiritual equation and determine what effect and impact they want to have on the worshipers who come into their services. The entire service is constructed with one predominant thought in mind: the needs and comfort of those attending worship services. The goal is to satisfy the "felt needs" of the religious consumers who are shopping for church.[1] However, if you ask the wrong questions, you will get the wrong answers. The biblical question is "Who is the object and focus of our worship?" The prophet Isaiah addressed this issue in his narrative at the time of King Uzziah's death during the middle of the eighth century BC (see Isa 1:1–18; 6:1–13). Jesus returned to this same issue in His dialogue with the Samaritan woman as recorded in John 4.

THE ISAIAH 6 MODEL

During the middle of the eighth century BC, the people of Israel repeatedly replaced heart worship with religious routine, often multiplying their sacrifices and offerings in order to placate God (Isa 1:11). Israel abandoned their exclusive audience of the Almighty God even to the point of despising the "Holy One of Israel" (Isa 1:4). In his grace, God spoke through the prophet Isaiah to invite His people back to true worship; then they would experience His free-flowing forgiveness that would target the central problem area, the human heart (Isa 1:18). In that age of spiritual indifference and material prosperity (Isa 2:7), Israel's heart had grown callous, their ears dull, and their eyes heavy. God interrupted their religious routine.

In Isaiah 6, God gave Isaiah, the people of Israel, and all future worshipers a divine model of what true worship entails. First, God is the one who takes the initiative in worship, and in this case, it was a revelation of God to Isaiah: "I saw the Lord seated on a high and lofty throne, and His robe filled the temple" (Isa 6:1). This revelation was

---

[1] Emerson describes the American church scene as a "religious mega-mall" which produces product variety or religious pluralism. Consequently, if the worshiper feels like his or her needs are unmet, then those needs will be met by other suppliers. It is impossible for all options to be offered by one supplier, so the worshiper will go where his needs are met most effectively. In fact, Emerson adds, "Nor can all options successfully be offered without ending in chaos." See *Divided by Faith*, 141.

personal, targeting only Isaiah; it was penetrating, for God's robes filled the entire temple. Along with the epiphany of the eternal King, angels were compelled to join in the chorus of praise. As an eyewitness to this heavenly display of the glory of God, Isaiah could only respond to the holy God with an acute confession of his sins. Rarely does Scripture record a worshiper in the visible presence of God apart from an overwhelming sense of reverence and holy awe from the one who sees God (cp. Luke 7:25; Acts 9:3; Rev 1:9–20). Isaiah's reason for the confession of his specific sin of an unclean mouth was due to this fact: "because my eyes have seen the King, the LORD of Hosts" (Isa 6:5). The sight of a holy God rendered Isaiah speechless, for his very breath had been polluted by sin. Following the pure praise of the angelic worshipers, Isaiah became intimately conscious that he was an alien and trespasser in the presence of purity, too wicked to worship. Isaiah was praiseless while all of heaven resounded with reverberations of adoration and worship of the one true God. Yet God immediately moved toward Isaiah's repentant heart with both the spiritual cleansing of his sin and a visible confirmation as an angel touched his impure lips with a burning coal (Isa 6:6–7). Instantaneously, God transferred His holy altar in heaven to the cleansed lips of Isaiah. After God forgave Isaiah, He called His true worshiper to His service and mission: "Who should I send? Who will go for Us?" (Isa 6:8). The one who received God's forgiveness eagerly made himself available to do whatever God wanted him to do. The final aspect of this worship model was God's commission of the worshiper to go with His Word as His official mouthpiece.

In the modern framework of what many religious leaders deem to be worship, there seems to be more of a focus on self than on God. Several questions are often asked, such as: Did I hear my style of music? Would people like me fit in this service? What has the church provided for me and my unique needs and tastes? Am I represented in the leadership or in the song selection? Are people raising their hands? Is the music lively enough or quiet enough for me? In sharp contrast to the emerging worship models, the biblical model demands that God be the primary focus, "lofty and exalted." Leonara Tubbs Tisdale offers this input in the context of multiracial worship: "Deep worship is focused both on the praise and glory of God and on the edification of the worshiper. The key issue is God."[2] Perhaps the reason people are not meeting God and experiencing true worship is that their spiritual lenses are somewhat out of focus because they are turned away from the eternal King sitting on the throne.

THE JOHN 4:24 MODEL

The ministry of Jesus offered another biblical worship model that signified and confirmed that the primary focus of our worship is God. Just as Isaiah learned that biblical worship starts with God and ultimately ends with God, the Samaritan woman also discovered the same truth. During His dialogue with the Samaritan woman, Jesus targeted her heart with the good news of the gospel. The more Jesus revealed to her about His identity and what He had to offer her, the more she either misinterpreted or deflected His comments. After Jesus told her about her living situation with a man who was not her husband, she attempted to focus on a controversial issue so that the attention might fall on someone else. She claimed, "Our fathers worshiped on this mountain, yet you Jews say that the place to worship is in Jerusalem" (John 4:20). Abraham first built an altar at this well upon his entrance into the promised land in order to worship God. She basically asked, "Which group is right, the Jews or the Samaritans?" Jesus did not ignore her question, but did not stop until He arrived at her heart. Worship really deals with the heart. From the Samaritan perspective, the city of Shechem overlooked Mount Gerazim and was the first place Abraham built an altar once he entered the promised land (Gen 12:6–7). Furthermore, Mount Gerazim was also the place where blessings and curses were shouted to the covenant community of Israel, so this mountain should have priority over Jerusalem, according to the Samaritans.[3] In contrast, everything the Jews did centered on Jerusalem, the focal point of King David's reign.

In the next few verses, Jesus revealed some very important truths concerning worship. The first is that the location of worship is not important (John 4:21). Debate is meaningless, for Jesus pointed

---

[2] See John 5:19–20; 18:13–14. Leonara Tubbs Tisdale, "Navigating the Contemporary Worship Narrows," in *Making Room at the Table*, ed. Brian K. Bount and Leonara Tubbs Tisdale (Louisville: Westminster John Knox, 2000), 175–88.

[3] During the time of Moses, the people of Israel shouted curses from Mount Ebal while they shouted blessings from Mount Gerazim. See Deut 27–28.

forward to a time of true spiritual worship when both the Jewish Jerusalem and the Samaritan Mount Gerazim would be bypassed. Each of
these locations represented a lengthy but segregated history. Whether
the worshiper was in a Jewish or Samaritan worship location was not
important. In our contemporary context, whether the worshiper is in
an all-black, all-white, all-Hispanic, or all-Asian location is not as
important as the primary focus on the God of all nations. The second
truth is that the object of worship is most important (John 4:21–22),
for Jesus clarified for her that the Samaritans worshiped whom they
did not know, while Jews worshiped whom they knew. The third truth
is that God seeks true worshipers (John 4:23). Who are the true worshipers? According to Jesus, they are the ones who worship God "in
spirit," which is the creative life-giving power of God, not just in outward form. In the Jewish religion, the worshipers often followed the
letter of law that eventually segued into the loss of spirit and vitality.
True worship comes as a result of receiving the free gift of salvation
through Jesus Christ: thus worship is the response of the recipient of
the matchless and unparalleled gift.

Worship in Spirit

What does the expression of this worship look like? Most impor-
tantly, the primary expression of worship must come from the heart
of the worshiper. Worshiping God "in spirit" might be better understood if we knew what it means not to worship "in spirit." In contrast,
worship that was not done "in spirit" but "in flesh" was described
by Jesus in this way: "These people honor Me with their lips, but
their heart is far from Me. They worship Me in vain" (Mark 7:6–7).
Obviously some expressions of worship can be done outwardly with
words and physical motions, but may not be acceptable to God. Worshiping God requires us to worship "in spirit." In addition, the phrase
"God is spirit" is a not a definition of God, but rather descriptive of
God's interaction with us as spiritual creatures. It is easy to get caught
up in the physical aspects of worship such as our attendance, singing,
raising of our hands, giving of our tithes and offerings, prayers, and
involvement in rituals, but Jesus calls us to something much more
meaningful and intimate. His Spirit calls us to connect through our
spirit in a way that transcends location, race, history, and tradition.
The writer of the Chronicles gives clear instruction of what God truly

sees: "The eyes of the LORD range throughout the earth to show Himself strong for those whose hearts are completely His" (2 Chr 16:9). In a multiracial worship service, the need to connect spiritually with God is even more evident because there are not as many outward or physical similarities among the different races.

Worship in Truth

Jesus added that this worship was also to be "in truth." This phrase calls and challenges the believer's worship to capture the significance of the reality of God that is revealed in Jesus Christ. Formerly the Samaritans worshiped falsely; now Jesus set the standard in spirit-worship: it must be done in truth. As we approach God in worship, we must come to Him in complete sincerity and complete reality. There are to be no facades, no pretensions, no reliance on outward forms, and no half-hearted approaches. Just come as you are. Spirit-worship and truth-worship are not two separate and independent characteristics, but essentially depict worship which is God-centered, made possible by the gift of the Holy Spirit, and in personal knowledge of and conformity to God's Word-made-flesh, the One who is God's truth.

AN OBSERVATION OF
CORPORATE WORSHIP AT WILCREST

In our previous book, *People of the Dream*, a chapter titled "Shadows" depicted many of the struggles Wilcrest endured in this painstaking journey of transforming an all-white congregation in decline into a growing multiracial congregation. In fact, my original recommendation for the title of that particular chapter was not "Shadows," but "The Dark Night of the Soul." There were so many setbacks, failures, departures, changes, unknowns, wrong decisions, untimely adjustments, perceived favoritisms, neglect of one or more groups, and misunderstandings. At the beginning of the "Shadows" chapter, an African-American, Lashawn, visited the "Ordination of the Seven" service (December 2002) and offered several of the following comments, primarily targeting our worship service and worship style,

> The choir was diverse. It looked to me to be about 1/3 to 1/2 nonwhite. But, the music was not only "white" but rather slow and traditional. I wondered why the nonwhite people

are part of the choir. Who selects the music? Are there non-whites who have input into the song and music selection? The worship style is not a least bit charismatic. There was very little clapping or raising of hands. Frankly, I could hardly hear people singing, outside the choir. I did notice a black woman in the choir holding up her hands (to about waist level) and closing her eyes during one of the worship songs. It struck me that it probably took some courage to do even that, considering what, from my perspective, was a very rigid and conservative style. The church also seems to have a number of older people who attend (50s plus). Is the church trying to be sensitive to the senior white people? Does this explain the conservative traditional white worship style? Do they have the most power, limiting what changes can be made? Overall, the church struck me as a WHITE church! . . . This makes me wonder why the nonwhite people attend the church. I am quite curious about this because there is really not much of anything that attracts me to the church and I cannot imagine what attracts Latinos. Personally, I was disappointed, even sad about the disconnect that I saw between what the church claims to be and what, from my visit, it was. People who are nonwhite are welcome, I am sure, but they don't seem to be appreciated for what they can uniquely bring to the church or really included at every level. Given what I saw and experienced, I would not be able to invite other African Americans to Wilcrest.[4]

This assessment was extremely painful but at many points accurate, especially coming from an African-American perspective. As a result of this piercing evaluation and a variety of other factors, the church and staff began to transition our paradigm of how we do worship, what music we select, who reads Scripture, who are the greeters, and how we implement different sounds from around the world. As discussed in the chapter "Giants in the Land," one of the primary barriers that we repeatedly attempted to cross from the inception of the multiracial vision was how to reach the black community effectively. James Darby helped us understand it was going to take much more

---

[4] *People of the Dream,* 132.

than just placing a black minister to students on our staff. He asserted that there would have to be a change in who made the decisions and how they were made, specifically in the areas of leadership and worship. Initially, many of our African-Americans related to me that they listened to gospel music on the way to church in their car because they knew they would not be able to sing or hear gospel music once they entered the doors at Wilcrest. After our worship leader's return in 2000, the ministry leadership team determined to implement worship that would reflect many diverse sounds, but especially the gospel sound from the African-American tradition. Our staff knew this change might also come with a cost, just as a prominent black pastor from North Texas contended, "If you sacrifice for one, you might lose the many." What he meant was that if the church sacrificed the worship style for the African-American community, the church might end up losing the multiple races that had already been incorporated into the fabric of the church.

A real racial divide exists not only in our society but also in our churches, and there is no greater visible divide than between blacks and whites. It has been a long struggle, but this chapter will show some of the steps that Wilcrest has taken to bridge this gap and cultivate a worship atmosphere in which every race is represented and celebrated. However, Lashawn's lengthy critique caused us to examine seriously every aspect of multiracial worship. This will not be a rebuttal of her critique point for point, but I will use her remarks to prompt pertinent questions concerning several pivotal aspects of multiracial worship followed by three possible models in which to express worship in a multiracial congregation.

ASPECTS OF CORPORATE MULTIRACIAL WORSHIP

Music

One of the most difficult areas of struggle in the transition from an all-white congregation to a multiracial congregation has been music. With the infusion of so many different musical backgrounds, each culture and tradition feels strongly that their heart expression of worship is the best expression, and sometimes the only acceptable worship form. In fact, any aspect of music that is not in line with their tradition is often deemed irreverent and an affront to God. The question is: How does a multiracial church express itself musically in worship? According to Kathy Black, one cultural value European-Americans bring to music is *harmony*, which is about singing together in the same language so we all sound alike. When different believers sing in different languages simultaneously, it sounds unharmonious, confusing, and chaotic. Rhythms are also different from culture to culture. The definition of harmony may change from one ethnic group to another. Some tap a foot or clap on the downbeat while others clap in threes to rhythms that have no up or downbeats.[5] This aspect has proved challenging to the Wilcrest choir, especially if some of the choir members are clapping on different beats. A clash of cultures can occur right in the middle of a praise song or a traditional hymn. According to Emerson, worship from the white culture primarily emphasizes melody over beat and rhythm, while worship from the black culture emphasizes a rhythm, a beat, and a groove.[6] At Wilcrest, harmony is in the process of being redefined and expressed. Leonard Sweet observed that as recently as fifty years ago:

> Congregational singing sounded much different than it does today. . . . Every congregation—no matter how large or small—sang in four-part harmony. Soprano, alto, tenor, and bass . . . blended together to create a rich, layered sound in each hymn. . . . When hymnbooks were precious and in short supply, children and newcomers learned the hymns by standing close by and listening to their neighbor. . . . When everyone got his or her hymnbook, the harmony began to flatten out. . . . Ironically, as everyone increasingly listened only to themselves, they all began to sound alike.[7]

When believers focus so much on their own racial expression of worship, their worship will flatten out and they lose their potential racial harmony. The church needs the fullness of the races to enrich the harmony of the heavenly choir. Mark Bangert adds, "Music has staying power; more than any other cultural characteristic it conveys and

---

[5] Kathy Black, *Culturally Conscious Worship* (St. Louis: Chalice, 2000), 69.

[6] *People of the Dream*, 136–37. Emerson adds that white worship styles and musical forms place mind over body while the black culture reflects an intertwining of the mind and body.

[7] Leonard I. Sweet, "Be an Energizer Bunny," *Homiletics* (January-March 1995): 12.

enfleshes the uniqueness of people. In a very profound sense music is the social text, the place where we can 'read' the community."[8] Martin Tel contends that "when we begin to listen to and in time sing one another's songs, we may have a new and renewed ecclesiology which will favor more and more unity."[9] God's multiracial choir singing in harmony announces to the world the harmony that He has brought to the fragmented races in the body of Christ. However, a clash will inevitably occur when so many sounds and styles of music converge in one place of worship. J. Nathan Corbitt confirms, "Singing is universal, music is not . . . because music is always bound to culture. It thus becomes a cross-cultural problem when one music is played in another context or culture."[10] Although music plays a vital role in the expression of one's faith within each individual culture, Christianity transcends all cultures. Music is a tool for the kingdom of God that ultimately serves to bring glory to God and to reconcile humanity to God and to each other.[11] In multiracial worship, the church gives the world an opportunity to see the glory of God as reconciled humanity sings in harmony.

Preaching

The preaching event stands at the center of biblical worship regardless of race. However, the expression of preaching often varies from culture to culture. For example, in some cultures, preaching behind the pulpit conveys a sense of authority of not only the preacher but also the Word of God. Other cultures which exercise the freedom to preach away from the pulpit may desire to convey a sense of informality, an attempt to break down the wall between preacher and laity. Speaking from behind the pulpit might be perceived as a sign of thoughtful preparation for some racial groups, while to others it might convey that one is unprepared and not open to the movement of the Holy Spirit. There are so many different styles of preaching, ranging from a monotone reading word-for-word of a manuscript to a

---

[8] Mark Bangert, "How Does One Go About Multicultural Worship?" in *Open Questions in Worship: What Does "Multicultural Worship" Look Like?*, ed. Gordon Lathrop (Minneapolis: Augsburg Fortress, 1996), 30.

[9] Tel, 167–68.

[10] J. Nathan Corbitt, *The Sound of the Harvest: Music Mission in Church and Culture* (Grand Rapids: Baker Books, 1998), 33.

[11] Ibid., 39–40.

totally extemporaneous, rhythmic, and interactive dialogue between an animated preacher and an engaged audience. One of the strategies at Wilcrest is to expose and expand our people to different preaching traditions and expressions. Over the course of the year, we offer a variety of preaching, backgrounds, training, and styles. Due to the diversity of cultures and ethnic groups, my preaching style shifted from a strong exhortation model to a dialogical approach, encouraging the congregation to interact with me.

Use of Greeters

When Wilcrest began to make the transition from an all-white congregation to a multiracial one, the most predominant need during the worship services was maintaining a reverence in the sanctuary. Due to the potential conflict and misunderstanding of the convergence of different races in one worship gathering, the question emerged whether we needed to emphasize freedom or order in our worship services. One of our early efforts to encourage a spirit of reverence included specific instructions in the worship bulletin indicating when people may leave, dealing with unsupervised children, and the amount of talking during the service. Not surprisingly, the written word often went unheeded. During this dilemma, God sent an African-American woman to my rescue. She subtly suggested that we might consider an usher or greeter committee that she would willingly enlist and coordinate. After several months of development, we dedicated more than 25 of our adults as greeters. I call these greeters our "spiritual bouncers" because no one can leave, get up, sit down, or re-enter without their supervision. This concept is deeply ingrained in the African-American church culture, but one that we desperately needed in our growing worship chaos.

The Time Factor

According to the Lilly mail survey, the average length of the worship services for predominantly white congregations is 70 minutes, for predominantly black congregations is 105 minutes, and for multiracial congregations is 83 minutes.[12] Upon my arrival at Wilcrest, the worship services were about 75 minutes, but now the average service

---

[12] Yancey, *One Body, One Spirit,* 81.

is approximately 90 minutes. In addition to the length of the worship service, punctuality is also a volatile issue. From the perspective of our whites, starting a service on time is an expression of respect, while some of our nonwhites perceive that such rigidity is an indicator of quenching the freedom of the Holy Spirit's movement. This continues to be an ongoing source of conflict, with both sides of the argument being expressed in spiritual terms. According to Emerson, each side claims "that their preferred style is more conducive to worshipping God."[13] One of our white men expressed the frustration to the laxity of punctuality of many of our nonwhites. One of our Hispanic members responded, "If you show up on time all the time, in their culture that is equated with thinking you are very important and have to be there for things to work. That's not a very Christian trait." Out of a sense of perplexity, the white member contended, "One culture thinks it offensive not to be on time, the other thinks it offensive to be on time. No easy solution there!"[14]

Expressive versus Quiet Behavior in Worship

In some ethnic and denominational cultures, worship is not worship without involving the entire body in praise to God. Moving, dancing, clapping, and tapping the feet are a natural part of worship.[15] In our mission trips to Cameroon and Nigeria, during the offering, people dance while moving to the front to give their offering to God. For others the tone of worship is more sedate. The body is involved and the mind is focused on the worship and praise of God, but there is little overt verbal or bodily participation unless it is scripted. According to Black, this may be due to denominational influence even more than any racial aspect.[16] Yet in a multiracial congregational setting, different expressions of worship occur simultaneously while focusing on the "audience of One."

---

[13] *Against All Odds,* 27.
[14] Quoted in *Against All Odds*, 53.
[15] Black, 80.
[16] According to Rhoads at Culmore United Methodist Church in Falls Church, Virginia, "Worship preferences of our congregation run the gamut: from mainline Protestant to charismatic, liturgical to revivalistic, stoic to emotive, sedate to enthusiastic, passive to full participatory. And as one might expect the inclusion of one element in worship that may please some always poses the threat to offend another." Rhoads, *Where the Nations Meet,* 175.

Use of Different Languages

With approximately 44 different nations represented at Wilcrest, the need to translate the worship services into different languages becomes more pressing. At this present time, Wilcrest utilizes simultaneous Spanish translation via transmitter to receivers that our worshipers wear. Another approach has been adopted by the Mosaic Church of Central Arkansas, which intentionally provides both Spanish and English for every aspect of their worship services, including putting both languages on their overhead screens. Although Wilcrest uses simultaneous translation of Spanish, there is a strong effort to incorporate other languages into the fabric of the worship services. For example, choruses are often sung in English and then in Spanish. The Scripture is read in both English and the native tongue of the reader. During my fifteenth anniversary, 12 different members read Psalm 117 in 12 different languages, including: Douala dialect from Cameroon, West Africa, French, Indonesian, Vietnamese, and Teluga from India, Portuguese, and Housa from Nigeria, Spanish, Korean, and Hindi from India, Fanti from Ghana, English, and even the Cajun dialect from south Louisiana.

MODELS OF HOW TO LEAD A MULTIRACIAL WORSHIP SERVICE

Many of the different aspects of multiracial worship are an ongoing struggle, but the following models offer different forms of expressing worship in a multiracial congregation. These three models are adapted from Kathy Black.[17]

Assimilation Model

In this model, new people are expected to assimilate into the already existing worship style of the majority culture. The majority culture invites others to join in, learn, and adopt their style. The burden of learning new music is placed on all the newcomers. This model desires and sometimes assumes that the music of the majority culture will become a means for those of other cultures also to access God. It may be perceived and assumed that the majority music is preferred and superior to others. For example, if new members

---

[17] Black, 92–97.

come into their church, they assimilate into their sound and music.[18] This assimilation process welcomes new people from different racial backgrounds and worship traditions but encourages newcomers to integrate into the majority system. Although the worship style may be somewhat new, the majority group is patient with the new worshiper. Over a period of time, the new worshiper is expected to adjust in order to fit into the accepted style of worship that is expressed by the majority group.[19]

Model of Using Music That Is New to All Cultures

This model discards the traditions and histories of all people groups in order to create a new shared memory through music. It does attempt to treat everyone equally. The lyrics and musical composition of praise choruses are usually limited in nature. This model also focuses on the present. History and tradition are absent and released in search of a common present. Mosaic Church in Los Angeles and Brooklyn Tabernacle are good examples of this method, for they compose their own music and have their own fresh and distinct sound. The songs and drama skits are often written by their own people reflecting their own church's unique composition and vision. With so many cultures converging, they want to develop their distinct sound and worship culture, so that everyone can come in on equal ground. Yancey adds that this approach projects equality in social status for members of all races because everyone is beginning at the same entry point.[20] In theory, this approach sounds ideal, but people rarely leave their tradition, experience, and preferences at the door. One variation of this model is finding the common bond that already exists between different cultures. For example, there are some songs that all groups perceive to be meaningful to use in honoring and praising God. This model may lean too heavily on the past in the search for a shared

---

[18] According to Bernard Adeney, there are three stages of assimilation that a person experiences when arriving as a stranger in a new culture: (1) the preliminary stage, which is characterized by formality and tentativeness; (2) the transitional stage, when the immigrant is no longer treated like an honored guest and reality begins to set in of being an outsider and he seeks to find his identity in relation to this new culture; (3) the incorporation stage, when the individual is fully integrated into the new culture so much that it has become a part of the person. See Bernard T. Adeney, *Strange Virtues: Ethics in a Multicultural World* (Downers Grove, IL: InterVarsity, 1995), 133–36.

[19] Ibid.

[20] Yancey, *One Body, One Spirit*, 74.

memory as it values the histories of each of the cultures represented in the congregation. Yancey adds that this common bond or representation may only be a single song and therefore not enough to satisfy each racial group.[21]

Culturally Conscious Worship Model

In this final model, the diverse ways that people of every culture offer praise to God and receive inspiration from God through music are welcomed. This is best received when a particular song is attached to a personal testimony of its impact and meaning to that person. The church can use familiar hymn tunes with different lyrics that allow for a common history through the tune and a new start for all different racial groups through the lyrics. This model also seeks to utilize the music of all the cultures represented in the congregation to become an instructive means for each culture to access God in a new way. Yancey notes that one variation of this type of worship is when a church rotates the racial nature of their worship style. A church plant in Seattle utilized a rotation system of six totally different worship styles, each with their own band and worship leaders. Yancey argues that if the church is using a worship style that an individual worshiper does not enjoy, "the discomfort allows that person to rejoice that someone else is getting to hear what he/she wants to hear that Sunday."[22]

As new races integrate into multiracial congregations, the process may be compared to the Hebrew people, taken captive and living in Babylon, a foreign land. While there, they sat down and wept, "How can we sing the LORD's song on foreign soil?" (Ps 137:4). Is this what new immigrants feel as they come to the United States? For this reason, many choose to find homogeneous congregations where they can sing songs with people like themselves. Multiracial congregations provide a place where persons born in other countries can "sing the Lord's song in a foreign land."[23]

---

[21] Ibid., 75.
[22] Ibid.
[23] Black, 97.

KEY BREAKTHROUGHS IN MULTIRACIAL WORSHIP

In the journey at Wilcrest, learning what multiracial worship should look and sound like is a continual process. God taught Wilcrest through several different channels: (1) the biblical models of Isa 6 and John 4:24; (2) the experiences of our worshipers from different cultures and backgrounds; (3) the process of attempting different styles and methods by trial and error; and (4) the interviews and on-site visits with other churches globally concerning how they lead and express their worship. Yet in the development of Wilcrest's unique expression of worship, two key events occurred that served as breakthroughs in our understanding of what God wants for us.

The "Vision" of Hasan Khan

In July 1995, our church received a foretaste of what God was going to do on a larger scale in the future. After this day, I realized that our church could not handle all that God could do in one day, so He has taken us one step at a time. Our church body gathered for a prayer meeting on a Wednesday night, and God placed a heavy burden on my heart to pray for our multiracial youth group traveling on a mission trip to several of the inner cities in the Deep South.

In that audience, there was a young twenty-five-year-old man named Hasan Khan. Hasan was a Muslim who grew up in India. Over the previous months, Hasan regularly attended our church with his girlfriend from the Assembly of God tradition. They both told me that they came to our Baptist church because it was a middle ground between the Muslim faith and the Assemblies of God. I found their deduction most interesting. Hasan and I became friends and engaged in multiple conversations concerning the similarities and the differences between the Islamic faith and Christianity. The conversations were very open and dialogical, but I did not sense any tangible headway being made. After that particular prayer meeting, Hasan asked if he could speak with me. I did not think that his request was anything unusual, so we met in my office.

Hasan began the conversation with the most shocking words that I have ever heard spoken to me about one of our prayer services. He said, "Pastor, I saw a vision tonight." Our church is not known for our worshipers having visions. In fact, I thought at first he was not serious, but his eyes said that something had happened. So I responded, "Hasan, what exactly did you see in your vision?" He said, "While you and the rest of the church were praying, I saw four crosses right behind you. From these crosses, the Holy Spirit came down and embraced me." I quickly asked, "Is there anything else?" He replied, "No pastor, but what do you think this vision means?" Right at that moment, I prayed a prayer I had never prayed before. I asked the same God of Joseph and Daniel to grant me help concerning the interpretation of this "vision." I have never had words come out of my mouth with so much ease and at the same time not knowing what my next word would be. I turned to Hasan and asked, "How many crosses were outside of Jerusalem on the day Jesus was crucified?" He quickly answered, "Three." I then added, "That is correct, but perhaps the fourth cross in your vision was your cross." Hasan and I had shared on several occasions about the historical facts of Christianity and the life of Jesus. I always emphasized that God's love was most clearly expressed by Jesus dying in our place. The cross was not originally designed for the sinless Son of God, but for the condemned sinner. Then I continued, "Perhaps the Holy Spirit coming down from the cross and embracing you was God's sign to you that He wants an intimate and personal relationship with you." I knew from our conversations together that the Islamic faith did not emphasize a personal relationship with their god. Right at that moment tears began to stream down his face. Turning to me, he said "I want that personal relationship with Christ." Hasan then prayed to ask Christ to come into his life.

There are many other denominations and expressions of the Christian faith in which Hasan's vision would not be unusual, but for our church the experience represented a pivotal breakthrough. Not only was he our first convert from India, but he was one of our first Muslim converts. Following the mission pattern in the book of Acts, God often used supernatural events to help bring the gospel across new racial, ethnic, or cultural barriers. For example, God used many signs through Philip to reach across the Samaritan barrier (Acts 8:4–8,25), a vision to both the apostle Peter and the God-fearer Cornelius to cross the Gentile barrier (Acts 10), and the healing of a lame man in the city of Lystra to reach the uneducated Gentiles (Acts 14:8–18). One of the purposes of miracles is to confirm visually what has been spoken verbally. Hasan's experience provided validation for him of the spoken gospel and an encouragement as he stepped into his new faith in Christ, but it also instilled motivation for the church that God wanted to reach all the nations regardless of any perceived barriers. To Wilcrest, a Muslim from India was out of our accustomed realm of ministry, but God planted a seed and gave indication that it was not impossible for Him to use the church to reach all people groups.

Being Slain in the Spirit

Another worship service that altered our perspective on multiracial ministry occurred outside our familiar confines of Wilcrest. On one of the youth choir mission trips, our youth were involved in a ministry with a black congregation in Mississippi. During one of the worship services, the speaker encouraged our youth to experience "being slain in the Spirit." This involves a traumatic yielding of the entire self to the power of the Holy Spirit in which the individual ultimately falls to the floor as if slain or knocked down by the Holy Spirit. This phenomenon is difficult to explain, but it is an important part of the spiritual experience for many Christians. However, our youth as a whole had never been introduced to this concept, much less to the experience itself. A few of our young people engaged in this experience, while the majority of our youth simply observed with either a sense of confusion or apprehension. Some of the young people reported that it was an exciting movement of God, but they did not fully understand all of the ramifications. In fact, as they returned to Houston, the confusion seemed to increase as they compared that service with the services they were regularly experiencing at Wilcrest. Some of them initially concluded that Wilcrest was not as spiritual or exciting as the black church in Mississippi. As the youth began to express more of their feelings, the parents became quite concerned over this development.

As the conflict seemed to intensify, the issue crystallized into a sharp division between the exciting and spiritual black service and the boring and cognitive white service. In fact, the emotions escalated to the point that I called a joint assembly of all the young people who had gone on this trip and their parents to deal openly with this issue. This was an extremely difficult time for me because I had entrusted James

with the spiritual care of the youth and the parents' perception was
that their children were exposed to something extremely dangerous.

As I look back at this particular incident, I am so thankful that
James provided this opportunity for our youth to experience what
they did. However, at the time, I felt I had to address the entire group
to reassure them of our direction and practice at Wilcrest. I felt that
James thought I had possibly undermined his leadership by diminishing the experience of several of the youth by telling the entire group
why we did not practice "being slain in the Spirit" during our worship services at Wilcrest. If I had to do it all over again, I would simply recognize that our youth were stretched and exposed to another
expression of faith, but I would still walk them through a clear understanding of Scripture on the matter.

There are so many valid expressions of worship throughout Christianity in homogeneous congregations, and when the multiracial element is incorporated into the fabric of worship, the variables increase
exponentially. Donald H. Juel accurately observed, "The challenge
in multicultural worship is singing and praying, eating and drinking, with people who are genuinely different, in such a way as to
become the body of Christ." He adds that he "does not envision a
community in which differences disappear but one in which they
are not separate."[24] Accompanying the possibility of experiencing and enjoying different expressions of worship from a variety of
racial backgrounds, there is also a possibility that this diversity may
cause confusion and chaos. According to Kathy Black, "Worship is
clearly a communication event, and in multicultural congregations,
miscommunication and associated problems can arise when communicating cross-culturally."[25] We will now look at several ways that
Wilcrest attempted to bridge these inevitable gaps in a multiracial
congregation.

DIFFERENT APPROACHES TO BRIDGE THE GAP

Transitioning from an all-white congregation to a multiracial
congregation has required Wilcrest to experiment with different
approaches in the area of worship, such as testimonies from a vari-

---

[24] Donald H. Juel, "Multicultural Worship," in *Making Room at the Table*, 50.
[25] Black, 6.

ety of racial backgrounds, reading Scripture in multiple languages, singing in both English and Spanish, simultaneous translation of the entire worship service in Spanish, artistic expressions from all over the world, display of flags from the different countries to which we sent missionaries, and a variety of symbols that either celebrate different cultures or transcend them. Many of our attempts at bridging the racial gaps have resulted in temporary setbacks, but each failure laid the groundwork for future success. All of the difficulties, misunderstandings, failures, and adversities are worth the eternal investment after hearing the following testimony from one of the members from Wilcrest:

> It just blew me away to see that worship service. There were Africans with their traditional clothing, youth with hip-hop clothing, Mexicans, whites, South Americans, Asians, American blacks, blacks from the Caribbean, and they were all speaking English with accents or in their native language. You know, what really caught my attention was seeing this mass of people talk to each other as if they had grown up together. I had to come back to see what was goin' on here. I had never seen anything like it before.[26]

This testimony reminds the body of Christ of the value of seeing all the nations come together to worship the same God. In fact, a church-wide survey conducted in May 2002, reports that the primary reason why people came to Wilcrest was its worship services.[27] The worship service plays a pivotal role in any congregational setting, but in a multiracial church, worship will either unite or divide the different racial groups. Bridging the racial gap in worship will not only announce the multiracial vision but also sustain it.

CONCLUSION—A LITTLE OF HEAVEN ON EARTH

After a grueling ten years of seeing God move a homogeneous congregation to a multiracial one, the church celebrated my ten-year anniversary with a little of heaven on earth. Several components in

---

[26] *People of the Dream*, 108.
[27] There were 275 responses to this survey. The reasons that were given for coming to Wilcrest included: worship (40%), personal relationships (23%), location (22%), diversity (18%), friendliness (15%), and programs (11%). See *People of the Dream*, 105–10.

this worship celebration put me in awe of how far God has brought the entire church body and me along the path toward becoming a multiracial congregation. From our church body, five believers quoted our mission statement in their native tongue: French, German, Spanish, Cantonese, an African dialect; and then the entire church said it in English. A spiritual mariachi band sang a popular Christian Spanish song and a chorus sang in both Spanish and English. Our worship leader then had people stand as their country was announced. To hear the 40 countries named and to see each group from that country stand provided a powerful portrait of the multiracial vision reaching fruition.[28] I did not think that I would ever see 40 different countries represented in a Wilcrest worship service when I first arrived at the ninety-eight-percent white congregation in 1992. This service announced to the world that the nations had gathered in southwest Houston in preparation for the final worship service around the throne of God.

DISCUSSION QUESTIONS

1. What are the key elements of the Isaiah 6 and John 4 worship models? Compare and contrast the Isaiah 6 model with the John 4 model.

2. What are some key aspects of corporate worship in becoming a multiracial congregation? Which of these characteristics might prove to be the most challenging in your church and why?

3. Of the worship models presented, which model would best describe your church? Why?

4. What are some forms of expression or approaches that would help your church bridge the gap to other cultures in your worship services or your worship center?

5. Have there been any unusual expressions of worship that you or your church has experienced across racial lines in your local context or on the mission field? If so, what kind of impact has that had on you or your church? What do you believe God is trying to teach you through these potential breakthroughs?

---

[28] See appendix 4.

CHAPTER 11

LEADERSHIP IN A
MULTIRACIAL CHURCH

"He who leads, [let him lead] with diligence"(Rom 12:8, NASB).

J ust as the Marines popularized the slogan, "We need a few good men," the multiracial church cries out, "We need a few good leaders!" In any church, discovering and developing leadership is a daunting challenge. Whatever leadership dynamics and difficulties a homogeneous church may encounter, these seem to multiply exponentially with the convergence of several races and cultures. Several questions emerge. If you are good leader in a homogenous congregation, does that automatically mean you are a good leader in a multiracial congregation? Are the qualities of an effective leader in a homogeneous church the same as in a multiracial church? If there are any distinctive characteristics of a multiracial leader in the multiracial context, what are they? What leadership traits are absolutely essential in a multiracial congregation? Before we could assess the difference between leaders in a homogeneous and a multiracial congregation, Wilcrest had to locate and train new leaders. In addition, during the early part of the multiracial transformation process, we established worship and leadership as our two highest priorities due to the impression that they would make on any newcomer.

THE NEED FOR LEADERS

Since Wilcrest's membership had been declining since the mid-eighties, the number of qualified leaders had also been decreasing. Only a few key leaders carried much of the ministry burden, and therefore morale was diminishing. In order for the church not only to survive but also experience a racial transformation, we had to find new and trained leaders. Our first approach to remedy this dilemma, while crossing racial lines, was to call James Darby as our minister to students. However, his arrival did not bring an immediate surge of people from different people groups. We concluded diversification would come through new converts who had little or no religious or church background, not the transfer of believers from other homogeneous churches. As a result, the vast majority of our new members were either new believers or believers who had been out of church a long time; the immediate training of qualified leadership would be overwhelming.

We had several believers of different races come and visit for a period of time, but they would eventually leave. Due to so many quiet departures, I conducted informal exit interviews and asked why people were only remaining with Wilcrest for a brief time, especially the strong believers. The most obvious reason for their exodus was voiced by African-Americans who did not perceive that our changes in worship were enough to bridge the gap between races. Others said the church was so different from the ones to which they were accustomed. Through these interviews, I discovered that very few people joined Wilcrest from other evangelical churches. In fact, for several years, the ratio of baptismal growth to transfer growth was three-to-one.[1] In reality, our church had become so different that if a person was already acclimated to the style and composition of a homogeneous church, the multiracial church often proved too much of a contrast for them. With this discovery, we began to focus on not only converting unbelievers from all people groups, but tackling the laborious task of developing them into effective multiracial leaders. The church considered this to be a positive characteristic because this kind of growth would be true "kingdom of God" growth, not simply "sheep-swapping" between different evangelical churches.

The focus on unbelievers became a factor in our leadership because there were few nonwhites who were qualified leaders when they initially arrived at our church. At first, the only key nonwhite leader was James Darby, our minister to students, who was paid to be there. As the church began to disciple all our new believers, we began to see several of our nonwhite members assume leadership positions. The discovery and development of nonwhite leaders has

---

[1] See appendix 2 and appendix 3 for a detailed overview of the additions to Wilcrest.

been the most difficult part of the journey for me as the pastor of a multiracial congregation. At the present time, we have several leaders in the Awana ministry (children's ministry), yokefellows (those who assist the deacons in their ministry), committee members, and choir members from different races. Yet this racial transformation of our leadership was a process that had a mixture of a few successes and multiple setbacks, constantly battling the transitory nature of our people and our area. For example, we had an African-American deacon, ordained at another church, who served as the vice-chairman of the deacon body but relocated because of his job. At the time of his move, he was nominated to be the chairman of our deacon body. The church needed to raise spiritually effective leadership from each racial group on our congregation.

WHAT DOES THE BIBLE SAY?

In each church, there are primarily two areas of leadership within the local church: lay leaders who come from the general church family, and the vocationally called ministers. Both of these groups are essential for the proper working of the church's ministry. As Paul said earlier in Rom 12:5, "In the same way we who are many are one body in Christ and individually members of one another." Consequently, there is interdependence among the different parts of the body of Christ, regardless of role or ministry. When the apostle Paul sent his coworkers, Timothy and Titus, to help establish lay and pastoral leadership in the churches of Ephesus and Crete, he gave specific guidelines for determining who could serve in each of these leadership positions.

In 1 Tim 3:1–12 and Titus 3:1–10, these traits are listed in detail. These qualifications are not so much a job description as they are a heart description of the potential leaders. In 1 Tim 3:2, Paul began with the word *must*, which means God mandates it and none of these qualifications are an option. Some of the qualifications for pastors include being "beyond reproach," which conveys the absence of acts or habits that would give occasion for attack or criticism[2]; "temperate," which means sober, clear-headed, and free from the influence of

---

[2] George W. Knight III, *The Pastoral Epistles: A Commentary on the Greek Text* (Grand Rapids: Eerdmans, 1992), 155. Walter L. Liefeld adds that this quality does not depict a person totally without sin, but "one who is morally careful and responsible"; *1 and 2 Timothy and Titus,* NIV Application Commentary (Grand Rapids: Zondervan, 1999), 118.

intoxicants and any rash actions[3]; "prudent" or having a sound mind and self-control[4]; other qualifications include being "the husband of one wife . . . respectable . . . able to teach, not addicted to wine or pugnacious" (NASB); a pugnacious person is one who may quickly and violently strike out against another person[5]; further qualifications include being "gentle, peaceable, free from the love of money, one who manages his own household well, not a new convert," and having "a good reputation with those outside the church" (NASB). The most interesting characteristic concerning the multiracial congregation is that the pastor is required to be "hospitable," which literally means "lover of strangers," approachable, and gladly open-hearted.[6] A qualified pastor is one who intentionally demonstrates the love of God to those who are different from him regardless of their religious, racial, social, and economic backgrounds. Since the apostle Paul had already commanded all believers to love strangers and show hospitality (Rom 12:13), the pastor should set the example of loving strangers.

The other key leadership position in the local church is the deacon, which originated from the word describing a table-waiter who kicked up dust in eagerness to serve.[7] Some of their qualifications include being men "worthy of respect" who are serious about the spiritual task of serving others; "not hypocritical, not drinking a lot of wine, not greedy for money, holding the mystery of the faith with a clear conscience"; "blameless . . . husbands of one wife, managing their children and their own households competently." Overall, the deacon must exercise self-control and moderation in the areas of alcohol, money, temper, and tongue. In regard to his family, the deacon must be faithful to his wife and able to manage his children. His relationships, inside and outside the church family, must be hospitable, gentle, and highly esteemed. Finally, in regards to his faith, he must hold fast to the truth and be gifted in teaching. These core qualities are required of Christian leaders. The vast majority of these characteristics focuses on the character of the leader, but also entails

---

[3] Thomas D. Lea and Hayne P. Griffin Jr., *1, 2 Timothy and Titus* (The New American Commentary; Nashville: Broadman, 1992), 110.

[4] Knight, 159.

[5] Lea and Griffin, 111.

[6] Ibid., 110.

[7] See Philip H. Towner, *The Letters to Timothy and Titus,* New International Commentary on the New Testament (Grand Rapids: Eerdmans, 2006), 261.

a few areas of competency. God concerns Himself with qualified leadership in His church.

In addition to the biblical qualities that Paul clearly set forth for the leaders in the first-century church, there are some helpful and sometimes necessary traits for leaders of the multiracial churches. Just as there was some sense of evolvement from the priests and Levites of the Old Testament to the pastors, elders, and deacons of the New Testament, there is a need to define clearly the requirements in a multiracial church context.

CHARACTER SKETCH OF A MULTIRACIAL LEADER

1. Exposure and Experience with Multiple Races

It is extremely difficult for leaders to lead where they have not been, or to take followers through a transformation that they themselves have not experienced. When the leader personally experiences the multiracial context, knows the people's struggles, the potential failures and dead-ends, and the sacrifices that must be made to gain the rewards, then others will be more likely to follow. The most powerful expression of this type of identification and actually "getting into the skin" was when "the Word became flesh and took up residence among us" (John 1:14). God became like us so that Jesus might explain God to us (John 1:18). Furthermore, Jesus was able to identify with our weaknesses and was "tested in every way as we are, yet without sin" (Heb 4:15). In fact, this qualified Jesus as our priest and our leader. In Paul's desire to win different groups to Christ, he often attempted to become like one of them: "To the Jews, I became like a Jew . . . to those who are outside the law, like one outside the law . . . " (1 Cor 9:20–21). This is described as *incarnate leadership:* to get into the flesh and soul of the people to whom you will minister. On the day the church voted to call me as their pastor, one woman came up to me and said, "I know God wants us to be a multiracial congregation, but we never had anyone to lead us." The people of God are not asking that the leaders have all the answers, but they do need someone who is one step ahead of them in this spiritual journey.

A helpful example is a secular study done at the University of Michigan. This university is one of the most diverse of any large university in the Midwest, with minorities making up more than 25 percent of the 36,000 students. The university had compiled data on its students that indicated that five years after graduation, collegians who were exposed to a diverse student body were more likely to work in integrated settings, live in integrated neighborhoods, and have friends of another race. For example, 92 percent of the white students grew up in segregated neighborhoods, and more than 80 percent of the white seniors reported some level of interaction with Asian students, and 65 percent of white seniors said that they had substantial or some level of interaction with black students.[8] If this kind of impact exists among those who live in the secular world, the people of God who intentionally share the love of God across racial lines should see this integration become a reality.

The multiracial leader is the kind of person who can interact and build bridges to multiple races. According to the historian and contemporary American analyst David Hollinger, five major racial melting pots or groups are in the United States: Indian/Native American, African-American/Black, European-American/White, Hispanic/Latino, and Asian-American.[9] Emerson proposes that another group of individuals operates outside of the realm of their own racial melting pot in most aspects of their social relations. He identifies this group as *Sixth Americans* because they live in multiple melting pots simultaneously. Their lives are so radically different from most Americans who live in a racially homogeneous world; their world is "racially diverse with a little homogeneity sprinkled in."[10] Emerson adds that the pastor of a multiracial congregation will be more likely to be led by a *Sixth American* who is from a mixed racial background, such as being interracially married, reared in a mixed-race environment, and involved with other cross-race experiences.[11] The *Sixth American* mind-set must be established in the church in order to raise up a future generation of multiracial leaders.

2. A Strong Biblical Base

This biblical foundation will be the only defense in the face of enormous adversity when the church begins to move towards the

---

    [8] Steven A. Holmes, *Houston Chronicle,* 5/14/99.
    [9] See David Hollinger, *Postethnic America: Beyond Multiculturalism* (New York: Oxford Press, 1995).
    [10] *People of the Dream,* 99.
    [11] Ibid., 88. Twelve percent of multiracial congregations are led by a senior pastor of a mixed racial background compared to one percent of uniracial congregations.

reality of becoming a multiracial congregation. As the leader of a multiracial congregation, the ultimate authority on which we stand is the authority of the Bible. Numerous obstacles will be thrown in one's path, but the Bible provides a pattern and an encouragement to those who walk this less-traveled path. One of the primary obstacles will be church or cultural tradition, and only the Bible will serve as the ultimate standard against generations of tradition. It is helpful to understand that when the apostles diffused a volatile racial division between the Hellenistic and the Hebraic widows in the early church of Jerusalem, they were called to give more time and devotion to prayer and to Scripture (Acts 6:2,4). Any time a racial conflict occurred in the early church, Scripture was used as a reminder and instructor on exactly how to proceed. When the conflict came up between Peter and Paul concerning Peter's withdrawal from table fellowship with the Gentiles, Paul reminded him of the equity of both the sinfulness and the salvation for Jews and Gentiles alike. Even in the Old Testament, when the Jews neglected or refused to include the Gentiles in God's salvation, a Word from God would correct and remind His chosen people that they were instruments to reach the entire world (see Jonah 4:9–12; Isa 49:6). The Bible reveals God's heart toward the different races and gives encouragement to the leaders during difficult days.

3. An Evangelistic Heart

The biblical mandate for all disciples of Christ is to be witnesses to the world and make disciples of all nations (Matt 28:19–20; Acts 1:8). This call to evangelism is not optional for any believer. In fact, evidence that one is connected and rooted in Christ is that he is bearing fruit, meaning not only reproducing the character of Christ but also reproducing other Christians. In the early church, when the believers were filled with the Holy Spirit, they spoke the Word of God with boldness (Acts 4:31). The apostle Paul contended that if a person truly believes, he will also speak (2 Cor 4:13). It is impossible to walk with Christ and not share your faith with those around you. Surprisingly, we have discovered that the most effective way to grow a multiracial congregation is through the conversion of new believers. This seems to be somewhat elementary, but the American church often calculates its growth by the number of people added to the membership roll, regardless of whether they join from another congregation. Believers who are already a part of a homogeneous church have found integration into a multiracial congregation formidable. The fact that 93 percent of all religious congregations are at least eighty-percent homogeneous makes it extremely unlikely that new transfer growth will be from multiracial congregations. Consequently, at Wilcrest more than 60 percent of our new members have been new believers.[12] A leader must have an evangelistic heart for all races in order to grow the multiracial vision.

4. A Global Vision

This global vision is birthed through the study of the Bible that clearly reveals the heart of God for all the nations. Christ commands us in the Great Commission, "Go, therefore, and make disciples of all nations, baptizing them in the name of the Father and of the Son and of the Holy Spirit" (Matt 28:19). Prior to Jesus' ascension to the right hand of the Father, He adds, "But you will receive power when the Holy Spirit has come upon you, and you will be My witnesses in Jerusalem, in all Judea and Samaria, and to the ends of the earth" (Acts 1:8). Southern Baptists have done well in going to all the nations, but the increasing dilemma occurs when the nations come to us. One of our African women was so disappointed and confused when she arrived in the United States and discovered that not all American Christians were missionaries. In her experience in her own country, every Christian whom she encountered was a missionary. Her assumption reflects the desire of her heavenly Father.

In 2002, the church called Gihee Yoon as our minister to children. She was previously on staff at an all-Korean congregation. During her first month at Wilcrest, she spent a week at camp with a very diverse group of youth and a week in Mexico on a mission trip. Gihee continued to immerse herself in the various cultures of our children. She observed, "I can't believe I have not been involved in a multiethnic ministry before now. Before Wilcrest, I never thought outside the box and did not know it could be that exciting. I love receiving and giving hugs to people from all around the world." By her own admission, she formerly targeted other Koreans when she was in a multiracial context in order to feel a connection and find a place to belong. Now

---

[12] See appendix 2. See appendix 3 for a detailed breakdown of those who have joined Wilcrest.

she cannot wait for each Sunday to arrive and interface with the entire world in one location. This global vision begins in our backyard and does not stop until the gospel reaches the ends of earth.

5. A Teachable Spirit

God calls all believers to make disciples (Matt 28:19), but if we are to make disciples we first have to be disciples. The word *disciple* refers to a follower, a learner, or a student of another, and in the case of Christians, we are to be students of Christ. It also implies that a disciple of Christ is required to be in a continual learning mode. When the apostle Paul called the church of Corinth to "be imitators of me, as I also am of Christ" (1 Cor 11:1), he clearly stated that as he had learned and imitated Christ, so he wanted them to mimic his example. Even in the Jewish tradition, when a student studied under a rabbi, the rabbi would whisper into the ear of the student, and then the student would quote verbatim what his teacher instructed him to say. In a multiracial ministry, the learning curve is extremely steep and constant. A lack of models exists today. Therefore these conclusions result from extensive research of the Scriptures and other conglomerating church examples, while maintaining a willingness to experiment with unproven methods. Oftentimes, the only model is your own and the only concrete data is your few successes and multiple failures. Even after 17 years of leading a church to become a multiracial congregation, I find that there continues to be a dearth of information that is available to assist the multiracial congregation. The barrenness in this area has driven me to seek out those who can help, because I continue to encounter unknown situations. How I led an all-white congregation of 200 is radically different from how God wants me to lead a congregation of 500, representing 44 different countries. What works in a homogeneous congregation may not work as effectively in a multiracial one, and vice-versa.

6. A Forbearing Spirit

This trait is taken directly from Phil 4:5, which states, "Let your forbearing spirit be made known to all men, for the Lord is near."[13] A forbearing spirit is the attitude which gives others permission to be

---

[13] Author's translation.

different. The apostle Paul wrote this letter while in prison in Rome to a group of believers whom he introduced to Christianity. In the church at Philippi were a wide variety of people including Jews and Gentiles, but in order to ensure unity within the body, there would have to be a spirit within each believer that permitted others to be different. In the same way, the multiracial leader sets the example of permitting all different cultural groups to be who God called them to be in the body of Christ. This type of spirit cannot be taught as effectively as it can be caught by example. At Wilcrest, both our expressive cultures and our reserved cultures are learning to be patient with one another. The key verse in this delicate interaction has been Prov 27:17: "Iron sharpens iron, and one man sharpens another." Most of our members are enrolled in "Cultural Sensitivity 101" every week. Not one week passes that we do not experience some sort of misunderstanding due to cultural or racial differences and perceptions. Since we do not normally gravitate toward people who are different than we are, we ought to position ourselves strategically in a place where we are interacting with a variety of people groups. It is nearly impossible to "love strangers" or "pursue hospitality" (Rom 12:13) if we are never around strangers or people who are different from ourselves.

7. Advocate of Shared Diverse Leadership

Leadership is such a critical but fragile dynamic in the multiracial congregation. The church took a bold step forward when they called James Darby as minister to students to an all-white congregation. In September 1998, James Darby felt a call to an itinerant ministry of preaching and speaking across the country. His departure enabled the church to shift its resources from one full-time minister to students to four different part-time ministers or interns. The church called a part-time preschool minister, a children's intern, a youth intern, and a college minister. In addition to James' departure, Monty left for a church in Alabama about eighteen months later, so our original three vocational staff scattered in different directions. Although this was an extremely difficult and lonely time, it also afforded us the opportunity to open a new chapter in this multiracial pilgrimage.

In the spring of 2000, the personnel committee began to look seriously for an associate pastor either in the area of worship or youth. When I spoke to the committee, I was emphatic that this person should be a person of color for the following reasons. First, the leadership should reflect the growing diversity of believers. The church also was at a place where we needed to state boldly the future of the direction of our vision to the church and to the surrounding community. As a whole, the church continued to become more diverse. Even during this time without any full-time ministerial staff other than me, the choir began to become more diverse. It seemed that God was sending signals through every possible conduit to remind me how vital it is to incorporate a multiracial staff.

During this search process, some vocal members of the church did not share my passion to fill the vacancies in our staff with nonwhites. The basis of their argument was that we should enlist the most qualified person regardless of the individual's race. However, that line of reasoning from an all-white congregation usually meant being qualified by standards set by the majority white group. In addition, with the church becoming more diverse, the need to have qualified representation from different races would send a powerful signal to each racial group within the congregation. To the non-Anglos, diverse staff leadership would enable them to connect with those who made decisions in the church and would also encourage and empower them to step up in a leadership role. To the whites, diverse staff leadership would reinforce the direction of the multiracial vision and, at the same time, teach them how to follow nonwhite leadership. Consequently, I began to ask several of our nonwhite members concerning this issue. Their feedback was extremely important to me at this pivotal point in our spiritual journey. Their answers surprised me. To them, the color of the staff person's skin was not as important as the color of their vision. Did the new potential staff possess a multiracial heart? One of our Hispanic leaders encouraged and exhorted me by saying, "It does not matter if this person is green with only one eye in the middle of his forehead; if he is willing to pursue our vision, we need to hire him." I was encouraged by their response, but at the same time somewhat torn. I really thought that the next person on our ministerial staff should be a nonwhite. As I discovered through this deliberate and painful process, there is no way to predict the future.

One of the mainstays that kept alive the vision for multiracial representation in the leadership was the depiction of the church at Antioch, which had representation of both racial and economic diversity.

Luke mentioned Simeon, who was called "Niger" (Acts 13:1) meaning "black." Simeon probably was called "Niger" because he was a black African.[14] Not only had an African become fully incorporated into the church, but he was also a vital part of the leadership team of the church that served as the primary mission base for the first-century church. There is not another mention of Simeon who was called Niger, but the fact that Luke added his name to this leadership list reminds us how much value God placed on diverse leadership.[15]

From Emerson's extensive research of multiracial congregations, he deduced, "Organizations that have a diverse leadership staff are more able to satisfy multiple constituent groups within the organization, thus lessening the overall level of conflict."[16] Racially shared leadership is not only one of the primary means by which to propagate the multiracial vision, but it is also one of the most effective ways to avoid conflict in the multiracial setting.

The Ordination of the Diverse Seven. Another key event that indicated that the church was moving toward a shared diverse leadership paradigm occurred on December 8, 2002, when Wilcrest ordained seven deacons, three of whom were Hispanic. During the previous ten years, the church had ordained a total of ten deacons, all Anglos. In the thirty-year history of Wilcrest, the church had never ordained a non-Anglo deacon until this pivotal and moving day. All the prospective deacons and their wives went through a rigorous screening process that began with a total of 13 candidates. After a period of time, the initial group of 13 men was reduced to 7 men. During the ordination service, each candidate was asked to respond to a question in front of the entire congregation during the morning worship services. The last candidate, Fernando Medina, from the Dominican Republic, was asked about how being in the first class of diverse

---

[14] Hays, 177. See also F. F. Bruce, *The Book of Acts* (Grand Rapids: Eerdmans, 1988), 244–45; J. Stott, *The Spirit, the Church, and the World: The Message of Acts* (Downers Grove, IL: InterVarsity, 1990), 216.

[15] In sharp contrast to the shared diverse leadership model, the legacy of the conquistadores in Latin America advocates a model that has affected many of the Caribbean and Latin immigrants. This model emphasizes: (1) power and control over inclusion, (2) hierarchy over equality, and (3) status over humility. See Carol Hoffman-Gusman, "Cross-Cultural Leadership and Participation in the Local Church" (working paper, Miami Urban Ministries, Miami, FL, 1995). Rhoads contends that those who come from nondemocratic backgrounds find it difficult "to adapt readily to the more egalitarian and democratic decision-making structure of the U.S. church." Rhoads, *Where the Nations Meet*, 174.

[16] *Against All Odds*, 161.

deacons at Wilcrest would impact both himself and the church as a whole. He replied, "Imagine walking into this sanctuary and all the chairs, the walls, and the roof were totally white, or totally black, or totally brown; wouldn't that be extremely boring?" Another one of the Hispanics who was ordained was Ricardo Pineda, originally from Honduras. He was the first deacon that we ordained whom I had also baptized as a new believer. Both of these men also served as leaders in our Hispanic ministry. The final Hispanic was Henry Pineda, a Mexican-American, who has a heart to minister across all cultures.

The primary charge for our newly ordained deacons was from Acts 6:1–7, which described the early church also setting aside seven men for the ministry of the feeding of widows. However, the problem was much deeper than simply overseeing their diet. The reason the church selected these seven men was to deal with a cultural and ethnic problem between the Jews who grew up in Palestine and the Jews immersed in Greek culture. It is possible that there was a language barrier, but there was definitely a cultural barrier between the Hellenistic widows and the Hebraic widows. The predominant Palestinian Jewish leadership was ministering to the Hebraic Jewish widows, but the apostles selected seven Hellenistic Jews to minister specifically to those who had been neglected.

In the same way, three non-Anglo deacons were selected to minister to our entire church family, which at that time consisted of less than 50 percent Anglos. In my mind, the seven who were set aside by Wilcrest closely paralleled the original seven men who had been set aside by the first-century church. The stimulus that prompted the apostles to select "seven men of good reputation, full of the Spirit and wisdom" was the potential cultural and ethnic division within the church at Jerusalem. Wilcrest also selected men with the same qualifications to address the growing need of different cultures within the same local body. For the last 30 years, the deacon body has consisted of mostly Anglos, while the racial composition of the church changed dramatically. The church needed to implement an important biblical principle in the area of cross-cultural conflict. This principle involves the empowering of non-Anglos in the leadership realm, which simultaneously produced an overwhelming celebration. Many of our non-Anglos voiced their excitement and a true sense of finally being represented in the spiritual leadership of the church.

8. Seasoned Facilitator in Conflict Resolution

I was under the false impression that once we moved toward becoming a multiracial congregation that the majority of our conflicts would be behind us. However, the number of conflicts has not necessarily decreased but has differed. One of the potential conflicts is in the area of our physical facility. Many of our white members understand that our facility is more than 30 years old and is in need of repair and remodeling. However, many of our believers who have come into the body at Wilcrest have come from the third-world environment, and our physical building is far better than the ones to which they were accustomed. Consequently, the urgency of the need for a new or remodeled building is not a priority. If the multiracial leader was unaware of this background information, he could easily perceive that the whites were more focused on the material needs instead of the spiritual needs or the third-world members simply did not care about God's house. In our particular congregation, neither of these perceptions would be accurate, but in church conferences or business meetings, the leader needs to be aware of the cultural backgrounds and religious history.[17] This past year, the same debate surfaced again concerning whether our money should be spent on missions or to repair and maintain our building. Each person advocating the financial support for the building was strongly passionate that the physical structure of the church should be our best. Yet the argument for missions came from our unique calling to send a missionary to each of the countries represented by our membership. How could reaching the nations with the gospel not take priority over a temporary and earthly structure? In this particular instance, I did not have to stand up and say anything because several of the lay leaders permitted the people to speak out of the passions of their hearts, yet they continued to bring the people back to the vision. One lay leader contended that both the building and missions are vital expressions of our home base and our vision to reach the nations, and they should not be set against one another.

---

[17] Joseph Henriques contends that multicultural leaders have three roles in dealing with tradition and culture: leaders are to be (1) sustainers of cultural traditions that promote and help God's work, (2) breakers of those traditions that hinder, (3) and blenders of the traditions of cultures represented in their church. See Joseph Henriques, "Clouds in Our Community," in *Cultural Change and Your Church: Helping Your Church Survive in a Diverse Society* (Grand Rapids: Baker, 2002), 53.

Eric H. F. Law introduces a process called "mutual invitation," which helps the multiracial community in communicating and handling conflict. The process begins with the leader sharing his thoughts and feelings without projecting that he is an expert. The leader then invites someone else to share. After that individual has spoken, then the person speaking can invite the next person to share. Each person has the option to pass the privilege of speaking to any person they desire to choose. The release and reception of the privilege to share one's thoughts or viewpoints "decentralizes the power that is usually held by the designated leader."[18] This technique is a helpful tool in handling conflict among a wide range of racial and cultural backgrounds.

9. Person of Passionate Prayer

The Word of God commands believers to "pray constantly" (1 Thess 5:17; cp. Luke 18:1). In Jesus' teachings to His disciples in the Sermon on the Mount, Jesus assumed they would pray— "Whenever you pray . . . " (Matt 6:5–7)—just as Jesus often did throughout His ministry (Mark 1:35; Luke 9:18,28). One of the distinguishing marks of the vibrant early church was their devotion to prayer (Acts 2:42). Prayer was the stimulus that prompted the Spirit of God to come down in power at Pentecost (Acts 1:14), and the basis on which the apostles spoke with boldness (Acts 4:31). Prayer places a believer in a spiritual posture of absolute dependency for the power of God in the midst of our weakness.

When I came to Wilcrest, one of the priority items in the area of reaching across racial lines was the discipline of persistent prayer. I grew up in an extremely prejudiced area, and my previous pastorate was also in an area that was racially segregated. I came to Houston with a hope that integration among different races in a local body would be much easier. Yet there were some major obstacles upon my arrival. The only way there would be a God-sized breakthrough would be a movement that was so powerful that only God could receive

---

[18] Law, 83. Duane Elmer offers principles for cross-cultural conflict resolution. Some of these include: (1) The degree to which shame, face, and honor are core cultural values will determine how important it is to choose an indirect method. (2) All forms of confrontation should occur in private, if possible, so as to minimize any loss of face. (3) Build a close relationship with a host-country person who will be able to help you interpret confusing situations. (4) Scripture is the final judge of all cultural forms; prayer and discussion may be required before some cultural expressions are embraced. See Elmer, 181.

credit. On a regular basis, our church gathers for prayer on the first Saturday night of each month, in which the only focus is the spiritual awakening in our church, area, state, nation, and the world. One of my passions is the study of the history of spiritual awakenings across the world. The last comprehensive movement of the Spirit across America was in the early 1900s, sweeping across America and breaking down denominational barriers. Wilcrest's conviction is that the next major movement of God in this country will dismantle racial and cultural barriers. God has called Wilcrest and other multiracial congregations to serve as prototypes for other churches to follow whenever He eradicates racial barriers and demonstrates His power to overcome any obstacle and His love for the nations. If our church and others can work out some of the details before this great movement comes, it may make the other churches' transformation a little easier.

Another goal of praying for awakening on these Saturday nights is for our people to understand clearly that a multiracial church is not a human or social activity, but an intense spiritual activity that only the Holy Spirit can accomplish. It is no accident that the greatest movement of the Spirit of God recorded in Scripture was the day of Pentecost. Prior to this day when God poured out His Spirit, there was an intense ten-day period of nonstop prayer in the Upper Room. God exploded on Pentecost in response to the prayers of the disciples. God's Spirit stretched across language barriers, and 3,000 souls were added to the church in Jerusalem in one day. Consequently, our church continues to pray for a modern-day Pentecost.

During the last 15 years in the congregation, there were seasons of unusual spiritual movements when two- or three-hour confession or testimony services would occur. On September 17, 1995, 80 of our adults were in Bible study that emphasized encountering God with an open and repentant heart. During this session, one of our white women confessed that she did not have a heart for the immediate community, even though we had just conducted a prayer walk the previous Saturday. In fact she stated, "Just because we walked through the community for one day does not mean that we really care for the people." I asked her to share her heart with the entire congregation during the evening services later that night. After she spoke to the body at Wilcrest, an invitation opened for the people to respond. Several people approached the front and prayed at the altar. Then one lady stood and publicly confessed her sin of racial prejudice, so I asked four of our black members to come and pray over her. Then God placed on my heart to call the entire church body to the altar for a time of corporate confession for our apathy and unwillingness to reach the community with His heart. I also explained that some of our people might not be guilty of this sin individually, but if one part of the body is guilty, then we are all accountable to God as one body. In the same way, Ezra and Nehemiah prayed and confessed the sins of the entire nation of Israel, of which they were an integral part (cp. Ezra 9:1–10; Neh 1:4–11).

Subsequently, the entire congregation of 150 persons came forward to kneel at the altar for prayer. Furthermore, several guests came forward to join us at the altar. I led them in a prayer of confession, phrase by phrase, naming the sins of apathy, partial obedience, controlling our own agenda, and prejudice. Then several people prayed as representatives of their race, further confessing their sins of racism and prejudice. The entire group stayed on its knees in prayer for the next hour, and then many of them returned to their seats and waited for more. I have read and studied biblical and historical accounts of corporate confession, but to see this type of confession unfold before my eyes is wondrously incomprehensible.

One of the most powerful indications of how prayer has changed the church's spiritual fabric occurred during our January 2003 Cottage Prayer Meeting. We saw God cross another barrier in regard to race and language of different cultures. One of the participants that night was a young lady from Mexico named Carmen, who had just married one of our young men two weeks before. She and her new husband came to pray even though the wife spoke little English. During the intense prayer time, I felt led to pray for Carmen, who happened to be sitting next to me. As I began to pray, no English words came to my mind or my mouth. I had already been silently praying for Carmen and Juan, her husband. As I began to pray, however, only words in Spanish (I know some of this language) came out of my mouth for several sentences, and only later, English words. I did not think too much about what had happened until one of our members from Columbia introduced a friend she brought to the Cottage Prayer Meeting from England. This young woman spoke Spanish fluently and understood my prayer. I began to talk with her about her faith in Christ, and she disclosed her spiritual pilgrimage to me. After a period of discussion, she made the decision to become a Christian. In this process, I discovered that her name was also Carmen. God had called me to pray for Carmen in Spanish, not only for the young lady sitting next to me, but apparently also for another Carmen across the room who needed a personal relationship with Christ.

THE NECESSITY OF THE NINE

These nine qualities are necessary for any spiritual leader to possess and demonstrate as they set the example and pace for their congregations, but they are nonnegotiable in leading a multiracial congregation. Personal exposure and experience are what initially open the eyes of the leader to the need for multiracial ministry. Yet once this need for multiracial churches becomes visible, then the leader begins to read and study the Word of God through racial lenses. After the Word of God is firmly rooted inside the leader, the leader's heart begins to see the need to evangelize each racial group around the globe. In this journey, the needs will be greater than the knowledge or experience, so it is necessary to develop a teachable spirit. As the leader encounters multiple races, it will be mandatory to demonstrate a forbearing spirit, giving people of other races permission to express their faith without passing judgment. If the leader wants to sustain this multiracial vision, it will be essential to share leadership among the different races. As new leaders explore and expand their new responsibilities of leading a multiracial congregation, conflict and tension will be inevitable. In the same way that King David led with "skillful hands" (Ps 78:72), the multiracial leader will have to acquire competency in solving conflict across racial lines. All of these characteristics are vital in becoming an effective multiracial leader, but the one trait that must permeate every area is prayer. By utilizing this constant connection with God, the wisdom and power of God will flow through the leader to the rest of the body of Christ.

PRACTICAL APPLICATION

James Furr, Jim Herrington, and Mike Bonem's eight-step change process proved to be one of the most helpful tools that our church and staff utilized through this transformational process.[19] This next section applies their proposed change process to the context of the multiracial congregation.

1. Making Personal Preparation

The proper spiritual foundation through personal Bible study, prayer, accountability, and other spiritual disciplines prepares the leader for a leadership role. In assessing the life and ministry of King David, the psalmist wrote, "He shepherded them with a pure heart and guided them with his skillful hands" (Ps 78:72). His spiritual integrity enveloped soundness of heart and the sense of being totally given over to God. When God spoke to Samuel concerning the king who would replace King Saul, God was clearly seeking "a man loyal to Him" (1 Sam 13:14). God found that heart in David, one who had spiritually prepared himself to lead the people of Israel. Before Jesus embarked on His public ministry, He spent 40 days and nights praying and fasting in the wilderness as an integral part of His spiritual preparation. After the vision on the Damascus Road, the apostle Paul withdrew from the public stage for several years before he left on his first missionary journey out of Antioch of Syria. These spiritual leaders in Scripture were preparing themselves before God moved them into places of visible leadership. The personal spiritual preparation of the leader in a multiracial church is also mandatory, for the challenges are too overwhelming without an intimate connection with the God of all the nations. In addition to the spiritual preparation, King David had also shepherded the people of God with "skillful hands" (Ps 78:72). The word *skillful* means to have some understanding or discernment of how to lead the people. Consequently, the leader of a multiracial congregation needs to have some competency in this area of ministry. It would serve the potential leader well to be connected or under the tutelage of a leader or ministry that has experience in reaching across racial barriers.

2. Creating Urgency

There are two primary and distinct elements in creating a sense of urgency that will prompt and propel a church in the direction of

---

[19] James Furr, Jim Herrington, and Mike Bonem, *Leading Congregational Change Workbook* (San Francisco: Josey Bass, 2000).

multiracial ministry. The first involves giving a clear and accurate picture of the current reality, including demographics, spiritual status of the church, willingness of the people to move into this direction, traditions and patterns that characterize the group, problem areas, and perceptions of race and prejudice. The second aspect is on the other end of the pendulum, dealing with the issue of where God is leading the church. This part answers the question, "What is the vision for the church?" A careful study of Scripture, the church force, and the community is essential to discover a God-sized vision. This vision should be so far beyond human ability that there is no way to see and experience the fruition of the vision apart from the work of God. Once you grasp both the current reality and the future vision, there will be a persistent tension between what is and what can be. Jesus conveyed this same sense of urgency as He described the kingdom of God being in the midst of His disciples (Luke 17:21), while at the same time teaching that the day of the Lord will come to usher in the kingdom of God (Matt 24:1–51). This tension between the two comings of Jesus is often called "already but not yet." During this time, the people of God are to act as if Jesus might come back at any moment, thus creating a sense of urgency. At Wilcrest, a major part of the current reality was that our all-white church was in decline in a racially transitioning community and something needed to be done. The God-sized vision included that all nations could worship the same God at the same time at the same place because of the work that Christ accomplished in tearing down the walls between Jews and Gentiles (Eph 2:14). Scripture teaches that all the nations will be around the throne of the Lamb of God in heaven, but while we are on this earth there is still a division between the nations. We have a spiritual tension between what is to come in heaven and what we are experiencing now.

3. Establishing a Vision Community

Once the leader has taken the first two steps, then it is imperative to identify and include the believers who are called to this God-sized vision. Jesus established His vision community with His disciples, and the early church developed theirs with the elders, deacons, and missionaries. The sense of community can be developed through venues, such as worship services, small group times, retreats, Bible studies, prayer meetings, meals, and training sessions. It is critical that the people gather around the mission and not the leader. The vision is always more comprehensive than the individual person, especially in the multiracial ministry. Each member of the vision community can be compared to the individual members of the body: although each part is unique, each is essential for the proper working and implementing of Christ's vision for the body (1 Cor 12:12–31). The mission requires each member of the vision community to do his or her part, even though it might reach fruition during the next generation. Many of the changes that will be necessary will often take longer than the tenure of one leader, because the racial barriers have existed much longer than one generation. One interesting observation from seeing the ongoing transformation of a homogeneous church to a multiracial one is that the called leaders for this journey may not be the ones who are perceived to be leaders in a homogeneous congregation. The leader in a multiracial congregation fully understands and embraces the vision to reach all nations.

4. Discerning the Vision and Determining Its Path

Once the vision and the vision community have been established, the vision is then brought before the entire vision community for feedback. This step also entails the setting up of priorities, objectives, and action plans to accomplish what God has called the church to do. For instance, Paul's missionary vision called him to go to several cities and plant new churches and place key believers in leadership positions to oversee the new work. There were guidelines and qualification for the new leaders who would assist Paul's co-workers (1 Tim 3:1–13; Titus 1:5–9). When problems emerged, Paul would address the conflict by letter, representative, or in person. He had a clear picture of what a New Testament church should look like and laid out the essential steps of how the church would move in the multiracial direction. One of the primary elements of Jesus' vision with His disciples was that the kingdom of God would be established on earth through His church. One of the key teachings on how this vision will be accomplished was described in the Sermon on the Mount (Matt 5–7). In the multiracial context, the vision path may get somewhat confusing as believers from different cultures offer suggestions from clashing perspectives. This is why it is vital to have a vision community that is already committed to the multiracial vision, so when it comes to these details, there will be more of a consensus on what steps the church should take.

5. *Communicating the Vision*

When God gives a leader the multiracial vision, unless the vision is clearly and repeatedly communicated to the vision community and those who are interested, the vision will become hazy. An essential part of the communication process is the development of metaphors, analogies, and symbols. At Wilcrest, we portray the multiracial bridge to communicate that we are to incorporate the different nations into the body of Christ. In addition, we utilize artwork, such as through the mural in the sanctuary depicting all the nations gathered around the throne of God, other paintings and pictures that are displayed throughout the facility, the church's letterhead, publicity, Web site, and the literature. Our goal is to communicate the multiracial vision in every possible visual format, such as baptisms, weddings, baby dedications, choir, persons who are reading Scripture, the greeters, music selection, and the ones who preach in my absence.

Not only is the vision to be communicated through a variety of conduits, but it needs to be communicated regularly. John P. Kotter contends that in order for the leader to transfer the vision effectively, it "almost always relies on repetition."[20] When Paul addressed the church at Corinth, he understood the importance and the impact of repeating the simple and vital truths of the Lord's Supper: "For as often as you eat this bread and drink the cup, you proclaim the Lord's death until He comes" (1 Cor 11:26). There is no greater foundational truth in Christianity than the death, burial, and resurrection of Jesus, and Paul knew that it was vital for the church to keep the Lord's Supper as the primary vehicle for communicating what Jesus did for all believers. In the early days of implementing the vision at Wilcrest, many in our vision community often questioned the need to repeat the vision constantly to the people, implying that they had already caught the vision. We discovered that if the multiracial vision is not a priority, people have a tendency to move away from it by gravitating toward people similar to them. The call to multiracial ministry chal-

---

[20] John P. Kotter, *Leading Change* (Boston: Harvard Business School Press, 1996), 94.

lenges the believer to live out of the homogeneous comfort zone and bridge the divide between different races.

6. Empowering the Vision Community

This step includes both delegating responsibilities of implementing the vision to the key leaders of the vision community and training them to ensure that they are effectively prepared. For some leaders, it is difficult to release control to others, but without empowered and shared leadership, the vision will remain within the parameters of one leader. At the other extreme, some leaders release control but do not adequately equip the vision community, which will ultimately result in frustration and failure. In the multiracial congregation, as the leader delegates and empowers a diverse leadership, it will ensure that the vision for all the nations will be seen comprehensively. It is impossible to have an accurate multiracial perspective with only one race in leadership. Not all the individuals within the community connect at the same pace or in the same manner, especially when believers are from all over the world. At Wilcrest, there are times when different ethnic groups need to slow down and wait for others to process the decisions or changes within the vision. Certain people groups gravitate toward one aspect of the vision while at the same time are hesitant about other expressions. The early church in Acts practiced shared leadership in the delegation of the seven Hellenistic Jews who had the responsibility of feeding the Hellenistic widows who were being neglected by the Palestinian Jewish majority (Acts 6:1–7). The church of Antioch also demonstrated the empowering of a racially diverse leadership team (Acts 13:1–3). Jesus sent His disciples out on mission to preach, teach, and heal in His name. Later, Jesus sent out 70 of His disciples as His representatives to "the lost sheep of the house of Israel" (Matt 10:6). After the resurrection, Jesus told His disciples, "As the Father has sent Me, I also send you" (John 20:21). The Scriptures indicate that all people groups must be empowered to implement God's vision in order to spread His kingdom across all nations.

7. Implementing Changes in Congregational Life

In this step, the leader releases the vision community to carry out the action plans that have originated from the vision path. The individuals or teams have the responsibility to make necessary changes along the way as the plans are being implemented and evaluated. All of the changes or adjustments must be made in light of the overall vision as found in Scripture. At Wilcrest, change is constant. In our worship services, we added new instruments, started singing in English and Spanish, made available a simultaneous Spanish translation, added a team of diverse greeters, offered a second Sunday morning service, encouraged members from different races to read the Scripture, utilized diverse music, and changed the style of preaching from proclamation to a more dialogical approach. All of these ideas came from a wide cross-section of members through surveys, verbal input, and brainstorming sessions. Similarly, the early church had to implement numerous changes in the different churches, such as organizing a structure with the selection of elders and deacons (1 Tim 3:1–13), adopting a process to handle church discipline (1 Cor 5), sending out missionaries (Acts 13:1–3), addressing new doctrinal questions (Acts 15), and dealing with racial conflict between Jews and Gentiles (Eph 2). Many of these issues only emerged as the church grew and expanded into new territories and new people groups.

8. *Reinforcing the Momentum and Direction of Transformation*

When all the previous seven steps have been implemented, it is tempting to sit back and enjoy the results. However, this step reminds the leader that it is imperative to maintain a sense of urgency by revisiting the vision and developing new action plans as the former ones are accomplished. It is also helpful to identify the pockets of resistance during this time because the progress of the vision now provides spiritual leverage in order to challenge the believers who have not invested in it. The success stories serve as motivation for the entire church to be a part of what God is doing. Jesus' Great Commission, "Go . . . and make disciples of all nations," motivates Wilcrest to reinforce the momentum because we have yet to reach all the nations. This seems like an insurmountable task from an overall perspective, but each time our church sends missionaries to a new nation, we are one step closer. Each time a homogeneous church requests our church for help on how to begin the multiracial transformation, it reinforces what God started in us years ago and grants a sense of freshness and urgency. The book of 1 John reinforced the momentum of what Jesus instilled inside the apostle

John during the earthly ministry of Jesus. Jesus told His disciples the night before He was crucified, "I give you a new commandment: love one another. Just as I have loved you, you must also love one another" (John 13:34). John then wrote in his epistle 60 years after Jesus' crucifixion, "Dear friends, let us love one another, because love is from God" (1 John 4:7). The apostle John reinforced the momentum of the vision that Jesus had for the community of believers: They should love one another. Just as the early church passed on the key teachings to their next generation, each multiracial congregation must teach God's heart for the nations to those who come after us.

DISCUSSION QUESTIONS

1. Read 1 Tim 3:1–12 and Titus 3:1–10. What are the qualifications of the pastor or elder? What are the qualifications of the deacon? Do the listed qualifications place an emphasis on competency or character? Why?

2. Which one of the nine leadership traits discussed in this chapter is your strongest? How is this trait expressed? Which of these characteristics is the strongest in your church as a whole? How is that expressed churchwide?

3. Which of the nine leadership traits is your weakest? Which one of these characteristics is the weakest in your church as a whole? What is a possible plan of action to strengthen this weakness, both personally and churchwide?

4. Briefly describe the eight steps of the change process. If you are about to begin or have already started this journey toward becoming a multiracial congregation, where in the eight-step process are you? What is the next step for you to take in order to keep moving in this journey? What are the possible barriers that you might encounter in moving forward in this process?

5. As an individual, what steps have you taken personally to prepare for this multiracial journey?

CHAPTER 1 2

THE CALL TO THE NATIONS

"Go therefore and make disciples of all nations . . ." (Matt 28:19).

THE BIBLICAL CALL TO MISSIONS

In Jesus' "Little Apocalypse" in Matthew 24, He revealed to the disciples the signs that must take place before the Second Coming. In Matt 24:14, Jesus said, "This good news of the kingdom will be proclaimed in all the world as a testimony to all nations. And then the end will come." According to His clear instruction, the gospel of Jesus Christ will be preached as a witness to every nation, ethnicity, culture, and tribe before the end of this age and the establishment of the kingdom of God. Since this is such a vital part in the kingdom process, then the kingdom citizens must make this a high priority. Jesus' last words to His disciples before His ascension commanded them to make disciples and to be His witnesses to all nations (Matt 28:19; Acts 1:8). These last words give a profound sense of urgency to the disciples and to us concerning the call to the nations.

To be recipients of God's grace and citizens of the kingdom, God immediately calls believers to look outward to a world that desperately needs the love of God. One who has invited the "light of the world" into his life cannot help but shine God's light into a dark and lost world. As Christians, since we have the love of Christ dwelling in us, we cannot hold tightly to what has been so freely given to us. It is a contradiction against the loving nature of God to say that we love God but not the world that God so loved that "He gave His One and Only Son" (John 3:16). *To love God is to have a heart for the nations.* The essence of the gospel refuses to allow the good news to remain silent or motionless; it must spread to the ends of the earth. Just as the leaven cannot help but spread to the rest of the loaf of bread (see Matt 13:33), so the gospel must spread to a world that needs the hope of God's salvation. By its very nature, it is impossible for the gospel to become stagnant, for when God sent His Son from heaven to earth, the call to move out of our comfort zone resounded. God the Father did whatever was necessary to give the world the good news of salvation and hope.

THE COVENANT WITH ABRAHAM (GEN 12:1–3)

The call to reach the nations has resided in the heart of God from the beginning. When God established His people with the call of Abraham, an essential part of the formation of the nation of Israel was to be a blessing to "all the families of the earth" (Gen 12:3 NASB). The Hebrew word for "family" is frequently used for a smaller section of a larger group such as a tribe or a nation. The same word is used to describe either tribes or households. Based on this, Walter C. Kaiser contends, "Therefore the blessing of God given to Abraham was intended to reach smaller groups of people groups as well as the political groupings of nations."[1] Through the person of Abraham and eventually Israel, God's design was that His people would serve as His priests and representatives in order to be a channel of blessing to the rest of the world, from the smallest people group to the largest nation. To bless all the families of the earth was the ultimate reason for the call of God on Abraham; everything else was secondary, even the blessing of becoming a great nation or receiving the promised land.

Right up until the time of Abraham, all of humanity was in desperate need of the blessing of God. The curse of God marked and saturated the world after the fall of humanity with the sin of Adam and Eve in Gen 3. Both the serpent and the soil had been cursed due to the original sin. Subsequently, God cursed Cain for the murder of his brother, and Noah cursed Canaan. Finally, God scattered the people assembled around the tower of Babel because they failed to acknowledge their Creator who wanted to bless them. Abraham

[1] Walter C. Kaiser, *Mission in the Old Testament: Israel as a Light to the Nations* (Grand Rapids: Baker, 2000), 19. For an excellent discussion of the terms *tribe, clan, father's house,* and *household of God* in laymen's terms, see Rhoads, *Where the Nations Meet,* 109–10.

would now be the channel to allow God's blessings to flow to the cursed humanity.

According to Brueggemann, "The call of Sarah and Abraham has to do not simply with the forming of Israel but with the re-forming of creation, the transforming of the nation."[2] However, throughout Israel's history, they misunderstood the call of Abraham to be an exclusive call that separated them from any contact with the rest of the nations. They turned inward as God called them to go outward. The psalmist reminded Israel that God's anointed king will be the source of blessings of peace, justice, and salvation to all the nations (see Ps 72:1–3,18–19). In Jer 4:2, the prophet appealed to the covenant of Abraham to reiterate that the nations would bless God if Israel would return to God with a repentant heart and walk in His ways. The apostle Paul also emphasized the blessing of Abraham as an argument to include the Gentiles as recipients of God's blessings: "The purpose was that the blessing of Abraham would come to the Gentiles in Christ Jesus" (Gal 3:14). Earlier Paul insisted, "Now the Scripture foresaw that God would justify the Gentiles by faith and foretold the good news to Abraham, saying, 'All the nations will be blessed in you'" (Gal 3:8). The children of Abraham had been called and designed by God to reach the rest of the world with the blessings of God so that all the nations might glorify God.[3]

THE COVENANT WITH MOSES (EXOD 19:4–6)

The Gen 12:1–3 covenant planted the seed in Abraham and his descendants that they were the conduit of God's blessing to all the families of the earth. The Mosaic covenant further clarified how blessing other nations would be expressed in a tangible way. With the Mosaic covenant, God commanded that the nation of Israel was to be a kingdom of priests that would administer God's Word to the rest of the nations (Exod 19:4–6). According to Daniel C. van Zyl, the idea of being priests was not just to be separate and uncontaminated by the world around them; "priest and holy suggest separation and devotion to Yahweh, but in a functional way, oriented to service: they were to

---

[2] Walter Brueggemann, *Genesis* (Atlanta: John Knox, 1982), 105.
[3] James Chukwuma Okoye, *Israel and the Nations: A Mission Theology of the Old Testament* (Maryknoll, NY: Orbis, 2006), 46–54.

represent and mediate God, his glory and his goodness to others."[4] In the establishment of this covenant with Moses and Israel, God gives the reason why they are to reach the nations: "for all the earth is Mine" (Exod 19:5 NASB). Since the entire earth is His property and all of humanity is His possession, Israel is to be to Him "a kingdom of priests and a holy nation . . . Israel is commissioned to be God's people on behalf of the earth which is God's."[5] All of humanity is the object of God's concern and compassion. In fact, the Mosaic law stated that there should be provisions for the special care of the alien and stranger (see Exod 12:48; 22:21). The reason given for such support and encouragement for foreigners was that the Israelites themselves were at one time aliens in a foreign land.[6] God always had the nations in view, but His method for reaching the world would be through a nation of priests.

In the New Testament, since believers became descendants of Abraham by faith in Christ (Rom 9:6–13), the apostle Peter called the church "a chosen race, a royal priesthood, a holy nation, a people for His possession, so that you may proclaim the praises of the One who called you out of darkness into His marvelous light" (1 Pet 2:9). Peter assigned three functions of this new priesthood for believers: (a) to offer spiritual sacrifices; (b) to give testimony; and (c) to sing the praises of God who called you out of the darkness into His wonderful light. Thus in 1 Peter there is truth that "the missionary intention informs the very worship and the daily life of holiness of the Christian community; the Christian community incarnates God's holiness and glory in the world and draws others to God's holy presence."[7] What God started with the covenant with Abraham, He continued and clarified with His covenant with Moses and the people of Israel. They were to serve the nations so that the nations may know of the glory of God.

---

[4] Daniel C. van Zyl, "Exodus 19:3–6 and the Kerygmatic Perspective of the Pentateuch," *Old Testament Essays* 5.2 (1992): 264–71; 267.

[5] Terence Fretheim, *Exodus,* Interpretation (Louisville: John Knox, 1991), 212.

[6] According to Parker J. Palmer, the stranger is a "central figure in biblical stories of faith, and for good reason. The religious quest, the spiritual pilgrimage, is always taking us into new lands where we are strange to others and they are strange to us. . . . The very idea of faith suggests a movement away from our earthly securities into the distant, the unsettling, the strange." *The Company of Strangers* (New York: Crossroad, 1983), 56–57. The story of Ruth and Naomi concerns two women who become strangers by faith; one in the land of Moab due to the famine, while the other in the family of God due to what she sees in her mother-in-law, Naomi.

[7] Andreas J. Köstenberger and Peter T. O'Brien, *Salvation to the Ends of the Earth: A Biblical Theology of Mission* (Downers Grove, IL: InterVarsity, 2001), 65–66.

THE COVENANT WITH DAVID (2 SAM 7:9–11)

God promised David, "I will raise up after you your descendant, who will come from your body, and I will establish his kingdom. He will build a house for My name, and I will establish the throne of his kingdom forever" (2 Sam 7:12–13). The covenant that God established with David "contained important allusions to Gen 12:1–3 which suggest that what God has in store for David is a *reiteration,* if not a *partial fulfillment,* of what was promised to Abraham."[8] When God told David, "I will make a name for you like that of the greatest in the land" (2 Sam 7:9), it was an allusion to the promise that God made with Abraham (Gen 12:2). God then conveyed to David, "I will establish a place for My people Israel and plant them, so that they may live there and not be disturbed again" (2 Sam 7:10), which was a fulfillment of the promised land that God would show Abraham (Gen 12:1).

David understood the connection to the covenant that he received and how it would affect all of humanity in the future in his response to God: "You have spoken about the future of the house of your servant. And this is the charter for humanity, O Lord Yahweh."[9] The word "charter" translates the Hebrew word for "law" or *torah,* which means teaching or instructing, specifically here the charter or teaching for all humanity.[10] Therefore, the covenant with David has importance with all of humanity, both for the Jews and for the Gentiles. Consequently, David's covenant is in continuity with the Abrahamic and the Mosaic covenants, for David's descendant will function as Yahweh's representative as ruler over the nations. The promise of the covenant with David was ultimately fulfilled in Jesus Christ, the son of David, who was the son of Abraham, who was also the Son of God (Rom 1:3–4). The son of David, the Messiah will bring hope to all humanity.

COVENANT WITH THE CHURCH

All throughout the Old Testament, the covenants that God established with His people had one ultimate target: the salvation of the nations. God used Abraham to be a channel of blessing to the "fami-

---

[8] Köstenberger and O'Brien, 39.
[9] This is Kaiser's translation of the Hebrew text of 2 Sam 7:19. See Kaiser, 26.
[10] Kaiser, 27. See also Wilson, 244.

lies of the earth," while He called Moses and Israel to be a "kingdom of priests" to the nations around them; and finally, He promised that the Messiah who would bring salvation to the world would come through the line of David. As the Old Testament closed and the New Testament opened, the call for missions to the nations remained unchanged. In fact, the call intensified as Jesus called His disciples and the early church to reach the nations. In the same way, Jesus also calls the church today to cross national, racial, religious, economic, social, educational, and traditional barriers for the cause of the gospel.

In the American context, it is much easier and safer to address missions as a denomination or from the perspective of Christians as a whole. If a denomination has missionaries among a people group, or if a local church sends missionaries to the Middle East, or individuals can give money, then it is typically believed that those at home are free from any further obligation. The apostle Paul confronts this remote and impersonal mentality with his words, "I am obligated both to Greeks and barbarians, both to the wise and the foolish. So I am eager to preach the good news to you also who are in Rome" (Rom 1:14–15). The concept of obligation that Paul used in Rom 1:14 is the same mandate that John used to describe the fact that Jesus "had" to go to Samaria. This word in John 4:4 conveys a sense of a divine obligation or mandate that had been in the heart and mind of God before eternity. It is insightful that this word is used in the context of reaching people or nations that the Jews perceived to be unclean or unfit for the kingdom of God. Jesus crossed the barrier to the half-breed Samaritans, while Paul reached across the Gentile barrier. Since Jesus had to go to the Samaritans and Paul was obligated to the Greeks and the barbarians, believers have a mandate and model to reach the nations. Based on the Christ who lives and lords over the believer's heart, the call to reach all the nations becomes personal. Believers cannot experience any rest until we see the nations hear the gospel or until the second coming of Jesus Christ.

MY PERSONAL COVENANT

In my own spiritual pilgrimage, there had been a growing desire and demand to reach more people with the good news of Christ. In fact this issue surfaced during my interview process prior to my coming to Wilcrest. When I was struggling with the decision to accept Wilcrest's invitation to be their pastor in 1992, so many obstacles prevented me from immediately accepting the position; namely, they had asked their former pastor to leave and they intentionally established ethnic missions separate from the white congregation. However, right before I was going to call the committee and inform them that they would probably need to pursue someone else, my wife asked me, "Where do you want to be a year from now?" Without thinking, my first response was to be around as many lost people as possible. At that time I was serving as a pastor in a rural setting of a town with a population of approximately 20,000, while there were over three million in the Houston area. The call to an area that had more lost people was part of the realization that God wanted us to reach as many people for Christ in the shortest period of time. I knew that because of the call that God placed on my life through the reading and studying of Rom 1:14–16, I was obligated to the entire world with the gospel. Consequently, when God called me to be the pastor of Wilcrest, this call to the nations would spread to the entire church.

Presently, this call to missions bleeds through everything we do and seeps through every pore of our spiritual skin. Missions have now become a nonnegotiable mandate and core value. God instilled this vision for the nations at the foundational stage of the formation of the multiracial vision statement. As people seek to connect with Wilcrest, I now ask them the same question: "Do you feel that God has called you to Wilcrest, because with that calling comes a covenant to become a missionary?" Obviously when longtime believers who have been part of other ministries or churches hear this, their initial reaction is that they were just hoping to join the church. We let prospective members know up front that God has called each member of Wilcrest to be a follower of Jesus Christ who will intentionally reach across racial lines while in training to be a missionary. Interestingly, our new believers seem to have the least difficulty in perceiving themselves as missionaries; they think that every believer is a missionary. For example, an eight-year-old girl invited one of her Muslim soccer teammates to a sleepover in order to share Christ with her. The next Sunday, this little girl related her experience to me and asked, "Am I a missionary now?" To receive a call to be a part of the vision that God has given to Wilcrest is to receive the call to be a missionary.

COVENANT FOR ALL?

If Jesus "had to" and Paul was "obligated," does this mean each church and individual is obligated to reach all the nations? Some key questions concerning missions in a multiracial ministry emerge: Are the nations around the world or the nations around the local church our primary target? Are the different ethnic groups within the context of the local congregation your exclusive mission field? What role do the people from other nations who have integrated into the local church play in the international mission field, if at all? Does the church have any obligation to reach people from different nations other than the ones they reach locally? Does the church's call to missions look identical in a homogeneous congregation to the way it would in a multiracial one?

WHERE DO YOU START?

The call to missions is so clearly and emphatically laid out in Scripture. God initializes this call in the beginning and sends it forth to Israel as they carry out their priestly duties to the rest of the nations. Then, Christ's example and commands propel the call to missions to the early church and Paul, who devotes his life and testimony to the nations. The foundation for a missional beginning undoubtedly is the Word of God. After studying and reflecting on the key mission passages of Scripture for a six-month period, Wilcrest expressed the call for missions in a formal sense with its adoption of the vision statement, especially the last phrase, "transforming unbelievers into missionaries." A member at Wilcrest must be a missionary. Most of our members had no idea exactly what that meant or looked like. Honestly, neither did the staff. We knew we were supposed to do something different than in previous years, but the implementation of the vision statement was unclear.

A variety of responses emerged when God gave a call to the nations to a declining white church in a racially transitioning neighborhood. The vast majority of our people were extremely excited and energized by this God-sized task, while a few others were content to advocate the old paradigm: people reaching people just like them. This latter view translated into Hispanic churches reaching Hispanics, black churches reaching blacks, Asian churches reaching Asians, and white churches reaching whites. In fact, the paradigm of each race reaching their own race was advocated and implemented by Wilcrest in the establishment of a Chinese and an African-American mission. As we transitioned into the multiracial paradigm, I preached a series of sermons from the story of Jonah that boldly confronted this segregated view of reaching different people groups.

JONAH: A MISSIONARY TO ALL NATIONS

The book of Jonah and Isa 66:18–21 are the only two places in the Old Testament where messengers are specifically commanded by God to go to the Gentiles. Yet Jonah did not share the same passion for the nations as his God. A brief outline of the book of Jonah gives the reader clear direction and indication of God's message: (a) the pagan sailors are saved in Jonah 1; (b) Yahweh saved Jonah in Jonah 2; (c) Yahweh saved the Ninevites in Jonah 3; (d) Yahweh ultimately saved Jonah from his nationalistic exclusivism in Jonah 4.[11] God's call to His prophet Jonah was clear and simple: Go to Nineveh, the capital of Assyria, which was the center of oppression against Israel during that period (Jonah 1:1–2). The message to the Ninevites and to the rest of the world was that God's salvation was for all peoples and no one was excluded. God designed Israel to be His audible voice to those who were spiritually deaf and to be His visible form to those who were spiritually blind to the love of God. God claimed His love for all humanity through a series of events: the storm, the great fish swallowing Jonah, being spewed out on the shore, and the repentance of the entire city of Nineveh. It is provoking that the pagans were more receptive to God's Word than the prophet of God. After the calming of the storm, the sailors "feared the LORD even more, and they offered a sacrifice to the LORD and made vows" (Jonah 1:16); and after hearing the call to repentance, the city of Nineveh "proclaimed a fast and dressed in sackcloth—from the greatest of them to the least" (Jonah 3:5b). The last chapter of Jonah grants the most insight regarding how missionaries are to see the lost world around

---

[11] Okeye, 82.

them. Jonah's initial argument is that God did not have any right to have compassion on Israel's fiercest enemy, but rather they deserved divine retribution. God demonstrated compassion for Jonah by providing him shade from a plant that He grew overnight. Jonah did not ask for the plant nor did he deserve it, but God in His overwhelming grace gave it to His prophet. In the same way that God caused the plant to grow and shade Jonah in his discomfort, God also provided salvation to the city of Nineveh, who did not ask for help nor deserve it. It is neither up to Jonah nor to us to determine who will hear the gospel, but we must simply go where God has commanded.

MISSION TRIP TO MEXICO UNDER
JAMES DARBY'S LEADERSHIP

In the same way that Jonah needed an impetus to get moving in God's direction, God provided an impetus to Wilcrest with our African-American minister to students, James Darby. He eagerly embraced the Wilcrest vision statement that mandated all church members to become missionaries. One of James' primary expressions of what it means to be a missionary at Wilcrest was to lead our youth group on mission trips to different parts of the Deep South. He had a two-fold purpose with this endeavor: (1) to initiate our young missionaries to a mission field that was racially and culturally different than their comfort zone at home; and (2) to expose other areas of the Deep South to what can happen through a multiracial congregation. These mission trips targeted Louisiana, Oklahoma, Mississippi, Tennessee, and Alabama, as well as other parts of Texas. In fact, these trips provided the essential groundwork for the worldwide mission trips that eventually emerged.

The call to missions began to extend steadily beyond the borders of the United States as the church moved beyond its Jerusalem and Samaria. The first international mission trip that James Darby led was a group of twenty-eight novice missionaries to assist a rural church in the mountains outside Acapulco, Mexico, in 1995. This trip seemed to provide a monumental breakthrough both geographically, linguistically, and spiritually. This was the first international mission trip that Wilcrest took under the new vision statement. It was obviously more than a mission trip to Mexico to help people, but it was the beginning of the fruition of seeing the members of a multiracial congregation become missionaries.

MISSION TRIP TO KENYA

Another spiritual marker in the shaping of how Wilcrest was to help in the transformation of our unbelievers and believers into missionaries was my mission trip to Kenya in 1995. This was the first major mission trip overseas. Upon my arrival, a Kenyan missionary friend reluctantly relayed to me that he was robbed at gunpoint the previous week. He did not inform me before, because he thought that this would deter my coming. Whether he told me or not, God had something both frightening and memorable in store for me and my friend. After a seven-hour truck ride on dirt roads toward the northern border of Kenya in predominantly Muslim territory, my friend and I spent the night in a training center that had just recently been constructed. It was approximately 8:30 p.m. when the building was viciously attacked. My missionary friend quickly extinguished our Coleman lanterns, and we locked ourselves in a small closet at the rear of the building. For the next 45 minutes there was incessant screaming and beating with metal objects against the thirty-gauge corrugated metal siding. While in complete darkness, the missionary told me that this was probably a drug-related attack since we were the only whites in that entire region. During that long 45-minute ordeal, God took me through several stages, including fear, anxiety, panic, anger, and ultimately a resignation that I might die on the mission field. I knew that if I were to die, I would have brought honor to God doing what He had called me to do. My greatest fear and grief was for my family, but God showed me that having placed my trust in Him, I must trust Him to take care of every area of my life.

Eventually the Christians in the village made their way to the training center and drove the attackers away. I only wondered why it took them so long to get there. My resolution was that God took me through the "valley of the shadow of death" to teach me that He would never lead me or the body of Christ to a place He has not already been. During that seemingly eternal 45 minutes, I was soberly reminded of the time that God caused the army of the Arameans to hear "the sound of chariots, horses, and a great army. . . . So they had gotten up and fled at twilight abandoning their tents, horses, and donkeys. The camp was intact, and they had fled for their lives" (2 Kgs 7:6–7). In the same way that God had provided His protection in His perfect time for His people of Israel, He would do the same for us.

Upon my return home, I shared this story with the church body at Wilcrest. A lady excitedly approached me and asked, "What was the exact time that all of these events occurred?" I related to her that it was approximately 8:30 p.m. in Kenya on a particular date. She responded that God had impressed upon her during her lunch break on that day not to take lunch but spend that time specifically praying for God's protection over me. This heavy burden that was placed on her was the exact time that all of these events were happening in Kenya. The same God who was calling me to trust Him in Kenya was the same God calling the body of Christ in Houston to be a part of this powerful movement. That story forever changed the way the home base at Wilcrest prays for their missionaries while they are on mission trips.

MISSION MISFIRE

During the painful and parenthetical years of 1998–2000, I often thought of editing or revising our vision statement to change the last phrase, "transforming unbelievers to missionaries," to "transforming unbelievers to fully contributing and serving followers of Christ who will stay at Wilcrest for a prolonged period of time." The vision was becoming such a reality that many of our transformed missionaries were responding at an alarming rate to the call of God to move from Wilcrest and do their ministry on another mission field. This sizable departure affected morale, attendance, leadership, and the financial giving at the home base. I wanted to ask God if we could make it mandatory for all members to commit to a prolonged period of ministry at Wilcrest until we had reached a critical mass in the resource areas of people and finances. During the first eight years of my tenure, we rarely met budget, even though it was extremely conservative based on the constant flux of people. In these three trying years, we experienced the exodus of the two other full-time vocational staff members and numerous deacons and other leaders due to job change, relocation, or retirement. The decrease in visible leadership and resources caused a great deal of anxiety for me and the rest of the church. There were moments when we really did not know if or how we were going to make it through this turbulent period.

Throughout all of this tremendous shifting, God taught as that the vision was bigger than an individual or a budget. This exodus of key leaders and missionaries initially created a spiritual vacuum, but eventually drove the entire church body to an unprecedented dependence upon God for the fulfillment and fruition of His vision. I thought we needed a certain number of people and an amount of money to implement it adequately, but all we needed was God. Now I look back and see that God sent exactly what we needed when we needed it. This exacting lesson reminds me of the people of Israel wandering in the wilderness awaiting God's daily provision of manna, which eventually taught them a daily trust in a God who provides. Throughout this particular season, I often questioned God if we were on the right path and if we heard the right voice. The dilemma was if this vision belonged to God and was also God-sized, then why were so many of our key people moving away? Now I see that God was not shrinking or diminishing the vision but multiplying it over a wider area of influence.

GENERATIONAL MISSIONARIES

The first mission movement from within Wilcrest after my arrival in 1992 was among the youth led by James Darby across the Deep South. The mission strategy then began to expand outside of our Jerusalem (the U.S.) to our Samaria: Mexico, Canada, and Honduras. A few years later, God took us to the remotest part of the earth with several church trips to Africa. In addition, many of our individual missionaries began to travel all over the world, being commissioned and supported by their home base at Wilcrest. During this pivotal season in which God was transforming our believers into missionaries, our people responded by going on more mission trips to more countries. This rapidly increasing mission activity rendered clear evidence that our vision for the nations was reaching fruition. At the beginning of its implementation, our primary method of determining and gauging the growth of our missionaries was whether they had ever been on an international mission trip. The overwhelming majority of our people had never been on a mission trip until they joined Wilcrest, so when they returned home from another country, there was a measurable difference in the "before" and "after" picture of their spiritual lives. They simply were not the same people. It may be a part of human nature or a saturation effect, but our missionaries unknowingly began to gauge their spiritual growth by how many trips they had taken, how many different countries they had visited on mission trips, or how dangerous the country was in which the mission work was carried out. At the beginning of this process, it was not difficult to see the distinctive difference in how a person understood our vision statement of becoming missionaries based on whether or not they had ever participated in an international mission trip. When one of our members would leave the United States on mission, his mind-set would experience a spiritual reformatting on what it was to be a missionary in Houston. Yet as time progressed and more believers bought into this God-sized missionary vision, it became more challenging to determine or gauge the spiritual growth of our missionaries.

As a result of this dilemma of challenging our missionaries to grow, I developed different "generations of missionaries." All of these generations assume that the believer has gone on at least one international mission trip. These lines of demarcation are arbitrary, but I needed some form of spiritual evaluation to see our progress in this vision and where we needed to go. Initially I just wanted our believers to be involved in missions, but now I understand that God has called all of us to be missionaries first in our Jerusalem, then our Judea and Samaria, and then to the remotest parts of the world. God's call to missions does not just entail going to another country with the gospel, but the international trip has the potential to move us out of our comfort zone as one of the key steps on a lifelong journey.

The first group involves those people who have been exposed to a godless culture or a poverty-stricken environment while on an international mission trip. The *first-generation missionaries* (the first time in a different country) are those who are in awe of the amount of poverty in the third-world country and come back home with a deep appreciation for what we have in the United States. Their eyes are now open to how materialistic we are in the United States and how much we truly have. In turn, they now want to help those who have so much less. This attitude can be depicted in the following words: "I want to help those who are in need because I have so much. The nationals have so many needs and we have so many resources; we must assist them in every way we can." They often leave their clothes, shoes, or supplies, or provide support for specific needs of the nationals.

In addition, first-generation missionaries develop a heart to do similar work here in Houston. These missionaries have an eager willingness and insatiable zeal to serve those around them who are in desperate need. The need to serve also finds its expression in the performance of specific tasks and projects that need to be completed, such as teaching a Vacation Bible School class, participating in a construction project, preaching a sermon, prayer walking, and overseeing a soccer game. This increased desire to serve represents a major transformation from the focus being on one's own needs to the focus on others' needs. First-generation missionaries become extremely sensitive to the needs of those of different races and economic standing, which further instills the Wilcrest vision inside of them.

The *second-generation missionaries* (they have been on at least two international trips) are the leaders who oversee our first-generation missionaries. This missionary mind-set has now become an integral part of their maturity as believers as they incorporate a different way of living here in the States. They typically downsize or simplify their lives as well as increase their giving to missions. If they are unable to go on a particular mission trip, then they financially support someone else going. Their mind-set has been transformed from the first-generation missionary who sees and wants to help the nationals in dire poverty to seeing them as spiritual equals. Second-generation missionaries display a servant mentality, while not dishonoring them. The national believers are now seen to be on the same level spiritually as the missionaries, true brothers and sisters in Christ. These missionaries do not try to shape the mission field to look like home. This has often been challenging to our missionaries because they see a "better" or "more correct" way of doing things from their cultural lenses, but it is not as important as humbling themselves to the needs of the nationals. This stage refuses to look down on those who are being helped and now sees the nationals as fellow members of the body of Christ.

The *third-generation missionaries* at Wilcrest are those who take the initiative in leadership and development of different aspects of upcoming mission trips. These people insist on enlisting and mentoring others who have never been on a mission trip, thus multiplying the vision that all believers are missionaries. The concept of being a missionary has become such a reality; this missionary's comfort zone is the mission field. Third-generation missionaries want to learn from those in the mission field instead of exclusively trying to teach them or help them. This missionary willingly sits at the feet of the nationals in order to gain invaluable insight because learning occurs most effectively when one is completely out of a familiar and comfortable environment. The spiritual senses have been heightened in order to take full advantage of this intense learning environment that is free of any normal distractions. When the third-generation missionary submits to the nationals, then great honor is placed on the local believers.

All these mission trips have taught each one of these generations of missionaries what it means to be a racial minority on a personal and experiential basis. This may include that everyone around you is speaking a language you do not understand, or there are things happening that you have never seen. For one week, two weeks, or ten weeks, our missionaries have volitionally removed themselves from their own comfort zones in order to engage actively with another people group as ambassadors of Christ. Our missionaries then return to the home base with empathy and special lenses for those who enter the American culture for the first time. In addition, these mission trips have produced a burden and strong desire to see particular people groups or nations come to the Lord.

GOING ON MISSION TRIPS VERSUS
BEING MISSIONARIES

One of the primary complaints from members of our body at the home base has been "Why should we go to all these foreign countries if we have all these countries right here in our city of Houston?" From a human perspective, this input has some validity. It is less expensive and less work if we do all mission activities right here in our primary mission field. But many of those who make these comments are also less likely to be the first to volunteer to do any of the work here at home. The ones who are most motivated and excited about the work here are those who have done the work in a different country. So the question is not whether we participate in missions in the United States or embark on missions globally; the question is: Do we go on mission trips or are we missionaries? If we are missionaries, then we are missionaries *wherever* we are, whether in Houston or Honduras, Chicago or Cameroon, New York or Nigeria. God has called us to be missionaries to the entire world. We are under obligation both to the Greek and to the barbarian, to both the wise and to the foolish. God's economy and strategy of doing missions is strangely different from our way of doing missions.

As of 2008, our church has sent missionaries to 31 different countries, including the U.S., while at the same time we have more than 44 countries represented by our congregation. Every time we send a missionary or a group of missionaries to a new country, we hang that particular nation's flag in the worship center as a visible reminder of who we are and what our vision is. We have sent missionaries to the following countries: Mexico, Canada, Honduras, Chile, Venezuela, Guatemala, Costa Rica, Nicaragua, Peru, Haiti, Portugal, Kenya, Swaziland, South Korea, China, Taiwan, Australia, Germany, India, Kazakhstan, Afghanistan, Scotland, Ireland, Austria, Switzerland, South Africa, Nigeria, Cameroon, Ethiopia, and the Caribbean Islands, as well as several places across the United States. Now when a visitor comes to our worship services they will see people from all over the world in their native dress and see 30 different flags (sometimes theirs) in the place of worship for all the races and all the nations. This missionary-sending atmosphere has challenged and changed how many people who come to the United States as immigrants perceive the "American dream."

PURSUIT OF THE DREAM

Many of our international members came to the United States in pursuit of the "American dream," with all of the advantages, privileges, and freedoms. This dream encourages each generation to provide more opportunities and resources for the next generation. Yet the call of God often finds an alternative expression. For example, Abraham was a man of great wealth when he received the call from God to be a blessing to the rest of the nations. Yet his call resulted in leaving his family and land, and "he stayed as a foreigner in the land of promise, living in tents with Isaac and Jacob" (Heb 11:8–9). Abraham's pursuit of God's dream forced his next two generations to live in tents, sacrificing their permanent dwelling. Following God's vision often costs the entire family as they move out of their comfort zone and into the arena of obedience. God tends to touch our international members' hearts with this multiracial vision, and then they receive "God's dream" of returning to their Jerusalem as a missionary. One of our members from a third-world country revealed to me that of all the times he returned to his home country to visit his family, it never occurred to him that he was a missionary. Since then, he has gone with us on a mission trip to his country. He now states that he will see himself as a missionary in each of his subsequent trips back home.

When I first arrived at Wilcrest, I witnessed to a forty-two-year-old Vietnamese man in the fall of 1993. He told me he had to go back to Vietnam and ask permission from his parents to accept Christ and leave the Buddhist religion. In the spring of 1994, he traveled to Vietnam for the first time in 22 years and told his parents of his intention to accept Christ. Consequently, when he returned to the United States, he accepted Christ and I baptized him. Upon his return from this monumental trip, he realized that he had served as a missionary to his family. Another fact is that an elderly lady in our church, who felt a call to international missions as a young teenager, adopted this Vietnamese man and his family. Even though she never went on a mission trip, she fulfilled this call by providing a home for them. In the overall scope, she participated with the mission to Vietnam through this man into whom she poured the love of Christ. Consequently, this man's family from Vietnam did not hear the gospel from a white Southern Baptist missionary but from one of their own family members.

GO HOME AND TELL

In the same way that our Vietnamese missionary had to go home to share what Jesus had done for him, we discover the same pattern in the New Testament.

Story of the Gerasene Demoniac (Mark 5:1–20)

One of the first missionaries commissioned to spread the gospel was the Gerasene demoniac, from whom Jesus dramatically cast out a "legion" of demons. Jesus gave him the following initial assignment: "Go back home to your own people, and report to them how much the Lord has done for you and how He has had mercy on you" (Mark 5:19). Yet this new believer initially had insisted that he wanted to be in the safe and secure company of the physical presence of Jesus. The gospel, however, demands that we leave the safe confines of what is the most comfortable to go to the realm of discomfort. This demoniac had been away from his hometown and established his new residence among the tombs. He left his hometown in one condition, but returned completely transformed by the power of the gospel. Mark records that he returned and proclaimed in the Decapolis what Jesus had done for him. Since this was not a Jewish region, they had not heard firsthand who Jesus was and what He had done. This area needed to hear the gospel, and the most qualified person was a native who had been changed.

In the same way, many of the international people who come to our church arrive in one condition, yet they return to their country completely transformed. For example, Ricardo Pineda, who was originally from Honduras, came to our church and accepted Christ. After his baptism, he began to grow as a new believer and as a missionary. He departed from his home country as an unbeliever but returned as a missionary representing Christ and his new home church. He played a key role in our first mission trip to Honduras. Furthermore his involvement in the Honduras mission trip also accelerated his involvement in the Spanish ministry at Wilcrest. Sometimes he serves as a missionary in Houston, sometimes in Honduras, but always with the same call.

Pentecost and the Ethiopian Eunuch (Acts 2:1–11; 8:26–40)

When the Jews of the Diaspora heard the gospel on the day of Pentecost, they received Christ and returned home different than the way they had arrived. The Jews were Parthians, Medes, Elamites, residents from Mesopotamia, Judea, Cappadocia, Pontus, Asia, Phrygia, Pamphylia, Egypt, Libya, Cyrene, Rome, Crete, and Arabia (Acts 2:9–11). Luke tells us that 3,000 experienced salvation. This Scripture does not specifically tell us which ones accepted Christ, but it is likely that some of the original 3,000 conversions were from these countries listed in the same chapter of Acts, and they went home to share what God had done in them. The Ethiopian eunuch apparently had a similar experience. Scripture tells us that when he received the Christ that Philip was preaching that he went "on his way rejoicing." This eunuch who had been excluded from the full membership of the Jewish community because of his physical condition would not be prohibited from being fully incorporated into the family of God through baptism.[12] The phrase "on his way" implies that he went back to his home country of Ethiopia, which was the black African kingdom of Meroe, sharing what had happened to him. There is no biblical evidence that he was the first missionary to his home country, but by the fourth century Christianity had been firmly established in Meroe.[13]

In the Wilcrest story, there is one that closely parallels the story of the Ethiopian eunuch returning to his home country with the gospel. Vickie Lai, originally from Taiwan, was baptized in 2002. She is 25 years old. During a dialogue with me, she reflected on her return trip to Taiwan in which she visited family. She noted that this trip was extremely different from previous visits. During this trip, she was involved in a traditional family ceremony, which involved visiting the graves of her ancestors, in order to communicate with the dead that the living family members were healthy. She realized that this was the first such ceremony that she was asked to participate in by her family since becoming a Christian. She felt a tinge of hesitation and uneasiness and quickly prayed that God would help her. Right before she was to place something on the grave, her cell phone rang, and she received a call from a friend she had not heard from in years. The phone call lasted as long as the ceremony did. In fact, her sister accused her of adopting the ways of the United States and abandoning her heritage. Upon her return to the States, God used Vickie's testimony to help her sister come to Christ.

In August 2006, Vickie returned to Taiwan permanently because her student visa expired. She has been such a vital part of our choir and an embodiment of our vision statement. Despite wanting to stay

---

[12] J. B. Polhill, *Acts,* New American Commentary (Nashville: Broadman, 1992), 226.
[13] Hays, 176.

in the United States with her Christian family, she knew that she must return home where none of her family members were believers. Consequently, she perceived herself as a missionary to her family and to her country.

What is happening at Wilcrest is the same thing that happened in Scripture with the Gerasene demoniac and the Jewish pilgrims at Pentecost and the Ethiopian eunuch. People from all over the world come into contact with the gospel and it transforms their lives. The same Christ that has taken over their lives now calls them to share with their families, their villages, and their countries. It is the nature of leaven; the spreading cannot be thwarted. Understanding the potential missionary network is the key to fulfilling the Great Commission through the local church. Thom Hopler depicted the flow of missions in this way: "Every person is a doorway to a family, and every family is a gateway to a community."[14] Yet in a multiracial church, the flow of missions would be that each immigrant would be a doorway to a nation.

THE WILCREST EXPRESSION OF MISSIONS

One of Wilcrest's goals is to send missionaries to each of the countries that are represented by our church body. This passion comes from Acts 1:8, ". . . you will be My witnesses in Jerusalem, in all Judea and Samaria, and to the ends of the earth." The majority of our people's Jerusalem is Houston; their Judea is Texas; their Samaria is Canada or Mexico; and their "ends of the earth" are countries across the Atlantic or Pacific Ocean. However, there is group of people at Wilcrest whose Jerusalem is actually across the ocean. As our church sends missionaries to the ends of the earth, we will arrive in their Jerusalem. For example, in the summer of 2002, we sent a total of 25 people to Honduras, of which two were from Honduras. In addition to the two members who went to Honduras, we also have an additional 15 church members from there. Consequently, they are going to their Jerusalem and then return to the United States to do mission work in their "ends of the earth."

---

[14] Thom and Marcia Hopler, *Reaching the World Next Door: How to Spread the Gospel in the Midst of Many Cultures* (Downers Grove, IL: InterVarsity, 1993), 119.

MISSION TRIP TO NIGERIA

In the State of the Church Address in 2004, I made a covenant that if any of our people would lead a mission trip to their home country, I would go with them. Little did I know what a God-sized challenge was going to present itself over the next few years, and if I had known, I am not so sure that I would have worded that covenant exactly the way I did. One of our Nigerian believers, Alherry Dogonyaro, heard and responded to the challenge and worked fervently with her family back home to establish a connection to return to her home village in northern Nigeria. Over the next two years, we experienced two setbacks to take our first trip to Nigeria due to conflicts in schedule, visa and passport issues, and financial difficulties. However, in the fall of 2005, we set a firm date to go to Nigeria at the end of February 2006. At the beginning of February 2006, a Dutch cartoonist depicted Osama bin Laden as a character with a turban and a bomb attached to it. This portrayal caused an eruption of violence over the entire Muslim world, including northern Nigeria where Christians and Muslims have been fighting over the last several years. The vast majority of our members strongly encouraged me that our group of four should delay the trip until the trouble and violence subsided. The members also discovered that the United States State Department issued a travel advisory warning to Nigeria during this crisis. One other interesting factor was that many of our Nigerians from the Christian South came up to me and told me that they would not even go to the northern part of Nigeria because of the dangers to Christians and to missionaries from the Muslims. I came to a "crisis of belief" that challenged me to reevaluate my call and covenant to reach the nations regardless of the sacrifice and danger, and my source of security and safety. As our team of four left, I really thought that something would happen to us while we were there. In fact, I wrote letters to each of my boys to and my wife and got my house in order. Yet I left with an unusual peace that God was in control and we needed to be in Nigeria.

Upon our arrival in the northern part of Nigeria, it became evident why we were there. As we entered the home village of Alherry, the entire village came out to greet us. We ate together, worshiped together, shared testimonies and Scriptures together. Yet the most priceless memory for me was to see Alherry's face as she introduced her Christian family to her blood family and her home village. I taught a group of pastors in the very house in which she had grown up. I also had an opportunity to listen to a Nigerian pastor who had been in the middle of the Christian and Muslim fighting. In this town, we spent the night next door to a Muslim mosque. He shared that God had called him to establish a church on the Muslim side of town right after a season of severe fighting in which there were several thousand causalities in one single month. The Baptist seminary in Kaduna was burned completely to the ground along with several of the Christian churches. He added that there was not one Christian family who had not lost at least one family member in the crisis. He had been a pastor on the Christian side for several years, but God called him out of his comfort zone. I asked him how many members he had after these five years. He responded that they now had more than 250 believers right in the heart of the Muslim section of that town. God showed me how my sacrifice to come to Nigeria was nothing compared to this pastor's obedience to a simple call of God.

One year later, we had the privilege of returning to the same village with a mission team. The previous year I conveyed that the reason we were in Nigeria was due to Alherry's response to the challenge to return to the home country of any of our international members. This challenge touched a Nigerian pastor in such a way that he went back to his church in a large Nigerian city and challenged his members to lead mission trips to their home villages. Over the next year, this urban church led three mission trips back to the rural villages of his members. The call to "go home and tell" that is depicted with the Pentecost converts, the Gerasene demoniac, and the Ethiopian eunuch mirrors what God is doing with many of our international members.

SUMMARY

Jesus succinctly reminded His disciples the night before His crucifixion, "If you love Me, you will keep My commandments" (John 14:15). To love God is to have a heart for the nations. The call to reach the nations has always been in the heart of God, clearly depicted in God's covenants with Abraham, Moses, David, and ultimately in the life and ministry of Jesus. God's love for all people was evident in the life of the prophet Jonah. In spite of his resistance to call the city of Nineveh to repentance, God still provided the message of hope to the Gentiles. This biblical survey places the New Testament church under obligation to reach every person on the earth. Consequently, every believer then becomes a missionary, not just a believer who goes on mission trips. In developing an understanding of being a missionary, there are three generational missionaries mind-sets: (1) the first-generational missionary seeks to help the nationals because they are in such drastic need; (2) the second-generational missionary seeks to serve alongside the nationals as spiritual equals; (3) the third-generational missionary willingly submits to the teaching and example of the nationals. As believers in a multiracial church, there are mission fields all around you. Furthermore, one of the unique expressions of missions in a multiracial congregation is the transformation of an immigrant's "American dream" to the pursuit of "God's dream," reaching all the nations. One of the most powerful manifestations of the fulfillment of "God's dream" is when immigrants return to their own Jerusalems with the gospel. In the multiracial church, the flow of missions is that each immigrant will be a doorway to his or her nation.

DISCUSSION QUESTIONS

1. What role, if any, did missions play in the covenants with Abraham, Moses, and David? Read Gen 12:1–3; Exod 19:4–6; 2 Sam 7:9–11.

2. Read Matt 28:19–20; Acts 1:8; Rom 1:14–16. What is the biblical mandate for missions? What is the role of missions in your church? Have you participated in a mission trip, either locally or globally? If so, describe some of the changes that happened to you spiritually?

3. What is the difference between going on a mission trip and being a missionary?

4. If the statement is true that loving God means having a heart for the nations, what is your assessment of your love relationship with God?

5. Briefly describe the primary distinctions in each of the three
   generational missionaries, especially in their attitude toward the
   nationals. If you have been on an international mission trip or
   trips, into which generational missionary category would you
   place yourself and why?

CONCLUSION

CHAPTER 13

MULTIPLYING THE VISION

"Now to Him who is able to do above and beyond all that we ask or think—according to the power that works in you—"(Eph 3:20).

I s the multiracial church a biblical model? Based on the biblical evidence presented throughout this book, there is no doubt that God's purpose for redeemed humanity, both Jew and Gentile, is to "glorify the God and Father of our Lord Jesus Christ with a united mind and voice" (Rom 15:6). The next question is more challenging. Since the multiethnic church is a biblical model, is it the only model or one of many options that are available to the church of the twenty-first century? Since only seven percent of all religious congregations in the United States are at least represented by a twenty-percent minority racial group, are the ninety-three percent of all other churches missing the biblical target?[1] The beginning point should be that each church, at the bare minimum, reflects the racial diversity of the community. However, God calls the church to go beyond reflecting your surrounding community and to project the God of all people to the area around you. From Genesis to Revelation, the message resounds that God calls the nations together.

The multiracial congregation is the one voice in the wilderness crying out, "Prepare the way for the Lord" (Mark 1:3; cp. Isa 40:3) as it prepares for the final convergence around the Lamb of God as depicted in Rev 7. Since the multiracial congregation is a biblical model, one might ask if it can be sustained over a long period of time, and if so, what it would look like. Can the God "who is able to do above and beyond all that we ask or think" sustain this vision in spite of a litany of obstacles and barriers? Paul's prayer in Eph 3:14–21 is

---

[1] Emerson, *United by Faith,* 2.

in a context where "the Gentiles are co-heirs, members of the same body, and partners of the promise in Christ Jesus through the gospel" (Eph 3:6). Christ broke down the barrier of the dividing wall between Jews and Gentiles (Eph 2:14b), which represents the division among all the races. In the work of atonement through Christ's death, burial, and resurrection, we are not only reconciled to God, but now we are also reconciled to each other. Surely God would help those seeking to do this through a multiracial vision and community.

QUESTIONING THE VISION

Pastors, friends, family members, and believers have asked numerous times if I was sure that God had called Wilcrest to become a multiracial congregation. Due to declining attendance and finances, white flight, unstable and inconsistent leadership, departure of key leaders, loss of morale, constant concerns and frustration concerning the music and the direction of the church, I often wanted to quit. Yet God prevented me from leaving. I felt like the apostle Paul when he declared, "Woe to me if I do not preach the gospel!" (1 Cor 9:16). Woe to me if I dare abandon the call of God. The vision that God planted in my heart through my parents' inner-city ministry, my life experiences growing up in an all-black neighborhood, my marriage across racial lines, the Word of God calling me to reach all people with the gospel, the growing discomfort in an all-white congregation, all pointed in the direction of a multiracial ministry. My desire was to emulate the simple, biblical response from so many of God's leaders, "Here I am" (Abraham, Gen 22:1,11; Moses, Exod 3:4; Samuel, 1 Sam 3:4; Isaiah, Isa 6:8). Once the divine call is placed on one's life, there is only one right choice: obedience.

Jesus clearly states in the Great Commission, "Go, therefore, and make disciples of all nations, baptizing them in the name of the Father and of the Son and of the Holy Spirit, teaching them to observe everything I have commanded you. And remember, I am with you always, to the end of the age" (Matt 28:19–20). As a multiracial church, God commands Wilcrest to multiply this model to the ends of the earth. In fact, a multiracial model begins the fulfillment and fruition of the Great Commission in each local congregation as all the nations are becoming disciples within one context. As a multiracial church, we are to go where the people are, just as Jesus instructed His disciples: "But you will receive power when the Holy Spirit has come upon you, and you will be My witnesses in Jerusalem, in all Judea and Samaria, and to the ends of the earth" (Acts 1:8). We cannot wait for people of different nations to come to us. We must go to them with this mandated multiracial model (cf. Acts 20:21,27). Finally, we are to treat all believers as full members of the body of Christ. In Peter's report of his vision and experience with the Gentile Cornelius to the Jerusalem church, he testified, "As I began to speak, the Holy Spirit came down on them, just as on us at the beginning" (Acts 11:15). This statement is Peter's acknowledgment that both Jew and Gentile are recipients of the same Holy Spirit, and thus are equals in the family of God.

The biblical reference concerning the importance of seeing and implementing God's vision was written by Solomon. He contended that when there is no revelation, people wander aimlessly and without any direction (Prov 29:18). Although Wilcrest committed to a specific vision in 1993, we would quickly be lost in the midst of a barrage of tangents if the church failed to remain focused. Many detours, such as decreases in attendance and financial support, the departure of key leaders, and the transitional nature of the immediate area surrounding the church, constantly pulled the church away from God's vision. In spite of these difficulties, God provided everything we needed to accomplish His purpose of seeing the nations gather together. The essential groundwork was laid over the last 15 years, but the next 15 years will be just as vital, especially in helping other churches pursue this multiracial dream. Come, dare to dream with us.

VISION FIFTEEN YEARS FROM NOW

Before I can describe the vision for the next 15 years, it is paramount that I return to the beginning to see the fifteen-year vision initially presented to the Wilcrest family. On the day of the churchwide interview in March 1992, I painted the potential portrait of a multiracial church that could occur years into the future. One day Wilcrest would have black, white, Hispanic, and Asian members all singing the same songs and hearing the same message in the same place. What I originally described in general terms has greatly exceeded my expectations through multiple manifestations of this multiracial vision and ministry. One primary part of this dream was that the multiracial congregation would cease being an abnormality, but become the norm of churches in America. This was a dream 15 years ago, but today it is an emerging reality in one local congregation in southwest Houston. A strong affirmation that this dream could actually reach fruition occurred in an early episode with my oldest son, Austin. Three years after my arrival at Wilcrest, I spoke at a church in southeast Texas and my boys were with me. After the service, my seven-year-old asked us, "What is up with this church? Everyone here is white!" In that one simple question, it became evident to me that the multiracial congregation at Wilcrest was the norm for my son. It is the only church that he knows. Consequently, every other church has to pass through Wilcrest filters and lenses for my son. Now at the age of 19, he still makes the observation that something may be drastically wrong with uniracial churches. He continues to ask, "What's up with them?" I concur with my son and must continue to ask, "What is wrong with those churches that refuse to reach beyond their racial, cultural, social, economic, and denominational barriers that we ourselves have erected?"

In the next 15 years the issue of race will not be our predominant focal point. Our people will have had 30 years of experiencing the unity of the Spirit and celebrating diversity among the races. In the midst of diversity, the unity that we have in Christ will be the central focus that will move us into the next dimension. During the initial stage of the transformation process, Wilcrest had to make race an issue in order for race ultimately not to be an issue. During my interview with the pastor from Brooklyn Tabernacle Church, he also assessed that race is not an issue in his church because they have been a multiracial congregation for such a lengthy period. That sounds somewhat paradoxical, but the analogy of childhood would reinforce this concept. As parents, we persistently train our children in simple tasks such as personal grooming, eating, reading, and appropriate behavior. Our hope is that the child later carries out these functions without consciously thinking about them. I see the same pattern emerging in a multiracial congregation; we have incessantly taught that the norm is the multiracial model. Consequently, the believers who have matured under this teaching and model will think multiracially and see through lenses of love for all the races. Solomon affirms this truth when he asserts, "Teach a youth about the way he should go; even when he is old he will not depart from it" (Prov 22:6). We are depositing God's vision for the nations inside the hearts of the future generation. This training involves teaching believers that all races are created in the same image of God. Christ broke down the dividing wall between the Jews and the Gentiles, and all believers will be gathered around the same throne of God.

In the next 15 years, our church will serve as a training center for two different types of missionaries. The first type of missionary will be either a college or seminary student who expresses a strong calling to missions. If the student possesses a call to missions to a specific geographic area, there is a great probability that our church will either have a member from that country or from a nearby region. The family from that country will then adopt the student in order to teach the customs and the language that will equip the future missionary for later service. This approach will serve as a filtering process, to test and determine the strength and accuracy of one's call to missions. It would be inconsistent to claim a desire to go to the international mission field, but demonstrate an unwillingness to minister to the neighboring nations. This missionary-in-training would also serve as an intern to help him or her learn to work as a leader in a multiracial setting. The training period in the multiracial church context will encourage this missionary-in-training to interact with multiple races, often from the perspective of a racial minority. The church would serve as an intentional transition from a homogeneous background to the international mission field, allowing the missionary-in-training to acclimate steadily across racial lines.

The second type of missionary will be the immigrant who originally arrives from another country and then settles in Houston. Perhaps one comes to the United States searching for the "American dream" with the promise of education, riches, and success. However, God interrupts his or her vision of material wealth to transform it to a heart for the nations. These immigrant believers will be personally involved in the leadership and strategy of reaching their own countries, because of their connection with Wilcrest and participation in the passion to reach all the countries represented in the congregation. Initially they will serve as contact persons who will lead Wilcrest to their home countries for mission projects. After serving in this capacity, my dream is that many of these will return to their home countries as missionaries for continual short-term trips or even on a long-term basis. This strategy has already opened the door to Mexico, Honduras, Cameroon, and Nigeria, with many more countries in sight. Wilcrest could then serve as a home base of support in the area of training, finances, and enlistment of other missionaries to reach those particular countries.

Wilcrest then will become a home base and training center for missionaries to be sent all over the globe. The Southern Baptist Convention has successfully sent missionaries to most of the countries of the world, but how exciting would it be for the local church to step on the soil of so many different parts of the world? It is as if God's call to Isaiah, "Who should I send? Who will go for Us?" (Isa 6:8) will not be answered exclusively by a denomination but by each member of the local church. As a result of this God-sized vision, all believers see themselves as missionaries. The constant theme that is set before the missionaries of Wilcrest is not how many people are coming to our church, but how many people we are sending out to the mission fields around us. The training will include exposure and engagement with a multiplicity of cultures and races from the entire world, yet in one location. Members of Wilcrest will be able to experience simultaneously the balance of a unifying vision and the diversity of nations and cultures. This paradox keeps the multiracial church in a healthy and growing balance. Christianity has always been full of paradoxes, such as: the gentle will inherit the earth (Matt 5:5); you must die to self in order to have life (Luke 9:24); those who humble themselves will be exalted (Matt 23:12); and those who are weak are made strong (2 Cor 12:10); but now we can also experience true unity in Christ through the diversity of different races.

In preparation for the final gathering of all the nations, Wilcrest will be a reminder to the evangelical church that multiracial ministry is possible. This is not simply theory; it is real. As the apostle John claimed, "What we have seen and heard we also declare to you" (1 John 1:3). Secondly, if anyone sees what is happening and is moved to implement some of what they see, then Wilcrest will serve as an ongoing resource to provide feedback and support. The pathway to multiracial ministry is lined with multiple difficulties and obstacles. Help from others who have been there is invaluable.

A sense of urgency also keeps driving me to maintain the course. What we have seen in the southwest Houston area is the steady growth of each individual racial group to such an extent that whites are no longer the majority. Presently in Alief Independent School District, more than 70 languages aside from English are spoken in homes. Formerly, minorities desired to be a part of the mainstream white culture because of their need for jobs, houses, and schools. However, the larger each racial group becomes, the less they feel the need to be incorporated into the majority white stream. In fact, in southwest Houston, complete areas of shopping centers, banks, groceries stores, housing, and churches or religious centers cater to only one racial or cultural group. Consequently, the more diverse Wilcrest becomes, the more danger that each individual group will gravitate toward its own racial or cultural group within the congregation itself. In order to prevent this from occurring, there needs to be a continual casting of the vision and the structure that encourages each member to connect with all people groups. We only have a brief window of opportunity to project the multiracial congregation across the landscape of American Christianity. As Leonard Sweet has already noted, the United States is steadily approaching being a nation without any majority race by AD 2056.[2] In our religious marketplace atmosphere, when people are given multiple options in the choice of churches, they inevitably choose to worship with people who are most like them. Unless the biblical model is clearly presented and encouraged, we may return to the "separate but equal" mentality. To prevent this racial segregation, the church must remember our primary mark of identification of belonging to Jesus: "By this all people will know that you are My disciples, if you have love for one another" (John 13:35). Love among races will be difficult for the world to see if churches continue to segregate by the color of their skin.

POSSIBLE SCENE IN 2020 AT WILCREST

The leaders gather in a strategy planning session to evaluate the present condition of the church and to deal with one major void

---

[2] Sweet, 176.

in the ministry at Wilcrest. Where are all the white members? The church reviews the demographical history of the area surrounding Wilcrest. One of the key leaders notes that white flight started in the area surrounding the church in the mid-eighties and continued through the early years of the new millennium. In fact, in 2004, the Alief Independent School District reported 6 percent of the approximately 37,000 students were white. This closely paralleled Houston Independent School District during the same school year, which had more than 93 percent of its students as black and Hispanic. The racial ratio in the schools continues to make an enormous impact on the church. Although some are still connected to Wilcrest, the majority of the whites do not live in the immediate area. The first years of the implementation of the multiracial vision occurred when Wilcrest was completely white, and Alief School District was approximately 50-percent white. However, when Wilcrest reached the critical mass and the church became less than 50-percent white in 2003–04, the school district was overwhelmingly nonwhite. Now 15 years later, Wilcrest has almost 50 different nations represented in the congregation. However, whites represent only 10 percent of the congregation.

The question that seems to be on the mind of everyone in leadership is what to do concerning the lack of participation from the whites? Does the church continue to reach out to more nations and expand the vision? Does the church attempt to reformat the structure, leadership, and worship in order to reach more potential white members? One leader suggests that we start singing more "white music." Another one chimes in that perhaps we should lower the volume of the music. These suggestions prompt a deacon to recommend making our services shorter in order to accommodate the white members and guests. One of the staff members argues that there should be additional white staff hired to send a strong signal that all races are in visible leadership positions. One of the white leaders who had been with Wilcrest throughout the entire transformation process reminds the leadership team that the church is not a white, black, Hispanic, or Asian congregation, but a multiracial body that must learn to express itself in a multiracial paradigm. Although the church needs to be sensitive to all racial groups, the vision requires that each racial group sacrifices the need to be the dominant voice and group so that Wilcrest may reach all groups.

ANOTHER POSSIBLE SCENARIO

A multiracial congregation that has been on the journey for 30 years could possibly move in another direction, if the church determines that race is not a top priority. It could be that in the context of America, the race division will remain the same or increase and widen. Rebecca Y. Kim, a sociologist, reports surprising findings from her research of second-generation Korean-Americans. What she discovered might point in the direction of racial segregation in American congregations, if the church does not keep the issue of race at the forefront of its vision.[3]

The target of her study was second-generation Korean-Americans who were strong evangelicals, mostly from middle-class families. These Korean-Americans grew up in racially mixed suburbs, were familiar with mainstream culture and organizations, and were involved in Christian campus ministries. Within America's racially divided society, different Asian ethnic groups developed because they perceived they were treated differently primarily because of their physical appearance.[4]

In the safe retreats of their Asian-majority Christian organizations, they escaped a society in which race mattered. Kim discovered that these students were seeking some sense of community in the midst of "ethnic density and diversity," desiring "family away from family." When left with a choice, the homophylic forces also emerged and the students chose to be with those who are most familiar and similar to them and so would provide a strong sense of comfort. The second-generation Korean-Americans selected to participate in ethnically homogeneous Korean campus ministries in this open religious marketplace. In addition, these exceptional students who had gained access to elite university campuses felt they had earned the right to be treated like the majority for the first time instead of the minority. It seemed that these students had grown weary of constantly dealing with negative stereotypes, prejudices, and a variety of other misunderstandings simply by being Korean or looking Asian. Specifically in an all-Korean environment, these students experienced for the first time an opportunity for power and leadership that had not been read-

---

[3] Rebecca Y. Kim, "Second Generation Korean American Evangelicals: Ethnic, Multiethnic, or White Campus Ministries," *Sociology of Religion* 65 (Spring 2004): 19–34.

[4] *Divided by Faith*, 11–17.

ily available in panethnic, multiracial, or predominantly white religious settings. As they retreated to their own evangelical groups, the second-generation Korean-Americans' worship services looked very similar to mainline Christianity yet remained segregated from other groups.

This study shows that just because nonwhite Christians have been exposed and integrated in a multiracial environment, it does not guarantee that they will attach themselves to a multiracial Christian organization or a church. Although this study specifically deals with second-generation Korean-Americans who are active in Christian campus ministries, it undoubtedly raises the question of how a multiracial congregation can sustain its momentum and vision. As the religious marketplace continues to increase with multiple ethnic and racial options for Christians, this might mean that more people will still align with the ministry or church that looks most like them. The multiracial church must continue to discover how it can be a viable option in the American church marketplace.

BIBLICAL REMINDER

In Paul's letter to the Galatians, he addressed a group of Jewish converts who initially stepped away from the rigid Jewish legalism and all of its unrealistic demands and embraced Christ alone as their hope for salvation. Yet as time progressed, a group of nationalistic Judaizers began to influence these Jewish converts demanding that they had to place their faith in Christ and retain the Jewish law in order to become true believers. Paul's strong words of admonition and correction reminded them that they did not receive Christ through the law. The apostle added that they had been running so well in their faith, but what had hindered them in their progress of the gospel and the mission to the Gentiles (see Gal 3:2–6)? The return to the exclusive Jewish religion turned the Galatian believers' focus inward, excluding those who were racially and religiously different. However, from the inception of Christianity, the gospel has transcended all racial distinctions and ethnic boundaries. Although Christianity began with the Jews (John 4:22), it was to move from Jerusalem and Judea to Samaria and the ends of the earth (Acts 1:8). The divine direction of the church must turn outward to the nations.

In the contemporary context, the multiracial congregation begins to fulfill the Great Commission by reaching across all racial lines. However, if the next generation reverts to homogeneous safe gatherings, it will be moving against the divine direction of the gospel.

MISSION IMPOSSIBLE

Are there any exceptions to the call to become a multiracial congregation? In his book *United by Faith,* Michael Emerson and his coauthors propose three valid reasons why churches are uniracial: (1) many churches are not located in geographical areas where this goal is attainable, particularly in rural areas; (2) the lack of a common language; (3) the unique circumstances of first-generation immigrant groups.[5] There is a fourth exception or reason why a homogeneous church should not immediately move in the multiracial direction. The decision to become a multiracial congregation in some churches would actually be more destructive than the alternative of sending out some of the core members to plant a multiracial congregation. The transformation to a multiracial congregation from an unhealthy or weak homogeneous church base would require overcoming obstacles without the proper spiritual foundation and fuel. In the case of Wilcrest, although the church was in decline, the need for spiritual survival provided a healthy impetus to make whatever changes were necessary to transition into a multiracial congregation.[6]

However, what if the believer or the congregation is in an environment that is predominantly one race? How is it possible to reach across racial lines if the believer attends a uniracial school or lives in a uniracial neighborhood or works in a uniracial business or is connected with family and friends who are all the same race? Are there any practical steps that an individual or a congregation can take to reach across racial lines and be obedient to the call of God while still in the homogeneous context?

---

[5] *United by Faith,* 143. The first generation immigrants may find the challenge of crossing from their culture to another culture too difficult.

[6] Wilcrest was categorized initially as a "survival embracing" congregation, but eventually transitioned into a "niche embracing" congregation. Wilcrest's need and desire for survival was due to the steady decline over the previous decade (1980–1990). Over the next ten years (1992–2002), Wilcrest embraced the niche of targeting those who wanted to be a part of a multiracial congregation. See *People of the Dream,* 52–61, 73.

The first step that is necessary to move across racial lines is *expo-sure*. For an individual or church in a uniracial setting, it requires intentionally moving out of their familiar surroundings and placing themselves in a position to come into contact with other races. This may involve going on a mission trip to another section of your city, state, country, or across international lines. Even in the course of your daily life, put on intentional racial lenses as you look for people from different backgrounds with whom you can interact. Exposure to different races has a profound effect on how you perceive and interact as a missionary representing the God of all nations.[7]

The second step is *education*. Become teachable as you read from a variety of literature dealing with different races. In the bibliography, there are some resources that would help you understand different racial perspectives. In addition to learning from reading, it is vital to develop a personal relationship with a person from another racial background. If this person is in a peer relationship with you, both of you can learn together as you share this multiracial journey.[8] If this person serves as a mentor, your willingness to place yourself under the teaching of someone from a different race will enable you to understand what few can. In the early years of the multiracial transformation at Wilcrest, the whites who placed themselves under James Darby's leadership and teaching grew immeasurably in the area of racial reconciliation.

Another helpful tool in the area of educating believers to move out of their comfort zone was derived from one of the assignments for the students in my "Multiracial Church" class. I teach this class at the undergraduate level for Houston Baptist University and at the graduate level for Southwestern Baptist Theological Seminary. The assignment is twofold: the first part is to visit a church that is racially different than their own and write down their observations; and secondly, I asked them to interview a member of the pastoral staff from

---

[7] See chapter 11, which deals with the characteristics of a multiracial leader. The first trait is "exposure and experience with other races." In that section, I describe a University of Michigan study that validates the impact of students who have been exposed to different races. Emerson adds when whites are not as racially isolated, the race problem is real. See *Divided by Faith*, 83–84.

[8] For an example of this, see Raleigh Washington and Glen Kehrein, *Breaking Down Walls: A Model for Reconciliation in an Age of Strife* (Chicago: Moody, 1993). This work relates the personal stories of two pastors from different races coming together to form a cross-cultural friendship and church.

that church in order to gain their perspective on how they deal with race issues. Most of the students have grown up in a homogeneous church and have never visited a church where they were the racial minority. This educational exercise has proven to be insightful. One white student was amazed that the entire black congregation was "singing like a choir." He had never witnessed such an engaging and exhilarating worship service. One of the white students interviewed a black pastor who claimed that his church had "no desire to strive for multiethnicity because it would make the congregation feel as if outsiders were infringing upon their family." One white student went to an all-black service with more than 1,500 in attendance and not one person spoke to him. Most of the students did not encounter what they expected. Either the students received a lot more than they could imagine, or they felt extremely isolated and rejected. Until believers place themselves in situations where they are the racial minority, one level of learning will never be experienced.

On the congregational level, it would prove helpful to establish a partnership with a church with a different racial composition. This church does not necessarily need to be in your geographical proximity. By worshiping together or joining together in a ministry project, the two churches have the unique opportunity to connect at a spiritual level while engaging in a spiritual activity. If the connection is with a homogeneous congregation that is a different race than your congregation, both churches can sharpen one another as they are introduced to a different expression of Christianity (see Prov 27:17). In the Wilcrest experience, we have enlisted several all-white and all-black churches to join us in mission trips, youth camps, community projects, and shared worship services. In each case, the people from uniracial churches are exposed to a multiracial church. These joint endeavors serve both as an encouragement that a multiracial congregation is possible and as a challenge to get others out of their racial comfort zones.

The third practical step is *endurance*. When you place yourself in a position to be exposed to those of different racial backgrounds and in a learning relationship, it does not automatically mean that the road to racial reconciliation will be easy. If you are moving in the direction of racial reconciliation, you will always be going against the spiritual grain of contemporary society. Resistance will come from within the church as well as outside. The key is never to give up. The believer must do whatever is necessary to see this multiracial vision become a living reality in all areas of life. For example, some of our people have intentionally moved into neighborhoods where they are the racial minority. They have placed their children in schools that are either racially diverse or their children are the racial minority. Some have moved to homogeneous churches as missionaries to help instill the multiracial vision. This journey is not a hundred-meter sprint, but a grueling, lifelong marathon. As Martin Luther King Jr. said, "If you cannot fly, run; if you cannot run, walk; if you cannot walk, crawl, but by all means, keep moving." From the inception of the United States, racism and prejudice have resulted in a society that is saturated with the effects of racism.[9] This racial segregation did not occur overnight nor will it be healed overnight. However, it is worthy of our relentless pursuit because it honors and glorifies the eternal God of all the nations.

SUMMARY

For the last 15 years, Wilcrest embraced and implemented a vision of God transforming a homogeneous congregation to a multiracial one. The journey was filled with numerous setbacks, obstacles, heartaches, and failures, yet God remained faithful; nothing is too difficult for Him (Jer 32:27). Looking back on this process enables the church to see the future 15 years with more confidence and clarity. One of the goals of seeing this vision implemented in one local church context is that the multiracial model would be the norm for the church in the United States as the nation moves toward having no racial majority group by AD 2056. It would be a movement of God to see 93 percent of religious congregations consisting of at least 20 percent of a racial minority group. It would be strong evidence of God's activity to see only 7 percent of the churches in the United States be racially homogeneous.

Another goal of this multiracial vision is to have the multiracial congregation deal with the race issue so thoroughly that it is no longer

---

[9] Emerson identifies the effects of racism and prejudice in the United States as a "racialized society," which he defines as a "society wherein race matters profoundly for differences in life experiences, life opportunities, and social relationships." See *Divided by Faith*, 7.

the predominant focus. The world would see believers of all races loving each other in the local church and know they are connected to the Christ who loves the world. The multiracial church could also provide a home base and training center for a new global mission force. Believers who have learned and practiced reaching across racial lines at the local church level now will be adequately equipped to reach all racial groups with the gospel. The multiracial church would also be a catalyst for immigrants to return to their Jerusalem with a new network of Christian support. As the immigrants arrive in their Jerusalem on mission, they are leading a part of the body of Christ to the ends of the earth.

Whatever Wilcrest looks like in 15 years, the previous 15 years remind the body of Christ that God can do the impossible. Whether race needs to be the primary focus or not, God undoubtedly has given the American church a brief moment of grace to reach across racial lines in the local church context. It is difficult to foresee whether the religious marketplace will hinder the growth of the multiracial church, or the biblical model and mandate will override the felt need to worship in their own culture. The biblical projection for the final worship, however, establishes the heavenly model with every nation, every tribe, every tongue, and every people worshiping at the throne of God. The prayer of the earthly multiracial church is "Your kingdom come. Your will be done on earth as it is in heaven" (Matt 6:10). Let us enjoy heaven on earth.

DISCUSSION

1. Based on what God has been teaching you throughout this book, do you believe the multiracial model is a biblical model? Is it the only biblical model, or are there other models? What are the exceptions that would permit a uniracial model?

2. Do you think that since the United States is projected to have no racial majority by AD 2056, there is an urgency to establish multiracial congregations? If so, why? If not, why?

3. Do you think that race should be intentionally brought up for discussion by churches, or should we let whatever happens happen? What are the reasons you feel this way?

4. If you are living in a uniracial environment, what are the three practical steps that you can take as an individual or a church to move in the multiracial direction? If the uniracial context is your situation, what steps have you taken in the area of exposure? What are the two primary ways that you can educate yourself in the area of multiracial ministry and relationships? What steps are you willing to commit to take in the area of education?

A P P E N D I X 1

WILCREST BAPTIST CHURCH
SURVEY

1. What is your age?

   20–25 26–30 31–35 36–40 41–45 46–50 50–55 Above 55

2. What is your predominant race?

3. How long have you been a part of Wilcrest Baptist Church?

4. What are some of the rewards, benefits, highlights, etc., that you have really enjoyed about being a part of a multiracial church?

5. What has been the most difficult, painful, or greatest sacrifice you have experienced being a part of a multiracial church?

6. What have you had to forfeit from the previous church of your race to become a part of this church?

A P P E N D I X 2

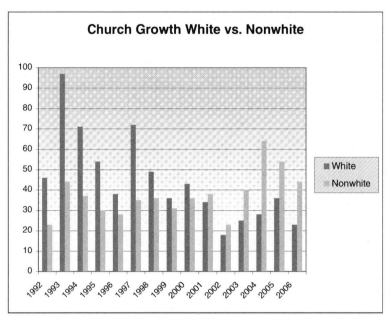

Church Growth White vs. Nonwhite

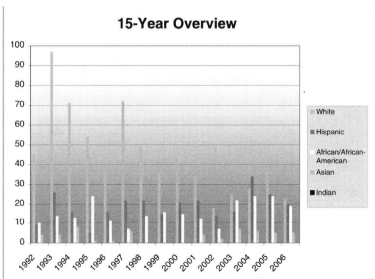

15-Year Overview

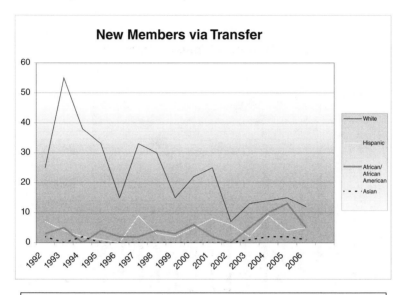

Via Transfer			
	White	*Hispanic*	*African/ African American*	*Asian*
1992	25	7	3	2
1993	55	4	5	0
1994	38	2	0	2
1995	33	1	4	0
1996	15	0	2	0
1997	33	9	2	0
1998	30	3	4	0
1999	15	2	3	0
2000	22	5	6	0
2001	25	8	2	0
2002	7	6	0	0
2003	13	2	5	1
2004	14	9	10	2
2005	15	4	13	2
2006	12	5	5	1

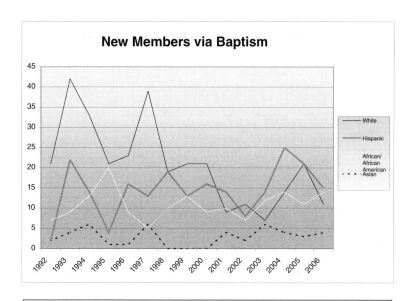

Via Baptism			
	White	*Hispanic*	*African/ African American*	*Asian*
1992	21	2	7	2
1993	42	22	9	4
1994	33	14	13	6
1995	21	4	20	1
1996	23	16	9	1
1997	39	13	5	6
1998	19	19	10	0
1999	21	13	13	0
2000	21	16	9	0
2001	9	14	10	4
2002	11	8	7	2
2003	7	14	12	6
2004	14	25	14	4
2005	21	21	11	3
2006	11	15	14	4

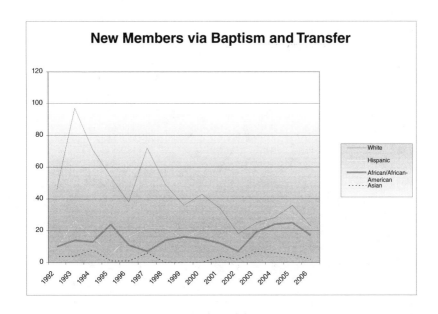

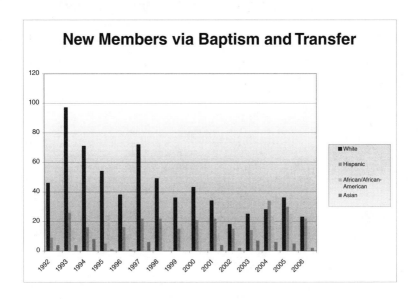

| | **Total** | | | |
	White	Hispanic	African/ African American	Asian
1992	46	9	10	4
1993	97	26	14	4
1994	71	16	13	8
1995	54	5	24	1
1996	38	16	11	1
1997	72	22	7	6
1998	49	22	14	0
1999	36	15	16	0
2000	43	21	15	0
2001	34	22	12	4
2002	18	15	7	2
2003	25	14	19	7
2004	28	34	24	6
2005	36	30	25	5
2006	23	22	17	2

AN OVERVIEW OF THE ADDITIONS
TO WILCREST (1992–2002)

I n 1992, Wilcrest had 180–200 people in worship on an average Sunday morning, with approximately 98 percent of the congregation being Anglo. In the early 1980s the church had grown to almost 500 in attendance, but with the oil bust, Alief had experienced a major shift in its racial mix. In my first two years here (1992–93), Wilcrest experienced an unusual period of seeing people open their hearts to Christ and follow up in believer baptism. Although the church baptized 75 new believers each of its first two years, there was still an enormous amount of turnover. The racial mix in the church began to change gradually, primarily through conversion.

During the last seven months of 1992, there were 32 baptisms and 42 who joined from another congregation. Of the baptisms, there were 21 whites, 2 Hispanics, 7 African or African-Americans, and 2 Asians. Of those who joined from another church, there were 25 whites, 7 Hispanics, 3 African-Americans, and 2 Asians. Of the 74 people who joined Wilcrest during my first seven months here, there were 46 whites, 9 Hispanics, 10 African or African-Americans, and 4 Asians.

In 1993, we had 77 total baptisms and 64 other additions to the church. Of those new believers being baptized, 42 were Anglo, 22 were Hispanic, 9 were African or African-American, and 4 were of Asian descent. Of those joining by transfer: 55 were Anglo, 4 were Hispanic, and 5 were African or African-American, and no Asians. Consequently, only 9 believers transferred into Wilcrest from another evangelical church who were non-Anglo. In 1993, there were a total of 141 new members: 97 of these were Anglo and 44 were non-Anglo.

In 1994, there were a total of 66 baptisms. Of the ones who were baptized, 33 were white, 14 were Hispanic, 13 were African or African-American, and 6 were Asians. Of those who joined from other churches, 38 were white, 2 were Hispanic, 2 were Asian, and none were African or African-American. Interestingly, there were only 4 non-Anglo additions to our church during that year. In 1994, there were a total of 108 new members: 71 whites, 16 Hispanics, 13 African or African-Americans, and 8 Asians.

In 1995, there were a total of 46 baptisms. From this group, there were 21 whites, 4 Hispanics, 20 African or African-Americans, and 1 Asian. In addition, there 38 other additions to Wilcrest: 33 whites, 1 Hispanic, 4 African or African-Americans, and no Asians. There were a total of 84 additions to Wilcrest: 54 whites, 5 Hispanics, 24 African or African-Americans, and 1 Asian.

In 1996, there were a total of 49 baptisms. Of these baptisms, there were 23 whites, 16 Hispanics, 9 African or African-Americans, and 1 Asian. There were also 17 other additions: 15 whites and 2 African-Americans. There was a total of 66 additions: 38 whites, 16 Hispanics, 11 African or African-Americans, and 1 Asian. During this time, we were seeing fewer people join Wilcrest from other churches. I believe the reason for this is that Wilcrest was becoming so diverse that it was too different for those who were acclimated to a homogeneous congregation.

In 1997, there were 63 baptisms. From this group, there were 39 whites, 13 Hispanics, 5 African or African-Americans, and 6 Asians. There were also a total of 44 other additions: 33 whites, 9 Hispanics, 2 African or African-Americans, and no Asians. There were a total of 107 people who joined our church in 1997: 72 whites, 22 Hispanics, 7 African or African-Americans, and 6 Asians. This was an unusual year of new believers who were Anglo coming into the body of Christ. This was also the year that there was an unusual movement in the area of assurance of salvation and many of these baptisms were individuals who really felt that they had gone through the motions of placing their faith in Christ but did not experience authentic conversion.

In 1998, there were 48 baptisms, with 19 whites, 19 Hispanics, 10 African or African-Americans, and no Asians. There were also 37 other additions to the church: 30 whites, 3 Hispanics, and 4 African or African-Americans, and no Asians. There were a total of 85 total additions to Wilcrest in 1998: 49 whites, 22 Hispanics, 14 African or African-Americans, and no Asians.

In 1999, we had a total of 47 baptisms and 20 other additions to the church. Of those who were baptized, 21 were Anglo, 13 were Hispanic, 13 were African or African-American, and no Asians. Of those believers who were joining by transfer from another church, 15 were Anglo, 2 were Hispanic, 3 were African or African-American, and no Asians. Of the total of 67 additions, 36 were Anglo and 31 were non-Anglo.

In 2000, there were 46 baptisms. In this group, there were 21 whites, 16 Hispanics, 9 African or African-Americans, and no Asians. Furthermore, there were 33 other additions: 22 whites, 5 Hispanics, 6 African or African-Americans, and no Asians. Throughout the entire year, there were a total of 79 additions: 43 whites, 21 Hispanics, 15 African or African-Americans, and no Asians.

In 2001, there were a total of 38 baptisms. Of these, there were 9 whites, 14 Hispanics, 10 African or African-Americans, and 4 Asians. In addition, there were 35 other additions: 25 whites, 8 Hispanics, and 2 African or African-Americans, and no Asians. There were a total of 73 additions to the church: 34 whites, 22 Hispanics, 12 African or African Americans, and 4 Asians.

In 2002 through the month of April, there were a total of 28 baptisms: 11 whites, 8 Hispanics, 7 African or African-Americans, and 2 Asians. There were also 13 other people who joined the church during the first four months of 2002: 7 whites and 6 Hispanics. During this period, we had 41 total additions: 18 whites, 14 Hispanics, 7 African or African-Americans, and 2 Asians.

The overall statistics for the 10-year period of May 1992-April 2002 are as follows. There were a total of 540 baptisms; there were 260 whites, 141 Hispanics, 111 African or African-Americans, and 28 Asians. Of those who were joining from other churches, there were 380 people: 298 whites, 47 Hispanics, 31 African or African-Americans, and 4 Asians. In that 10-year period, there were a total of 920 additions to Wilcrest: 558 whites, 188 Hispanics, 142 African or African-Americans, and 32 Asians. Out of 142 African and African-Americans, there are 60 African-Americans, 43 Africans, and 39 from various islands. One observation is that the more we become a multiracial congregation, the fewer the number of people who will join from other churches. In addition, the primary growth in our non-Anglo groups come from conversions and baptisms.

As a result of this 10-year study, it quickly became apparent that the vast majority of our non-Anglos connected with Wilcrest through salvation and baptism. Only 82 non-Anglos of the 380 total people joined Wilcrest from other evangelical churches. One key truth that also emerges is the fact that the primary way to grow a multiracial congregation is through conversion. The more Wilcrest has become multiracial, the fewer transfers we have from homogeneous churches. Over this 10-year period, we experienced a 3 to 2 baptism to transfer rate of growth.

Throughout this entire process, I assumed that the more we opened ourselves to different cultures, the more people we would be able to reach numerically. However in reality, the number of people who are actually open to come and visit a multiracial congregation is small. The vast majority of people feel more comfortable in a homogeneous church environment; thus, we are somewhat limited in the people who would come to Wilcrest. Theoretically, this did not make much sense, but practically we have discovered that a small minority is open to worshiping with multiple cultures. The multiracial model is a new phenomenon among most evangelical churches.

A P P E N D I X 4

COUNTRIES OF WILCREST

North America
1. United States
2. Canada

Central and South America
1. Mexico
2. Cuba
3. Honduras
4. Guatemala
5. Venezuela
6. Puerto Rico
7. Dominican Republic
8. El Salvador
9. Nicaragua
10. Brazil
11. Chile
12. Colombia
13. Guyana
14. Trinidad
15. Argentina
16. Uruguay
17. St. Thomas
18. St. Andrews
19. Jamaica

20. Bahamas
21. Haiti
22. Peru
23. Costa Rica

Africa

1. Cameroon
2. Nigeria
3. Ethiopia
4. Sierra Leone
5. Ghana
6. Liberia

Asia

1. China
2. Taiwan
3. S. Korea
4. Indonesia
5. Japan
6. Philippines
7. S. Vietnam
8. Malaysia
9. India
10. Nepal

Middle East and Europe

1. Lebanon
2. Iran
3. Greece

BIBLIOGRAPHY

Adeney, Bernard T. *Strange Virtues: Ethics in a Multicultural World.* Downers Grove, IL: InterVarsity, 1995.

Bailey, Kenneth E. *Poet and Peasant and Through Peasant Eyes: A Literary-Cultural Approach to the Parables in Luke.* Grand Rapids: Eerdmans, 1976.

Balz, Horst, and Schneider, eds. *Exegetical Dictionary of the New Testament.* Vols. 1–3. Grand Rapids: Eerdmans, 1990.

Bangert, Mark. "How Does One Go About Multicultural Worship?" in *Open Questions in Worship: What Does Multicultural Worship Look Like?* Ed. Gordon Lathrop. Minneapolis: Augsburg Fortress, 1996.

Barclay, William. *The Letters to the Galatians and Ephesians,* rev. ed. Philadelphia: Westminster, 1976.

Barnett, Paul. *The Second Epistle to the Corinthians.* Grand Rapids: Eerdmans, 1997.

Belleville, Linda L. *2 Corinthians.* Downers Grove, IL: InterVarsity, 1996.

Black, Kathy. *Culturally Conscious Worship.* St. Louis: Chalice, 2000.

Blount, Brian K., and Leonora Tubbs Tisdale, eds. *Making Room at the Table.* Louisville, KY: Westminster John Knox, 2001.

Bonhoeffer, Dietrich. *Life Together.* New York: Harper & Row, 1954.

Borchert, Gerald L. *John 1–11.* The New American Commentary. Nashville: B&H, 1996.

Bruce, F. F. *The Book of Acts.* New International Commentary on the New Testament. Grand Rapids: Eerdmans, 1988.

Burge, Gary. *John.* The NIV Application Commentary. Grand Rapids: Zondervan, 2000.

Carroll R, M. Daniel. "Blessing the Nations: Toward a Biblical Theology of Missions in Genesis." *Bulletin for Biblical Research* 10.1 (2000): 17–34.

Carson, D. A. *The Gospel according to John.* Grand Rapids: Eerdmans, 1991.

Charlesworth, James H., ed. *The Old Testament: Pseudipigrapha.* New York: Doubleday, 1983.

Christerson, Brad, Korie L. Edwards, and Michael O. Emerson. *Against All Odds: The Struggle for Racial Integration in Religious Organizations.* New York: New York University Press, 2005.

Cole, R. A. *The Epistle of Paul to the Galatians.* Leicester, England: InterVarsity, 1985.

Corbitt, J. Nathan. *The Sound of the Harvest.* Grand Rapids: Baker, 1998.

Deddo, G. "Persons in Racial Reconciliation: The Contribution of a Trinitarian Theological Anthropology," in D. L. Okholm (ed.), *The Gospel in Black and White.* Downers Grove, IL: InterVarsity, 1997.

DeYoung, Curtiss Paul, Michael O. Emerson, George Yancey, and Karen Chai Kim. *United by Faith: The Multiracial Congregation as an Answer to the Problem of Race.* New York: Oxford University Press, 2003.

Dunn, James D. G. *The Acts of the Apostles.* Valley Forge, PA: Trinity, 1996.

Elmer, Duane. *Cross-Cultural Conflict: Building Relationships for Effective Ministry.* Downers Grove, IL: InterVarsity, 1993.

Emerson, Michael O., and Christian Smith. *Divided by Faith: Evangelical Religion and the Problem of Race in America.* New York: Oxford Press, 2000.

Emerson, Michael O., with Rodney M. Woo. *People of the Dream: Multiracial Congregations in the United States.* Princeton: Princeton University Press, 2006.

Fernando, Ajith. *Acts.* The NIV Application Commentary. Grand Rapids: Zondervan, 1998.

Fretheim, Terrance. *Exodus.* Interpretation. Louisville, KY: John Knox, 1991.

Furr, James, Jim Herrington, and Mike Bonem. *Leading Congregational Change Workbook.* San Francisco: Jossey Bass, 2000.

Garland, David. *2 Corinthians.* The New American Commentary. Nashville: Broadman, 1999.

Green, Amy. "Southern Baptist Surprise." *Christianity Today* 48.9 (September 2004): 54–56.

Grenz, Stanley J. *Theology for the Community of God.* Grand Rapids: Eerdmans, 1994.

Grudem, Wayne. *Systematic Theology.* Grand Rapids: Zondervan, 1994.

Gundry, Robert H. *A Survey of the New Testament.* 4th ed. Grand Rapids: Zondervan, 2003.

Hacker, Andrew. *Two Nations: Black and White, Separate, Hostile, Unequal.* New York: Scribner, 2003.

Hafemann, Scott F. *2 Corinthians.* The NIV Application Commentary. Grand Rapids: Zondervan, 2000.

Harding, Vincent, "With Drums and Cup: White Myths and Indian Spirituality: An Interview with George Tinker," in *America's Original Sin.* Washington, D.C.: Sojourners, 1995.

Harrop, Clayton. "Jewish Parties," in *Holman Bible Dictionary,* ed. Trent C. Butler. Nashville: Holman Bible Publishers, 1991.

Hays, J. Daniel. *From Every People and Nation: A Biblical Theology of Race.* Downers Grove, IL: InterVarsity, 2003.

Hays, R. B. "The Letter to the Galatians," in *The New Interpreter's Bible.* Vol. 11, ed. L. E. Kleck. Nashville: Abingdon, 2000.

Henriques, Joseph. "Clouds in Our Community," in *Cultural Change and Your Church: Helping Your Church Survive in a Diverse Society.* Grand Rapids: Baker, 2002.

Hoehner, Harold W. *Ephesians: An Exegetical Commentary.* Grand Rapids: Baker Academic, 2002.

Hollinger, David. *Postethnic America: Beyond Multiculturalism.* New York: Oxford Press, 1995.

Hopler, Thom and Marcia. *Reaching the World Next Door: How to Spread the Gospel in the Midst of Many Cultures.* Downers Grove, IL: InterVarsity, 1993.

Howard, David M., Jr. *Joshua.* The New American Commentary. Nashville: Broadman, 1998.

Huey, F. B., Jr. *Exodus.* Bible Study Commentary. Grand Rapids: Zondervan, 1977.

Hughes, Philip E. *The Second Epistle to the Corinthians.* New International Commentary on the New Testament. Grand Rapids: Eerdmans, 1962.

Juel, Donald H. "Multicultural Worship," in *Making Room at the Table,* ed. Brian K. Bount and Leonara Tubbs Tisdale. Louisville, KY: Westminster John Knox, 2000.

Kaiser, Walter C. *Mission in the Old Testament: Israel as a Light to the Nations.* Grand Rapids: Baker, 2000.

Kim, Rebecca Y. "Second Generation Korean American Evangelicals: Ethnic, Multiethnic, or White Campus Ministries." *Sociology of Religion* 65 (Spring 2004): 19–34.

King, Martin Luther, Jr. *Where Do We Go from Here: Chaos or Community?* New York: Harper and Row, 1967.

Kistemaker, Simon J. *2 Corinthians.* Grand Rapids: Baker, 1997.

Klein, Ralph W. *1 Samuel.* Word Biblical Commentary. Waco: Word, 1983.

Knight, George W., III. *The Pastoral Epistles: A Commentary on the Greek Text.* New International Greek Text Commentary. Grand Rapids: Eerdmans, 1992.

Koehler, Ludwig, and Walter Baumgartner. *The Hebrew and Aramaic Lexicon of the Old Testament,* ed. and trans. M. E. J. Richardson. Leiden, Netherlands: Koninklijke Brill NV, 2001.

Köstenberger, Andreas J., and Peter T. O'Brien. *Salvation to the Ends of the Earth: A Biblical Theology of Mission.* Downers Grove, IL: InterVarsity, 2001.

Kotter, John. *Leading Change.* Boston: Harvard Business School Press, 1996.

Larkin, William J. *Acts.* Downers Grove, IL: InterVarsity, 1995.

Law, Eric H. F. *The Wolf Shall Dwell with the Lamb: A Spirituality for Leadership in a Multicultural Community.* St. Louis: Chalice, 1993.

Lea, Thomas D., and Hayne P. Griffin Jr. *1, 2 Timothy, Titus.* The New American Commentary. Nashville: Broadman, 1992.

Liefeld, Walter L. *1 & 2 Timothy and Titus.* The NIV Application Commentary. Grand Rapids: Zondervan, 1999.

Maynard-Reid, Pedrito U. *Diverse Worship: African-American, Caribbean and Hispanic Perspectives.* Downers Grove, IL: InterVarsity, 2001.

Mitton, C. Leslie. *Ephesians.* The New Century Bible Commentary. Grand Rapids: Eerdmans, 1973.

Muddiman, John. *The Epistle to the Ephesians.* New York: Hendrickson, 2001.

Neal, William. *The Acts of the Apostles.* The New Century Bible Commentary. Grand Rapids: Eerdmans, 1973.

Nolland, John. *The Gospel of Matthew.* New International Greek Testament Commentary. Grand Rapids: Eerdmans, 2005.

O'Brien, Peter T. *The Letter to the Ephesians.* Grand Rapids: Eerdmans, 1999.

Okeye, James Chukwuma. *Israel and the Nations: A Mission Theology of the Old Testament.* Maryknoll, NY: Orbis, 2006.

Palmer, Parker J. *The Company of Strangers.* New York: Crossroad, 1983.

Peterson, Eugene H. *First and Second Samuel.* Louisville, KY: Westminster John Knox, 1999.

Polhill, John B. *Acts.* The New American Commentary. Nashville: Broadman, 1992.

Pollard, Alton B., III. *Mysticism and Social Change: The Social Witness of Howard Thurman.* New York: Peter Lang, 1992.

Reid, Alvin L. "The Zeal of Youth: The Role of Students in the History of Spiritual Awakening" in *Evangelism for a Changing World,* ed. Timothy Beougher and Alvin L. Reid. Wheaton, IL: Harold Shaw, 1995.

Reimers, David. *White Protestantism and the Negro.* New York: Oxford University Press, 1965.

Rhodes, Stephen A. *Where the Nations Meet: The Church in a Multicultural World.* Downers Grove, IL: InterVarsity, 1998.

Stott, John. *The Spirit, the Church, and the Word.* Downers Grove, IL: InterVarsity, 1990.

Sweet, Leonard. "Be an Energizer Bunny," *Homiletics* (January-March, 1995).

_____. *FaithQuakes.* Nashville: Abingdon, 1999.

Tenney, Merrill C. *New Testament Survey.* Rev. ed. Grand Rapids: Eerdmans, 1985.

Tisdale, Leonara Tubbs. "Navigating the Contemporary Worship Narrows," in *Making Room at the Table,* ed. Brian K. Blount and Leonara Tubbs Tisdale. Louisville, KY: Westminster John Knox, 2000.

Towner, Philip H. *The Letters to Timothy and Titus.* New International Commentary on the New Testament. Grand Rapids: Eerdmans, 2006.

van Zyl, Daniel C. "Exodus 19:3–6 and the Kerygmatic Perspective of the Pentateuch," *Old Testament Essays* 5.2 (1992): 264–71.

Vos, Howard F. *1 and 2 Samuel.* Bible Study Commentary. Grand Rapids: Zondervan, 1983.

Wagner, C. Peter. *Our Kind of People: The Ethical Dimensions of Church Growth in America.* Atlanta: John Knox, 1979.

Warden, Michael D., ed. *Experiencing God in Worship.* Loveland, CO: Group, 2000.

Washington, Raleigh, and Glen Kehrein. *Breaking Down Walls: A Model for Reconciliation in an Age of Strife.* Chicago: Moody, 1993.

Wenham, G. J. *Genesis 1–15.* Word Biblical Commentary. Waco, TX: Word, 1987.

_____. *Numbers.* Downers Grove, IL: InterVarsity, 1981.

Wilson, William. *Wilson Old Testament Word Studies.* McLean, VA: MacDonald, n.d.

Yancey, George. *One Body, One Spirit: Principles of Successful Multiracial Churches.* Downers Grove, IL: InterVarsity, 2003.

NAME INDEX

SCRIPTURE INDEX